Crafting a Curriculum of Coherence

Crafting a Curriculum of Coherence is a transformative guide that equips educators with the knowledge and tools to create a new kind of educational journey for children and young people, informed by the unique insights of Steiner Waldorf education.

Drawing upon years of experience, expertise and research, the authors present a step-by-step guide for curriculum renewal, design and delivery to create meaningful, coherent learning experiences that inspire and empower learners. The chapters offer a new way of conceiving skills as knowledgeable action with purpose, covering a potentialities and competencies approach, which makes learning truly holistic, and a layered curriculum model that moves from philosophy to classroom practice, enabling the development of coherent curriculum in any social or cultural setting. Featuring real-life examples, case studies, and thought-provoking exercises, the book encourages readers to think critically and creatively about education.

Exploring the interplay between curriculum design, pedagogy and assessment, this is an indispensable resource for educators who are dedicated to shaping a world where every child and young person can flourish.

Martyn Rawson is Professor for Waldorf Education in International Contexts at Alanus University of Arts and Social Sciences, Germany where he is responsible for the International Waldorf Master Programme, following 45 years as teacher and school leader in Waldorf education. He is co-editor of the English-language Waldorf Curriculum, a co-creator of a Waldorf e-learning platform (www.e-learningwaldorf.de) and the author of Steiner Waldorf Pedagogy in Schools and many articles on curriculum, learning theory, second language teaching and teacher education. He also teaches part-time in the high school at the Christian Morgenstern School in Hamburg.

Kath Bransby is the Education Coordinator for Waldorf UK and a board member of the European Council for Steiner Waldorf Education. With Martyn, Kath co-edited an updated English Language curriculum for UK Waldorf schools, and has co-written a number of articles. Kath also works as a senior lecturer in teacher education at Sheffield Hallam University, where she recently completed her Master's thesis, 'Why Waldorf?', an exploration of parents' and carers' reasons for choosing Waldorf education for their children.

Crafting a Curriculum of Coherence
Lessons from Steiner Waldorf Education

Martyn Rawson and Kath Bransby

LONDON AND NEW YORK

Designed cover image: Aristea Klanac

First published 2026
by Routledge
4 Park Square, Milton Park, Abingdon, Oxon OX14 4RN

and by Routledge
605 Third Avenue, New York, NY 10158

Routledge is an imprint of the Taylor & Francis Group, an informa business

© 2026 Martyn Rawson and Kath Bransby

The right of Martyn Rawson and Kath Bransby to be identified as authors of this work has been asserted in accordance with sections 77 and 78 of the Copyright, Designs and Patents Act 1988.

All rights reserved. No part of this book may be reprinted or reproduced or utilized in any form or by any electronic, mechanical, or other means, now known or hereafter invented, including photocopying and recording, or in any information storage or retrieval system, without permission in writing from the publishers.

Trademark notice: Product or corporate names may be trademarks or registered trademarks, and are used only for identification and explanation without intent to infringe.

British Library Cataloguing-in-Publication Data
A catalogue record for this book is available from the British Library

ISBN: 978-1-032-85504-2 (hbk)
ISBN: 978-1-032-85501-1 (pbk)
ISBN: 978-1-003-51847-1 (ebk)

DOI: 10.4324/9781003518471

Typeset in Sabon
by SPi Technologies India Pvt Ltd (Straive)

Contents

Introduction	1
1 Society or person? Different ways of seeing education	15
2 A (new) third way	39
3 What is curriculum?	54
4 A pedagogical anthropology	65
5 A developmental approach	86
6 Potentialities as a basis for dispositions and skills	114
7 Skills and dispositions	138
8 Teaching and learning: some generative principles	155
9 Teacher connoisseurship and pedagogical tact	180
Conclusions	192
Index	*194*

Introduction

Introduction

Curriculum has become a highly contested term, even another battlefield for the 'culture wars' in which various liberal and conservative, cosmopolitan and nationalist ideologies compete to shape education.

In a cultural environment where dark money drives political action and influence, and dark tech controls social media and artificial intelligence (AI) (dark because the processes are largely hidden and therefore mostly unrecognized), democracy is being reduced in value because it is no longer based on reliable information and science, critical thinking and social solidarity. In this battle zone, curriculum has a significant role to play in either perpetuating this system or changing it.

This, of course, makes education political. Education has never been neutral: it shapes – and is shaped by – ideas of what society, community and human happiness or wellbeing are, or what the adult world wants children and young people to become. The question is: who knows what education should do? As teachers, we would say that teachers, school leaders and teacher educators are the experts. After climate scientists, however, teachers are perhaps the profession least trusted by authoritarian governments and right-wing media, probably because they are generally interested in and committed to social equality, diversity and truth. But there are other stakeholders whose opinions are worth listening to. As Otto Scharmer recently put it in an analysis of the future of democracy, the two areas where change can be actually brought about by people is in business and in education, because these two fields actually get things done.[1] In fact what he recommends is that business leaders, civil society activists and educators should get together in "co-generating and embodying the change we want to see". Like Otto Scharmer, we believe that the way forward is not to go back to some 'imagined greatness', nor to hold on to what we have fought for (however worthy these achievements were).

We want to craft curriculum by "leaning into and operating from an awareness of the emerging future".[2] Scharmer cites Nobel prize-winner Ilya Prigogine's idea that "when a system is far from equilibrium, small islands of coherence in a sea of chaos have the capacity to lift the entire system to a higher order".[3] Crafting a curriculum is an act that could be described in these terms: it can create islands of coherence, especially when they link up to ecosystems of coherence within the educational world. Scharmer's methods involve realigning attention, intention and agency. His recommendations for the three major societal systems are:

1 Economies need to shift from running on ego-systems to eco-system awareness.
2 Democracies and governance systems must break their gridlock to become more dialogic, data-driven, distributed and direct.
3 Our learning systems must change from teaching for testing towards an education for human flourishing in ways that activate our deep capacities for co-sensing and co-creating the emerging future.

We see our approach to crafting curriculum as contributing to this agenda. In particular, we are interested in including a focus on human flourishing, adaptive problem solving, ethical decision-making and aesthetic perception, which the Organization for Economic Cooperation and Development (OECD) is investigating in its High Performing Systems for Tomorrow project, in which Otto Scharmer's Presencing Institute is involved.[4]

We want to move this debate on by offering an approach that integrates a focus on the development of the person with the cultivation of potentialities in the form of dispositions, habits of mind and knowledgeable skills that serve both the healthy development of the individual and society.

Transformative thinking

When new ideas, perspectives or terminology are imposed from outside or above, we think that teachers tend to respond by adding them on top of their existing tacit and explicit understandings. In many school systems, teachers are continuously asked to implement new policies and practices in the ebb and flow of educational discourse, so they get used to enacting the minimum change necessary. Many (if not most) leadership courses aim to overcome this tendency. As teachers ourselves, we think that our peers are intelligent, capable and well-intentioned people and therefore the best way to bring about change is to aim for insight and professional judgement. Insight requires us to go beyond or behind 'what works' to asking about *why* we do something.

If teachers have the space to express their pedagogical agency – and any intelligent education system will allow this – they might start with basic questions about the aims of education, and the nature of the developing human being. In our field of Steiner Waldorf education, we have always posed our colleagues the reflective question, "If what you are doing is a response to the learning and developmental needs of your students, what are those needs?" Or, to put it another way, "Why are you teaching what you are teaching – apart from the fact that it is indicated/prescribed by the curriculum? What are the deeper reasons?" It is always important to have this cascade of questions in mind, especially when planning either lessons or crafting curriculum:

- What is our starting point? The student's potential to develop as a person? Or the requirements of society and the economy? Both are important, but which has priority?
- What educational aims do we have?
- How can these aims best be achieved in a way that fosters – rather than weakens – human flourishing?

The first question may seem too philosophical and abstract for those working in schools and classrooms but we are dealing with human beings: education will have an immense impact on their lives, so we owe our students this consideration. *Whoever* designs curriculum has to start by taking a stance on the nature of the human being, the nature of society and the inseparable relationship between both. We are not educating children and youth in the abstract, but real people embedded in a nested ecological-social-cultural contexts, and therefore we need to take their actual needs into account and teach them in ways that strengthen their wellbeing and resilience. In our view, we can only answer these questions meaningfully, if we start with a pedagogical anthropology.

The anthropology we suggest in this book, mainly described in Chapter 4, may take a while to understand, because it is unfamiliar, not least because the need for a pedagogical anthropology itself is unfamiliar, so we have tried to build up the implications gradually throughout the book. Taking this perspective requires work and time, especially if we don't just add it on top of what we already practice. It permeates all levels of learning. Although it may seem pretentious to say so, it does require us to re-think educating from the inside out. In the end we may be teaching in similar ways, but we will almost certainly be doing so for different reasons and this, we believe, makes a significant difference. What we are suggesting is a major shift of perspective.

If curriculum is not just a complicated 'to-do' list for teachers to tick off, but reflects a comprehensive description of what teachers do, then it has to be thorough. Ideally, this book is a prompt for systematic reflection using whatever organizational structures you work within. We believe that the process of working through the layers of issues we mention can lead to a transforming of the way people think about curriculum and how they work with curriculum. Developing new ways of seeing and acting does not happen as a quick fix after a powerful presentation or even successful workshop, but through:

- being open to what is emerging,
- assimilating new ideas,
- putting them into your own words,
- allowing time for 'incubation',
- recalling and reconstructing them,
- applying them to your actual situation,
- using dissonance (deliberately thinking differently about these ideas, playing Devil's advocate, seeking other explanations),
- reviewing this application after a while.

The iteration of these processes eventually leads to new habits of mind with regard to curriculum practice.

Key features of the book

In this book we want to show how curriculum can be constructed (or reconstructed) in ways that serve both the person *and* the (global) community. We don't imagine that this is the only way to make curriculum, or even the best way, but we feel that it offers a perspective that may help in the current educational phase of transition from existing to emergent models.

We start with a brief history of education to show how the changing expectations, assumed functions and contexts of education have shaped what people understand as curriculum, which, if simplified, shows us two distinct, though often entangled strands:

1 The notion of *Bildung*, which has to do with the formation and self-formation of the young person, with the aim that they can subsequently develop and emancipate themselves.
2 The idea that education should prepare young people to be citizens that serve the state, the economy and civil society by learning sets of prescribed competences.

Because education is almost universally seen as a 'good thing' by adults, people value it for their children as personal, social and cultural capital. In modern times, most governments and transnational organizations, such as the OECD and UNESCO, have tended to see education as an investment in human capital. If we take a historical and international perspective, then despite the endeavours of educational philosophers, the primary functions of education are frequently taken for granted and reduced to questions of teachability (How can it be taught?) and learnability (How can it be learned?). Over the past few years, people have begun to realize that the world of work is radically changing through the application of artificial intelligence, that society, culture and political discourse are changing through social media, and that the geopolitical balance of power has fragmented and become multi-polar and unstable. In what way does all this change the role of curriculum?

Our argument is that we need to take up a Bildung perspective as a basis for common schooling and blend this with a revised idea about what skills and knowledge young people actually need to navigate their educational pathways and to equip them as persons for their lives after formal education. Our approach, which draws on the insights from Steiner/Waldorf education, is based on the following ideas. We will outline and explain each thread and then try to weave them into a coherent braid:

- Terms. We start by defining our terms, because we want to broaden the notion of curriculum.
- Historical overview. We give a brief historical overview of the two main educational approaches referred to above (Chapter 1).
- Educational aims. We discuss the possible educational aims which underpin curriculum (Chapters 2 and 3).
- Pedagogical anthropology. We introduce a pedagogical anthropology (in Chapter 4). Pedagogical means that it relates to the relationship between teaching and learning. Anthropology in this sense means an approach to understanding human beings from the inside, through self-observation and studying *with* people – children and young people – rather than external observation. This kind of anthropology is therefore participatory
- Human potentialities for flourishing. A basic assumption of this pedagogical anthropology is that every human being is born with a will to engage with the world and express and communicate their response to these experiences, which are the primary basis for potentialities. The processing of experience is what we call learning, and this leads to the development of dispositions, habitus, habits of mind, constrained and

unconstrained skills and abilities, which transform the whole person. This is what we call transformative learning. This has implications for how we describe progression in curriculum.
- A developmental approach. This approach to curriculum is based on a reading of the various developmental tasks facing students across the life course during their time in school education. These developmental tasks have various sources, some intrinsic, but most extrinsic and culturally situated and it is therefore the task of anyone designing or modifying curriculum to identify the nature of these developmental tasks at the local or national level. We offer various tools for engaging with this.
- A pathway of developmental themes. This developmental approach sees an interaction between the individual mind and its body, and social and cultural environment. However, we do not assume fixed natural stages, but rather present a model that maps out a qualitative developmental journey that we believe supports the development of the whole person and can thus have a stabilizing and harmonizing effect on the wellbeing of the student. Underpinning this developmental approach is a developmental psychology that takes the spiritual dimension of the human being into account (and we explain what we mean by this) and, in particular, how the agentic spiritual core of each person interacts with the body, with other people, with social and cultural structures and with the natural environment.
- Transformative learning. This means applying a Bildung perspective that sees learning as a process of transformation of the whole person, in the context of a series of developmental tasks.
- Generative principles for pedagogical practice. This pedagogical anthropology recognizes a number of generative heuristic principles, which can be used to construct practice, and in this case curriculum as practice. Heuristic principles are not set in stone but are living theory that can be modified by experience and subsequent research. These generative principles provide a conceptual framework for designing curriculum, and can be prioritized depending on the intentions, aims and context of any given curriculum process.
- Methods and subject didactics. Choosing teaching and learning methods that support strong learning and identifying how the various subjects can contribute to this overall development.
- Cultural perspectives. Each curriculum has to be anchored in the cultures of the communities it serves and at the same time enable students to become cosmopolitan citizens.
- Biographical intentions. Each person is engaged in a process of becoming that involves the construction of a coherent biographical narrative that gives expression to biographical intentions. It is a pedagogical task to recognize the signature of these individual biographical intentions and questions and create educational contexts that afford the person opportunities for biographical learning.
- Knowledge, skills and dispositions. We look at some of the overarching qualities that students may need to develop to meet a rapidly changing and uncertain future, such as resilience, courage, the ability to form judgements, the ability to engage in wicked problems, and intercultural and communicative skills. We look at how these can be woven into a braided curriculum (Figure I.1).

6 Crafting a Curriculum of Coherence

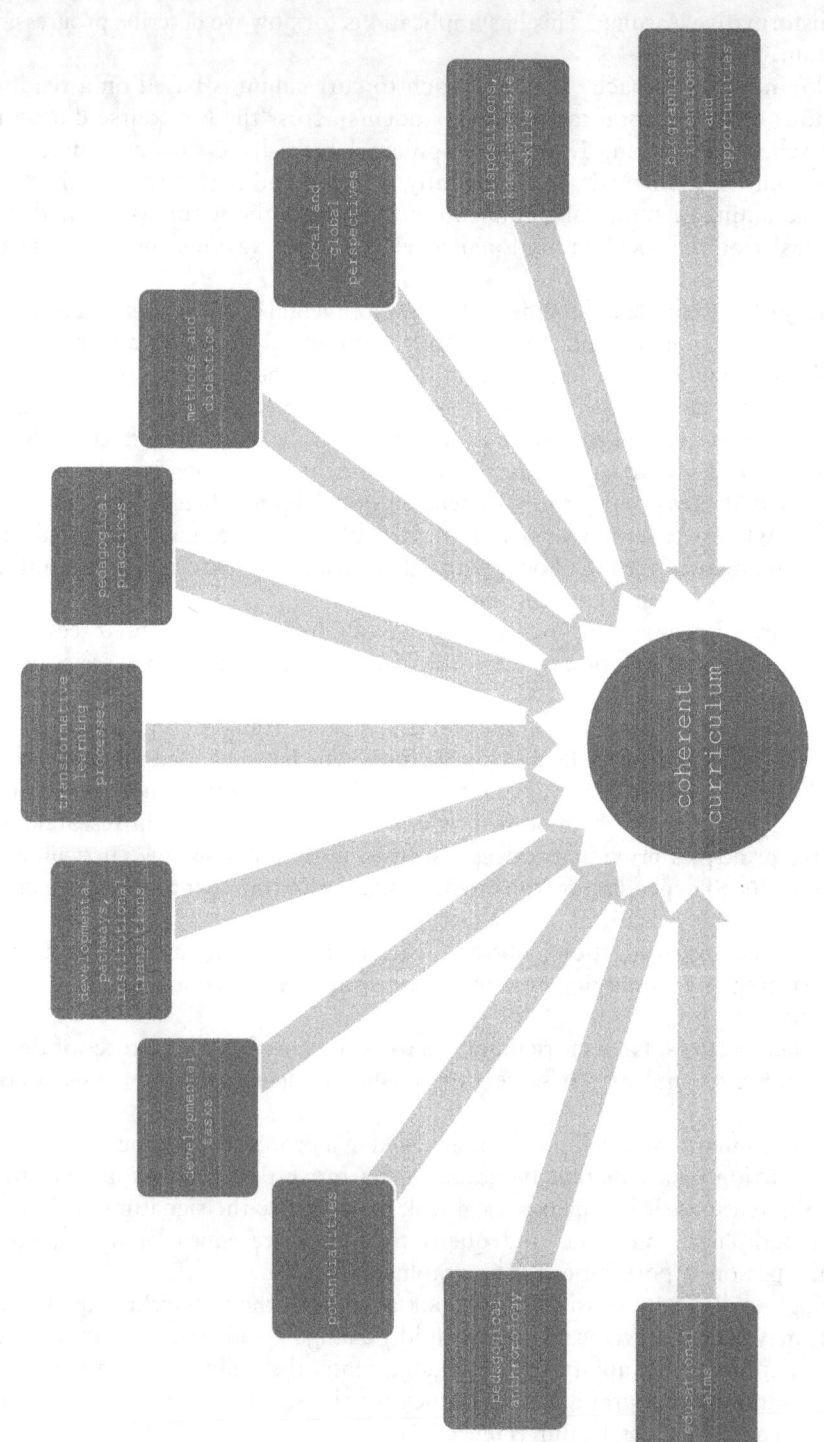

Figure 1.1 The strands that need to be braided into a coherent curriculum.

Steiner or Waldorf?

In 1919 the Austrian philosopher, esotericist, journalist, artist and well-known public speaker Rudolf Steiner (1861–1925) was asked by Emil Molt (1876–1936), entrepreneur, social reformer and owner of the Waldorf Astoria Cigarette Factory in Stuttgart in Southern Germany, to found a school for the children of the workers in his factory. In Chapter 2 we go into the background of this in more detail. The school was called the Waldorf School (*die Waldorfschule*) and Steiner always referred to the education as Waldorf (*Waldorfpädagogik*). The Waldorf School and its educational ideas soon inspired schools in other parts of Germany but also, even during the 1920s in Switzerland, England, the Netherlands, New York, Norway and Hungary. Since then, some schools are called Steiner schools (notably in Scandinavia) or Waldorf schools (e.g. Germany, USA and Canada). Countries like the UK have used both terms and even combined them as Steiner-Waldorf. And some countries use neither term. In the Netherlands, they are known as Vrije Schools – meaning independent schools. In the academic world, the education is usually referred to as Steiner education. Other schools are named after other interesting people (such as Martyn's school, the Christian Morgenstern School in Hamburg). The difference is whether one aligns with the man or with the educational movement that spread from the original Waldorf School (few appear to have qualms about naming an education after a cigarette brand). With due respect to Steiner, we prefer the name Waldorf. We use the terms Steiner and Waldorf in this context synonymously, however.

We both have a background in Waldorf education and mainstream education at early years, school and higher education levels. But we are basing this book primarily on our experiences of crafting curriculum within the international Waldorf community. We think we have something to offer both educational fields – Waldorf and non-Waldorf. Establishing Waldorf education in around 70 countries has been a remarkable achievement for the international Waldorf movement over the past 107 years, considering that it has no central, directing organization, with a masterplan for development and expansion. The Waldorf movement has grown rhizomically from an 'invisible' network of ideas and personal relationships and schools emerge wherever conditions are conducive (and often where they are not). Schools grow, divide, spread from initial hubs and, occasionally, wither for lack of resources. Though they all share a common educational vision, they interpret this in all kinds of culturally specific ways, often reflecting the ideals of the people who founded the school. But anyone visiting a Waldorf school – from Kathmandu to Cape Town, from British Columbia to Chengdu – will easily recognize the distinctive features of the education and when a thousand or so teachers from all over the world meet in Switzerland every four years for a World Waldorf Teachers Conference, there is a great sense of commonality and solidarity. In the Western world, there has sometimes been a suspicion of a secular education that is explicitly based on a recognition of spirituality, sometimes a fear that Waldorf schools are the front for a cult. They aren't and anyone who knows teachers, students and parents at actually existing Waldorf schools can verify this.

Waldorf education has largely kept its light under a bushel – an interesting biblical metaphor that implies that its inner spiritual light has been protected and shielded from too much exposure. This has mainly to do with the fact that Waldorf education is based on – and has grown out of – anthroposophy, or what its founder Rudolf Steiner also called spiritual science. It is this aspect that makes sceptical critics suspicious because they identify spirituality with religion and the esoteric with secret and hidden knowledge and thus with cults. This view is understandable when one looks at the translated titles of some of Steiner's work, such as *Occult Science*.

As Martyn has shown elsewhere,[5] until recently Waldorf education aligned itself with the whole of anthroposophy, and even referred to itself as anthroposophical pedagogy. This has led some critics, such as Professor Heiner Ullrich,[6] to advise Waldorf education that its anthroposophical theory is unscientific, despite considering it to be an excellent educational practice, based on his own empirical studies and those of other researchers,[7]. As Martyn and others[8] have argued, Waldorf education actually does builds on *some* elements of anthroposophy, but by no means all. Those foundations include Steiner's theory of knowledge and ethics (as outlined in his book *Philosophy of Freedom*), his pedagogical anthropology, his social theory and his lectures on education – all of which get a mention in this book. More importantly, the stance we take is that Steiner's pedagogical anthropology and its implications were the starting point of this educational approach, rather than the finished product, and that one hundred years (literally at the time of writing this sentence) after Steiner's death, this education has grown and evolved. The problem arises when some people identify the basis of Waldorf education as anthroposophy and define this as everything Steiner said or wrote (i.e. in the 350 volumes of his Complete Works).

What do we mean by curriculum?

Along with a broad spectrum of key educational terms – learning, development, competence, learning aims, learning outcomes, learning environments and so on – the term curriculum is remarkably culturally situated and also contested. This makes it necessary to define these terms when they are used in any international context. To this end, we offer the following explanation of how we use these terms.[9]

We understand curriculum as:

- What is taught. This covers specific curriculum content, themes and topics.
- How it is taught. This includes the methods of teaching and learning used, the learning environment and school climate, the activities that learners engage in and focuses on the way the learning is arranged and structured.
- When it is taught. This mainly refers to the age-relatedness of the pedagogy, which clearly differs between early years and high school, with many graded variations between. In a narrower sense, it takes the chronobiology (the science of biological rhythms) of learning into account and considers how time is a factor in the learning process, whether it is the time of day, the rhythms of learning over days, weeks, months and years, and even seasonal aspects (are levels of attention different in summer or winter?). All these factors relate to student receptivity and alertness, and whether learning is given time to mature, ripen, develop, consolidate, and so on. The quality of time is an important, often-intangible factor in learning, which does not assume that learning only occurs with fully-alert daytime consciousness but has periods of unconscious gestation, incubation, sorting, associating and enriching.
- Where it is taught. The location of learning plays an important role, whether this is in the classic frontal classroom, the arrangement of classroom furniture (e.g. facilitating group work, individual work stations etc.), or whether the learning takes place in specialist spaces such as laboratories, sports halls, art studios, theatres, craft workshops

etc. Perhaps the learning takes place in outdoor classrooms (i.e. workspaces outside), or in field trips in nature, in cultural spaces (art galleries, museums, public institutions) and through work placements and internships.
- Who teaches it. The who covers the whole range of persons in formal and informal roles from whom others may learn, including teachers in the classic sense of trained professionals but also people who take on the role temporarily in guiding the learning process, for example in the workplace, in museum pedagogy through educators or docents (US), and experts who come into school to share their experiences. It includes peers within the learning community and indeed the learning community itself, which provides a learning environment. There is another dimension to this, namely that of the person of the teacher. Ideally, teachers have high levels of professional skill and values that include a high respect for the students as developing human beings. The basic attitude that educators need is an awareness that every individual has potential that is not always apparent, but the active assumption that this potential is real can contribute to shaping learning environments in which this potential can be realized, at least in part.
- Why it is taught. Whatever teachers teach, how, where and when they teach it, it is because there are good reasons for doing so and that the teachers can express this in their own words if asked. In other words, all pedagogical practice is informed by theory – that is to say, there is a reason why it is being taught. Ideally, these reasons have to do with enabling the healthy development of the students and not simply because "it is prescribed in the curriculum". In effect, the reason why something is taught, the way it is taught (and where and when), that is, the intentions behind this choice of material or method, is known to the teacher. This knowing can be that of a novice or an expert, but there is a deliberate and conscious intention behind it, and that any unconscious intentions – what is known as the hidden curriculum – are brought to light.

We believe that curriculum needs re-inventing if it is to serve the actual needs of learners and society as a whole. Since we use a very broad definition of curriculum, this has major implications for schools. An 18-year-old student said to Martyn in school recently, "I don't think that the basic concept of school has changed in a hundred years – what do you think Mr. Rawson?" Martyn's short response was, yes that is fundamentally true, though there have been many changes in the way it's done.

Of course, it is important to bear in mind that we are always dealing with curriculum as intended, curriculum as espoused (for example, in policy documents or texts) and curriculum as practiced,[10] including the lived experience of those who 'enjoy' or 'suffer' it. The tensions between these different modalities are what makes the issue so complex. In order to narrow the gap between these positions, we suggest that curriculum should, firstly, offer orientation, secondly, be provisional in nature, and, thirdly, be under regular review.

Crafting curriculum

Initially, we were concerned that using the word 'crafting' in the title might lead the casual browser to think it was a book about crafts. However, there are compelling reasons for choosing this term, which was inspired by three main sources. The first is Richard Sennett's[11] book *The Craftsman*, which refers to the values that are associated with traditional craftsmanship, for which we suggest the gender neutral form, *crafting*. The essence of this approach is that if we want to make something as well as we can, then this not only improves the quality of what we make, but is also good for our wellbeing. Crafting also implies an interest in, even a love for, the materials and tools and for the sensory experiences connected to the activity. This idea is also closely aligned to Tim Ingold's[12] work on thinking through making and making as a social practice. Ingold shows how making creates knowledge and shapes environments and thereby forms the human being in body and mind, because we are sentient beings – that is, beings who live in a world of rich sensory experiences. Making influences the way we perceive the world, because it schools or educates the way we notice, observe, watch, listen and feel – in other words what we learn. Ingold speaks of the process of entering into a mutual relation of correspondence with the things we are working with or researching, a gesture which opens our perception of the world and which we can in turn answer to, in a way akin to craft work. The third source was Bernard Graves' book *Crafting: Transforming materials and the maker*,[13] which itself was inspired by traditional notions of crafting and making and emphasizes the aspects of transformation of the maker and the material, as well as the value of localization and sustainability. Crafting promotes an integrated approach to handicrafts that sources materials locally, uses tools with a long evolution, and which acknowledges how our language and our bodies have been shaped by what we make. Among the roots of these meanings is Aristotle's term *poiesis*, which means making things for a purpose. The term *autopoiesis* refers to the process of self-formation. Therefore, the notion of crafting implies self-formation through making and doing and the knowledge and culture we create by doing so.

Crafting a curriculum therefore means not just doing it, but also implies the ethos of crafting both in the making and its potential transformation of the curriculum 'material' and its makers. The crafting process is autopoietic (or self-forming) and this is a basic educational function of curriculum for the learners and the teachers.

Making or crafting something requires knowledge of the properties and qualities of the 'material'. Though properties of real (as opposed to metaphorical) materials are supposed to be objective and fixed, whereas qualities are deemed subjective, in practice materials can and do change their properties, so that even the properties of materials are not essential but historical, which means they have stories. In Ingold's words,

> In following their materials practitioners do not so much interact with them as correspond with them...Making, then, is a process of correspondence: not the imposition of preconceived form on raw material substance, but the drawing out or bringing forth of potentials immanent in a world of becoming. In the phenomenal world, every material is such a becoming, one path or trajectory through a maze of trajectories.
>
> (2013, p. 31)[14]

In our case we are not artisans making a physical object but educators making a curriculum, which may be documented on paper or digitally, but is a complex set of ideas. The 'materials' we are working with are people, activities, places, ideas and structures, but we still need to know them and understand the appropriate tools to work with them and their origins and contexts.

Connoisseurship

Another key term in this approach is connoisseurship. This was coined in educational contexts by Elliott Eisner to refer to the skill that teachers as reflective practitioners need to "make fine-grained discriminations among complex and subtle qualities... Connoisseurship is the art of appreciation."[15] Appreciation is the ability to recognize the meaning and value of experiences in context and is the basis for making judgements. It is a form of knowing-in-practice. In a wine taster, this skill is one of discernment based on acquired knowledge and the development of the relevant sensory processes in the palette and "high levels of qualitative intelligence", which enable the taster to compare the immediate taste and smell with other wines. It is a kind of knowledgeable perception, that starts with a heightened awareness in the moment of the experience. It is therefore an example of what the ancient Greeks called *aisthesis*, which referred to the knowing process in the act of sensory perception. Connoisseurship requires the ability to apply the right, which means appropriate, criteria to judge a situation. It is the ability, for example, to become aware of all the factors that influence students' learning, including understanding developmental tasks and an individual's biographical mythos.[16] Thus, connoisseurship is a quality that is needed to craft curriculum at all levels.

Some other key terms

Given the multiple sometimes subtle, sometimes distinct differences in the meanings of key words used in educational discourse internationally, we want to start by briefly explaining what we mean when we use the following terms, and we will revisit these throughout the book when they come up. A recent editorial in the *Asia-Pacific Journal of Teacher Education* pointed out that though English remains the *lingua franca* of international academic discourse in Asia, the question of translation in the age of AI requires careful handling. They cite the important German terms *Erziehung*, *Bildung* and *Ausbildung*, all of which are translated as education, which itself may be understood as schooling, though there are important differences between them.[17] Some terms are simply untranslatable but need explanation. Within each educational culture – another term we would like to define – these terms are often taken for granted, but anyone who moves between cultures and countries will find that we may use the term differently. Furthermore, the meanings of such basic terms as learning, competence or Bildung, change over time as they are co-opted by various political policies or because the educational philosophy shifts its focus. Sometimes these changes are deliberate, often not.

Bildung. We use this term a lot and it is slippery because even in German where it originates it has multiple meanings. The German term Bildung (and its longer form *Selbstbildung*) is usually translated as self-formation, though it can be argued that autopoiesis (literally self-making) contains all the senses implied by self-activity and self-formation,[18] and has a rich and diverse pedigree. The educationalist Christian Rittelmeyer[19] refers to the semantic field of Bildung as being like walking through a landscape; each time we stop to take in the scenery, we get a different perspective depending on our standpoint. What all the perspectives that the notion of Bildung offers have in common is the central idea of self-formation in a cultural context. As such, it is an idea with deep rhizomic 'roots' going back to Ancient Greece, Confucius, and Mencius in China, which is why the educational philosophy of Bildung is being taken up in transformed ways by contemporary neo-Confucian thinkers. Today in the German-speaking world it can be synonymous with education, as used in such terms as *Bildungsplan* and *Bildungsstandards*, where the formation of people implied is clearly institutionalized in schools, colleges and universities, though the word still has the wider sense of self-education or self-improvement through learning, which can and does happen outside of institutions. Some scholars argue that terms like *Bildungsstandards* are tautological, since the essence of Bildung is that it cannot be standardized, but is individual, as suggested in the term *Selbstbildung* – self-formation. Traditionally Bildung has been the educational philosophy of Central Europe, the German-speaking world, the Netherlands and Scandinavia, since the Protestant Reformation and the Age of Enlightenment, which saw self-formation as an act of emancipation from traditional Catholic religion through rationality and self-improvement.

Education. Education comes etymologically from the Latin *educare* (constructed from *ed* = ex = out + *ducere* = to lead, to draw out), therefore meaning to lead or draw out, and has always meant both upbringing and schooling, even if today this has become institutionalized as schooling. As Gert Biesta[20] has discussed, the relationship between the German terms Bildung and *Erziehung*, which has a meaning close to education in this sense of leading, highlights the distinction between Bildung, which is essentially self-activity and education/*Erziehung*, the basic nature of which is, someone teaching someone else something with purpose. In other words, it is intentionally relational *and* asymmetric, because the implication is that the one who is leading knows more than the one being led. However, Biesta's point is that the teaching can be better understood in a Bildung context as the teacher drawing the student's attention to something by pointing to it, in such a way that the student engages with it, forms a relationship to it and becomes transformed through the process.[21] The idea originated with the early 19th-century German educational philosopher Johann Friedrich Herbart (1776–1841). Thus, the learning process becomes one of self-formation rather than one of the students being formed, moulded or otherwise shaped and 'filled up' by the teacher and the school system, which is basically the aim of most school education today.

Pedagogy We use the term pedagogy in the sense of the art, craft and science of the relationship between teaching and learning.[22] Pedagogy (the last syllable being pronounced like *gee*) or pedagogics (which is often pronounced like Gog and Magog) is less commonly used in the Anglophone educational discourse. Even less common is the term for those who practice it, the somewhat awkward *pedagogue*. Perhaps its closeness to paediatrics, the medical term for treating children, which sounds technical or even the abhorred term paedophile (etymologically someone who likes children) is the reason for avoiding it. Even though it is less common in English, we think it is a useful term because it emphasizes the education-as-an-art-and-craft aspect of teaching and implies that teaching is a process of crafting learning situations involving connoisseurship.

Didactics Most dictionaries define didactics as systematic instruction or teaching and the intentions or purposes behind this. Thus, subject didactics refers to the reasons why particular school subjects, such as maths or geography, are taught, which usually go beyond simple facilitating knowledge of the subject. The aim of teaching something may be in order to instil a love for reading, or to cultivate a sense of cosmopolitan citizenship, or to school the powers of logical thinking. So, didactics is more than simply what is taught, it includes why it is taught and how it is taught.

Educational culture and discourse Culture is, of course, a very slippery and contested word. We use it in this book to refer to the set of educational practices and beliefs that are common to a certain group of people and the effect this has on those who experience this, such as students, teachers, parents and the general public. Of course, actual practices and the beliefs, philosophy or theory that inform these practices may not align and may be paradoxical or contested, but that condition also characterizes the educational culture – it always depends on the perspective. An educational discourse simply refers to the various ways people talk and write about the education.

The structure of the book

The kind of curriculum we are suggesting, and the processes involved in making (or remaking or modifying an existing curriculum), involves a number of factors mentioned above that we actually need to understand all at once. This doesn't really match the linear way books are usually organized, so we have tried to develop the idea in an iterative way. That means we start with an overall definition of curriculum, then explain in greater detail in successive chapters the background and implications of each factor, whilst looping what we have already said into the braid we are plaiting – an idea that may be easier to follow in practice than in this somewhat theoretical explanation. Though the chapters contain discrete contents, the process has to be thought of as something fluid and accumulative, like weaving a basket using willow. The succession of stages are merely snapshots of the whole.

The overall structure of our approach to curriculum follows the following sequence. After outlining a brief history of education to show why a new approach to curriculum is needed, we start the curriculum work with the idea of development by describing the nature of the human being from a holistic Waldorf perspective. As stated above, this draws on Steiner's pedagogical anthropology and how this has been adapted with the Waldorf discourse over the past hundred years or so. This leads to the more recent sociological idea of developmental tasks, which places curriculum practice into both a psychological and a sociological context. On the basis of this pedagogical anthropology and an awareness of the developmental tasks, we can draw up a set of generative principles that enable us to develop and evaluate practice. The next step is back to the human being, as it were, in order to account for the origins and development of potentialities, dispositions and knowledgeable skills. This takes us to steps of the learning process and the different modes of teaching and learning that this implies. The way we teach, or rather the learning opportunities that we create, have an impact on how students apply their energy and, on their wellbeing and resilience. It also influences whether students learn the self-efficacy, agency and courage that are primary requirements for navigating life today.

Pulling this together we arrive at our concept of a layered curriculum. Then we offer examples and guidelines for selecting the topics, experiences, subject knowledge and activities that make up the coherent curriculum – coherent because the parts 'hang together'.

Tasks for the reader

Before reading further in this book, it might be helpful to reflect and write down what aspects of crafting curriculum you think are important and why, and perhaps list them in terms of priority.

Notes

1 Scharmer, C. O. (2024). An emerging third option: reclaiming democracy from dark money and dark tech. Seven observations on 2024 and what's next. *Field of the Future Blog.* https://medium.com/presencing-institute-blog/an-emerging-third-option-reclaiming-democracy-from-dark-money-dark-tech-3886bcd0469b.
2 Cited from the article above.
3 Cited in the article above.
4 https://www.oecd.org/en/about/projects/pisa-high-performing-systems-for-tomorrow-hpst.html.

5 Rawson, M. (2021). *Steiner Waldorf Pedagogy in Schools. A critical introduction*. Routledge; Rawson, M. (2025). Types of discourses about Anthroposophy in relation to Waldorf education. In *Research on Steiner Education*, 16(1).
6 Ullrich, H.-. (2024). The Educational Discourse on Waldorf Education in Germany. In A.-K. Hoffmann & G. C. Buck (Eds.), *Critically Assessing the Reputation of Waldorf Education in Academia and the Public. Early endeavours of expansion, 1919–1955* (Vol. 1, pp. 22–46). Routledge.
7 The research is summarized in Tyson, R. (2023). Theoretical Research on Waldorf/Steiner Education – a Review in *Research on Steiner Education*, 14(2).
8 Such as Schieren, J. (2022). Anthroposophy under fire. *Art of Education Erziehungskunst*, May 2022. https://www.artofeducating.org/article/anthroposophy-under-fire.
9 We draw on the definition of curriculum offered by Dahlin, B. (2017). *Rudolf Steiner. The Relevance of Waldorf Education*. This definition is located within the landscape of Bildung and is also specific to Waldorf education.
10 This idea is borrowed from Ball S. J., & Bowe, R. (1992). Subject departments and the 'implementation' of National Curriculum policy. *Journal of Curriculum Studies*, 24(2), 97–115.
11 Sennett, R. (2008). *The Craftsman*. Penguin Books.
12 Ingold, T. (2013). *Making. Anthropology, Archaeology and Architecture*. Routledge. (Kindle edition), pp. 2–3. See also Ingold, T. (2025). *Old Ways, New People. Anthropology and/as Education* (second revised edition ed.). Routledge, p. 89.
13 Graves, B., & Code, L. (Eds.). (2019). *Transforming through Crafting. How traditional crafts and practical skills can enhance education*. Handson Press.
14 Ingold, T. Making: Anthropology, Archaeology, Art and Architecture. (Function). Kindle Edition, p. 31.
15 Eisner, E. W. (2017). *The Enlightened Eye. Qualitative Inquiry and the enhancement of educational practice*. Teachers College Press.
16 See van Manen, M. (2015). *Pedagogical Tact*. Left Coast Press.
17 Biesta, G.G, Takayama, K., Kettle, M. and Heimans, S. (2025). How to say in English what you cannot say in English? Dilemmas of 'global' scholarship and small steps forward. *Asia-Pacific Journal of Teacher Education*, 53(2), 135–137.
18 See Vinterbo-Hohr, A., & Hohr, H. (2006). The neo-humanistic concept of Bildung going astray: Comments to Friedrich Schiller's thoughts on education. *Educational Philosophy and Theory*, 38(2), 215–230.
19 Rittelmeyer, C. (2012) *Bildung: Ein pädagogischer Grundbegriff* (Bildung: A fundamental pedagogical concept). Kohlmeyer.
20 Biesta, G. J. J. (2021). *World-centred Education. A view for the present*. Routledge.
21 Biesta draws on the work of the German educational scholar Dieter Benner, who elaborates this meaning of Erziehung. See Benner, D. (2015). Erziehung und Bildung! (Education and Bildung!). *Zeitschrift für Pädagogik*, 61(4), 481–496, and, on Klaus Prange, (2012). Die Zeigestruktur der Erziehung. 2nd Edition. Ferdinand Schöningh.
22 We borrow this meaning the from the book by Nind, M., Curtin, A., & Hall, K. (2016). *Research Methods for Pedagogy*. Bloomsbury.

1 Society or person? Different ways of seeing education

Overview

Many approaches to curriculum today are pragmatic and instrumentalist and take for granted what the purposes of education are. In order to craft curriculum, we first need to locate it in a bigger picture of educational philosophy. With a very brief history of formal education in the West, we show how different philosophical perspectives have shaped curriculum design.

The present (im)perfect

Educational practice has mainly been shaped by people who were not teachers. This sentence contains the verb form present perfect (here appropriately in the passive mood – has been shaped by) which refers to a state of being that began in the past, continues into the present and is expected to last into the immediate future. The educational present has been, in our view imperfectly, shaped by the educational past, but the emerging future is summonsing quite a different education into being, one that could involve teachers, those responsible for teacher education and research far more. This new education has many precursors, including Waldorf education, and other innovative approaches, such as those of John Dewey, Maria Montessori, Martha Muchow, Lev Vygotsky, Margaret McMillan, Lucy Wheelock, Mary Jane McLeod Bethune, Harald Rugg, Jerome Bruner, Elliott Eisner, Guy Claxton, Ron Berger, Gert Biesta, and many others (to name some of our favourites, readers are encouraged to do an internet search on these interesting people).

Since the advent of public universal education (which for most Western countries began after the middle of the 19th century), education has been dominated by two contradictory approaches, each with multiple versions. The first focuses on the individual and their development as a person. The second sees education as meeting the needs of society – producing good workers, soldiers, citizens and administrators. Neither model is ideal for the demands of the present – hence imperfect.

Many education systems have elements of both these perspectives, but policymakers have tended to prioritize one. In order to understand why education needs re-thinking, we need to look briefly at the history of formal education.

A very short history of formal education (in the West)

Early history

Formal education is very much part of the narrative of progress. Indeed, it is seen as both a cause and a hallmark of progress, which is why people want it for their children and why they want the best possible version of it that money or their vote can buy. This also makes education highly contested. Since there are different versions of progress and civilization, so too there are different versions of what the best education is. Most people would agree that education should mirror the vision of society that they aspire to or wish to hold on to. The ideal society that they wish to be part of, or that they wish to maintain, is very much seen as requiring the right kind of education to maintain it.

But before we look at some of the competing visions of society and the kind of education they believe will serve the society they want, it is worth recalling briefly that over the course of 98% of human history, human culture did not have formal education. Margaret Mead,[1] the anthropologist, aptly described the transition from hunter-gatherer societies to farming and urban societies as a transition from learning societies to teaching societies.

Hunter-gatherer-pastoralist societies were generally egalitarian without power hierarchies and stratified social structures. Daily life was organized so that children were welcome to observe and join in when they were ready. The work was adjusted so that they could participate. Thus, children learned by doing, accompanied by narrative that gave context to all the complex things they needed to learn in order to contribute to their community. We should by no means underestimate the skills and knowledge required by nomadic forager-hunters to make the most of their environment, or to remember and understand the vast universe of myth, legend, tradition, custom, song and spirituality they inhabited, not to mention the usual complexities of human social life. And indeed, this method of informal and incidental learning through participation, supported by extensive narrative, remains a very effective way of learning many skills and much knowledge in certain situations even today. Many people working successfully in IT were not formally trained, not least because the systems and programmes change so rapidly. Their skills were acquired through participation in communities of practice, dispositions to reading the 'code', intuition, improvisation and no doubt a certain amount of trial and error.

Hierarchical, urban societies introduced a division of labour, meaning that people needed to be trained for their role in life. Literacy was required for administrators, priests and artists, but not generally for farmers, craftspeople or soldiers – and certainly not for slaves, who did much of the work in most ancient urban civilizations. Formal education was for the elites who already possessed significant cultural capital, which is why education for most of history has not been democratic but aristocratic. At a later stage in history, generally speaking during the Axial Age (starting around 500 BC) and coinciding with the emergence of Confucianism, Daoism, Buddhism, the Hebrew culture and Greek philosophy, the idea of education as part of the process of the development of the person was added. Becoming a wise person, capable of living and creating the 'good life' required the development of dispositions, habits of mind, cultivation of the body, and usually literacy. This tradition was continued within Christianity, especially in the monastic orders of the Middle Ages and within Islam in centres of scholarship.

The invention of the highly abstract technology of writing using an alphabetic code meant that formal education became necessary: this was a specific skill that could not be simply picked up by watching and participating. There is evidence from Mesopotamia, Ancient India, Egypt, China and Mesoamerica, that once writing became an essential cultural technique for state governance, chronicling important narratives, recoding meaning-giving myths and rituals, formal education was introduced. During the Global Middle Ages when the writing down of religious texts was important for the consolidation and spreading of religious ideas, there was always a tension between texts as a basis for orthodoxy, and their function of allowing access to other ideas and the transmission of powerful stories. The translation of texts, notably in those great cosmopolitan centres such as Gondishapur, Baghdad, Alexandria, Timbuktu, Padua and Toledo, was vital to intercultural Bildung. Mathematics became important once the quantity and complexity of numerical counting systems increased, and with this development, other applications of mathematics for astronomy, land surveying, navigation, inventories and divination also required formal teaching.

With the invention of flexible, relatively fast printing technologies and the expansion of widespread literacy in some societies (e.g. the Chinese imperial exam system, Islamic universities, England in the Age of Shakespeare) and the new access to classical texts, literacy became a more central part of education.

Modernity

The Reformation of Christianity led to new educational ideas. Protestantism taught redemption through self-improvement through literacy and education. There were actually two main streams of Protestant thinking relevant to education. The Lutheran version (Northern Germany and the Nordic countries) taught rationality and virtuous national citizenship, whilst the evangelical stream represented by reformers such as Ulrich Zwingli (1484–1531), John Calvin (1509–1564) and Comenius (1592–1670), who taught universal values through a universal education, spread from Moravia to Switzerland (and southern Germany) to Scotland and from there to the USA. Calvin's teachings influenced the Presbyterianism, Congregational and Reformed Churches and emphasized the virtue of work as a means to celebrate the good life, and this required knowledge and a dedicated education. This stream valorized piety and hard work (as exemplified by Weber's Protestant Work Ethic), individualism and the autonomy of the person, gilded with (often Quaker) philanthropism. Northern Protestantism via Martin Luther, however, taught obedience to the state, as seen in the Nordic notion of the social state.[2] Johann Friedrich Herbart (1776–1841) was influential, both in terms of establishing the modern study of psychology and in its relevance for education. For Herbart, Bildung as education involved the direction of attention by a teacher (or later self-direction) to what is important, to concepts that order and make sense of the mass of experiences. Such formative experiences will be most effective if they make a lasting emotional impression that leads to the formation of dispositions that accumulate to form a tableau of inner images that give structure and meaning to the biographical sequence and thus a sense of self. We will take up Herbart's theory of aesthetic judgment later.

In the 19th century, Comenius' ideas about education became highly influential, including structuring education systems into early years, elementary, secondary and tertiary levels. Drawing on the ideas of his contemporaries, Francis Bacon and Rene Descartes, he advocated for an understanding of the nature of the developing human being identified by rational, scientific observation. He also emphasized subject matter as didactics and the importance of teaching methods such as immersion in the language, and observation of phenomena, starting with what is familiar to the child, and learning about the child's actual world, not just through texts and classical literature.

In this respect Comenius anticipated the work of Rousseau, who sought to protect childhood innocence, Pestalozzi, who is famous for wanting to balance the work of head, heart and hands, and Fröbel, who created the notion of *kindergarten* and argued that nature was the ideal environment for children to develop their senses and awareness of the world around them through practical and meaningful tasks, and who also emphasized the importance of play.

Comenius' ideal that everyone should be educated is very much still a theme in UNESCO's drive for education towards sustainability, which specifically includes gender equality in educational opportunity, something which has not yet been globally achieved, and in the multiple ways that people are disadvantaged in education.

The Nonconformist and Dissenter traditions of England in the 17th and 18th centuries contributed even more radical ideas about education, by virtue of their belief that the spirit manifests in everyone, including women, children and the poor. The practice of subversive 'hedge schools', in effect hidden free schools, was a counterbalance to state-controlled education, and particularly against the dominance of Church schools. Later, hedge schools were subversive in promoting a non-British colonial education in places like Ireland (where they were known as scoil chois claí, scoil ghairid and scoil scairte) and were either Catholic, when Catholic Irish nationalism was being suppressed, Presbyterian or otherwise Nonconformist. This tradition continues in home schooling and the small-school movements that wish to avoid state control.

In many ways the Reform School movement in Germany at the beginning of the 20th century grew out of this tradition, also influenced by John Dewey's (1859–1952) ideas that educational should be both experiential and democratic. Dewey also emphasized the importance of communication and dialogue in education and of creating environments as close to real life as possible, in which children could make discoveries accompanied by strong affects and guided by teachers but generating meaning through dialogue. He also emphasized the need for children to develop habits of mind and dispositions to learning through and from their experiences.

Education for society

With industrialization and the emergence of nation-states from the 18th century onwards, education began to be seen by the authorities as the way to producing an educated workforce and loyal national citizens. Settler-colonial nations such as the USA needed mass education to support the assimilation of mass immigration through a common language, common values and a new patriotism. Colonial nations in Europe needed education to reinforce their national/imperial identity and subsequently to colonize and 'civilize' the peoples in their colonies, once these had been suppressed, and emergent new nations needed universal education to establish national identities and a common national language. The rise of workers' power through trades unions, socialist political parties, the women's rights and civil rights movements contributed the notion of education for all as a means to emancipation, as promoted by Marx and Engels and leading socialists such as Rosa Luxemburg, Margaret McMillan and Antonio Gramsci. Rudolf Steiner's motives for Waldorf education also reflected his wish to emancipate (in his terms) the proletariat through a free education.[3]

Neoliberal policy technologies

In the 1960s and 1970s, education in many Western countries was characterized by progressive ideas related to social justice and emancipation and a pluralism of approaches, with a smaller core of traditional humanist, often private institutions. During the Thatcher (1979–1990) and Reagan (1981–1989) years, education became a neoliberal project run along the lines of a business, using the policy tools of standardization, performativity and managerialism.[4] Across the globe, this has led to national curricula with specified learning outcomes and standards, often controlled by inspections and measures of school quality, and marketized through league tables. The OECD Programme for International Student Assessment (PISA) became an international league table that compares systems as different as Finland and Denmark with their high levels of teacher autonomy, with systems with rigidly controlled standards, such as South Korea and Singapore. Politicians have argued direct links between curriculum policies and PISA results. In England, with its detailed National Curriculum, statutory testing and tightly controlled regulatory and inspection systems, there have been rapid and ongoing revisions, modifications, and prioritizations. Research shows both improvements (increased standards in literacy and numeracy, and a corresponding ascent of the PISA tables) but also deteriorations (the unhappiest students[5] and a reduction in the number of children reading for pleasure – only 2 in 5[6]).

In an age of neoliberalism, two ideological forces have been at work in education. The first is cost saving for the state through managerialism (running schools like businesses), standardization (of teaching material and curricula) and privatization of provision (charter schools, academies who contract to run 'state' schools, prisons, hospital welfare services, border controls, public utilities etc.). One of the most radical examples of this is in Sweden, where profit-making privatization of public education has been allowed. This leads to an increasing commodification of education, where schools compete for pupils through their success in national examinations and league tables, through their branding and PR, and also through their ability to provide their pupils with some sort of advantage (for example, through extra-curricular activities and facilities). Educational ideals that might be considered more broadly worth striving for are often neglected. The OECD's governance of schooling, which emphasizes transnationally valid generic competencies, also exemplifies the movement towards a certain functional performativity (Uljens, 2022, vii)

The second ideological force is the notion that education should serve the needs of the economy, driving economic growth and international competitiveness. As 'knowledge economies' become more prevalent, their employment markets require flexible workers who can change jobs and even professions regularly – no more jobs for life in an industry or civil service. This means a focus on science, technology, economics and lifelong learning. Following the collapse of the Soviet Union and the emergence of many small nations (some new, some old), education was also seen as vital in the creation of national identities. Even those of the left began to see the necessity of a neoliberal 'third way' (e.g. in the UK New Labour period 1997–2007), which sought to blend social democracy with market-orientated policy tools.

Ideological influence in practice

From 1945 up until the late 1970s, anglophone and many other Western countries had innovative, progressive education systems as part of a welfare state set up for war veterans, their families and their offspring, the baby-boomers. This education also gave voice to civil rights, women's rights, anti-war and anti-nuclear movements, and the optimism of the Age of Rock and Roll and Woodstock. There was much experimentation and even a de-schooling/home schooling movement. The rapid growth of the Waldorf movement in this period was part of this mood of optimism and the sense that we could change the world.

In schools, teachers generally had considerable autonomy. Local authorities had an influence and government funded it. The downside was a lack of cohesion, poor leadership, patchy quality and parents having little say in the education of their children (leading to many founding their own schools). The whole thing cost more than the state could afford, especially after the oil crisis of the early 1970s, when 'Third World' oil-producing countries used their postcolonial powers and consciousness to make the West pay so that they could develop. In the US, Reagan, and in the UK, Thatcher (joined by New Zealand, the Canadian province Alberta, and the Australian state of Victoria), reacted and introduced market processes into state education alongside national minimum standards. This did not lead immediately to improvements, but generally to more competition between schools, tensions between schools and government inspectorates, stress between schools and parents and much resistance on the part of teachers who felt the loss of their autonomy and challenge to their professionalism.

This phase was followed by the full-blown top-down introduction of educational market forces and standardization. This was no longer only the response of the political right but was led by people like the US Democrat president Bill Clinton, though such policies became globalized through transnational organizations such as the World Bank and the OECD. This major second phase of education was characterized by increased competition within schools, between schools, between countries driven by league tables and rankings based on testing, a prescribed, detailed content curriculum, with key stage testing regimes and school inspections, with threats of school closures or 'special measures'. The professionalism of teaching was undermined by moving away from academic teacher qualifications to increased school-based training and a bonanza for the educational publishing industry which was invited to provide fine-grained, step-by-step teaching materials.

The benefits of this approach are, by most objective accounts, minimal; some standards improved but marketizing education only exacerbated the trend towards those with money being able to access the 'best' education, as measured by exam results. The more measurements for success that were introduced, the more people, both students and teachers, ended up being losers and failures. There was a massive reduction in levels of professional enjoyment and motivation in the teaching profession: school became about getting grades, and teacher recruitment and retention became an increasingly important issue.

Inevitably, there was a transition to a 'third way' which sought to combine quality and standards by way of partnerships between the state, private institutions, businesses, foundations, parents and the voluntary NGO sector. The aim was to find local solutions that met needs and enhanced community and democracy. 'Third way' systems in the Canada, the UK, Australia, to some extent in the US since the Bush Administrations, and also increasingly in developing countries, have stabilized education systems to some extent, modifying the more extreme elements of standardization and showing that the challenge of education is not met by either–or binaries, but requires more complex blends of ideas and practices. However, third way education remains largely top-down and prone to ideological push-and-pull factors: too much bureaucracy, too little funding, often leading to muddle and mediocrity. Success stories include Finland and the other Scandinavian countries, the Netherlands, Singapore, South Korea and China, all of which have in common less centralized, standardized curricula, more local school- (or city-)based autonomy, and greater professionalism of teachers – meaning they get better training and are encouraged to make professional judgements based on observations. The overemphasis on standardized data as a basis for pedagogical judgements is a major weakness, which remains part of the bureaucratization of education.

Beginning in Belgium in the 1990s, and now a central theme in European Union (EU) policy, competence-based curricula are ultimately focused on modelling children and young people to fit into the existing social structures, as these are understood, and therefore tend towards a kind of functionalism. This includes notions of happiness, wellbeing and resilience – the future citizen should be made resilient so that they can better cope with the rigours of an insecure world and be less of a drain on health services. Cynically one could argue that governments are saying: we can't guarantee you a secure future, access to health care and housing, so we need to make you resilient. Therefore, neoliberal policies require people not only to have the required skills to make a useful economic contribution (to an increasingly de-skilled workplace) but also to have the necessary social competences to fit in and be compliant. The rhetoric may be different and talk in terms of empowerment, active citizenship, and social and ecological responsibility, but the message communicated by the system is the opposite.

However, as the Belgian psychologist Paul Verhaeghe[7] has commented, neoliberal competence-based curricula foster personality schemata that dispose young people to seeing education as a competition that has to be won at all costs, since no one want to fail and be a loser. There is neither sympathy nor tolerance for failure, despite failure often being 'baked into' the system. This cultivates the attitudes of selfishness over solidarity, individualism rather than collaboration and teamwork; it panders to narcissism and envy, nurtures anxiety and a fear of loss of status, which frequently translates to blaming the other, xenophobia, and anti-immigrant attitudes. The rise of the far-right wing movements across Europe and America, fuelled by an ideological and polarized political system, is exactly what you get if people are continuously told that they will lose their privileged status, that they will lose out to 'unfair' competition. As Verhaeghe said more than a decade ago, there is no such thing as competitive solidarity, and the fear and loathing is only going to get worse. If we add to this toxic brew an almost complete loss of rationality in which fake news can easily tip the scales of behaviour from common sense to common nonsense, driven by social media algorithms that amplify and accelerate the process, then even metaphors like the medieval *Ship of Fools* seems understated.

It is ironic that the 20th century began with an all-out assault in the colonial West on irrationality (including religion, spirituality, and traditional social structures) in a drive to replace these with positivist science, imperial capitalism, and yet also mass democracy. When the Berlin Wall fell in 1989, and with it the Soviet empire, the ideological battle for hearts and minds between the capitalism of the 'free world' guaranteed by a *pax americana* versus collective state communism appeared to have been won. Now, in the 21st century, beginning with the bang of 9/11, the tables have turned on the 'free world', democracy has been hollowed out, the West's 'wars on terrorism' have disastrously failed, destabilizing whole regions and creating conditions that mean that millions of people have no economic or survival choice but to become migrants and refugees, thus fulfilling the prophecies of the far right and playing into their hands (as we have seen in a tragic sequence of democratic elections in Europe). The tables have fully turned on the achievements of the liberal West: emancipation, multiculturalism, ecological awareness, social justice, and the possibility of intelligent science providing creative solutions to the wicked problems of life (health care, renewables, technology, ecology, social sciences, the humanities, jurisprudence, and educational science). The world is being driven by authoritarian narcissists making up the rules as they go along and weaving their own powerful narratives that appeal to base human instincts and illusory visions of nationalist greatness – and not only in the United States. As Bob Dylan sang in a previous age "it's easy to see without looking too far, not much is really sacred".

So how can education keep up with this, particularly when in so many countries the space to do so is getting tighter and tighter? In general, the ship of education, whether state or private, cannot easily be turned (though it is generally not a ship of fools, and the crews are motivated by a genuine desire to do the good). The economy, the climate, the technology and the geopolitical situation all change faster than education can keep up with. Nobody really predicted in the 1990s what economy or society would really need in the 2000s, and no one can reliably predict what the current generation of school children need to know or be for the next decades.

Today, debates in education generally, and curriculum in particular, seem to centre around the question of whether curriculum should be knowledge-rich or competence-based, and to what extent curriculum should support the aims of diversity, inclusion and social equity. The culture wars have increased in education with arguments about decolonizing, what history should be taught, whether race theory has a place in the curriculum, and, generally, with what kind of society education should valorize. As we said at the beginning, curriculum is hugely contested.

In conclusion, the trend towards standardization is also one that denies pluralism and cultural diversity. It leads to a widespread homogenization of educational provision, on the assumption that the state knows best and 'one size fits all'. The arguments for biodiversity, which are also too easily set aside in the interests of a free market, can easily be applied to education, especially in a rapidly changing society and one in which cultural uniformity is no longer the norm in most countries. If education was once seen – and by conservative nationalists is still seen – as the primary means for reproducing society and its dominant cultural values – its *Leitkultur* – , then the question today is: which cultures are included and which excluded?

Education, because it aspires to be universal, has to be inclusive in the widest sense. That means, among other things, that it cannot represent, let alone impose, a unified world view. It has to include a range of imaginaries, in the sense of the web of meanings, structures and values that provide a society or segment of society or community with its cultural coherence and identification. These social imaginaries comprise assumptions, hopes, ways of seeing, norms, attitudes, gestures, systems and practices, that may manifest in the exclusion of certain others, or suggest desirable lifestyles. In a multicultural world, and a multi-medial world driven by influencers, the idea that education can ignore this and offer a prescribed social imaginary, is entirely illusory.

Most teachers, we believe, would agree that a certain amount of standardization is needed – minimum standards in relevant areas such as teacher qualifications, common national educational aims etc. However, in order to allow innovation in educational ideas, a measure of diversity in approaches and structures is needed. Crucially, these different models need to be facilitated or even required to explain and justify themselves and provide objective and appropriate research. In these open and equitable conditions, difference and diversity can only be to the general good.

Unsurprisingly, hybrid cultural forms proliferate in liquid modernity,[8] with its continuous interactions and flows of ideas and aspirations. We may regret the loss of stability, but we can't seriously claim that the existing older cultural forms are possible to hold onto anymore. Shifting and permeable boundaries are healthy in the educational and wider cultural sphere, precisely because this diversity generates innovation, yet this is often perceived as a threat to the controlling tendencies of the "there-is-no-alternative" instincts of many governments, struggling to demonstrate their possession of all the relevant answers. Trying to define what makes America, Russia, China, Britain, France, or little Hungary, Slovakia or Serbia great again makes no sense by imagining the past in the present. The only way forward is via the future and what it brings towards us, and the future is without doubt diverse and complex. We should celebrate this fact, not suppress it.

Education for the individual

A humanistic approach

The term humanistic should not be confused with *humanist*, which is a secular movement that rejects all aspects of spirituality and emphasizes positivist science and rationality. A humanistic approach takes the whole human being into account and grants the emotional and volitional aspects of the human being as much significance as cognitive aspects. It focuses on the process of becoming, self-actualization, personal growth and human fulfilment. In education, humanistic approaches emphasize wellbeing as important to learning. Humanistic methods of assessment for learning are generally formative and try to take the context into account. Humanistic approaches also see education as a path to emancipation, a view Paulo Freire famously articulated,[9] which values participatory practitioner research. If education is perceived as purely functionalist – an instrument to reproduce a certain kind of society and citizen in the service of the economy or to sustain a political ideology – then it tends to be based on behaviourist or neurological versions of the view that human beings can be programmed like smart machines to serve the existing interests of power and/or conceptions of what the economy needs in terms of skills to be competitive. In contrast, a humanistic approach values the importance and complexity of human development as a source for social development and renewal.

Bildung

Preceding – and also parallel to – developments in the Anglophone world and emergent nations, education in Middle Europe (including Germany, Austria, Scandinavia, The Netherlands, and much of Eastern Europe) was shaped by the educational philosophy of Bildung. The core idea of Bildung is essentially that of a relational self: that we come to our subjectivity through engagement with the other and that this process is transformative. In this sense it aligns with *Ubuntu*, the southern African notion that a person is only a person through other people.[10] As the philosopher Julian Baggini [11] puts it, "Its relational aspect is emphasized by the fact that it is a gerundive, a verbal noun. Ubuntu implies movement and action; it is not a static 'ism' and is thus also opposed to any kind of dogmatism. It is a humanistic concept, which like relationality in China, sees society, not God, as the transcendental source of value" (2018, p. 201).

Bildung has had its influence in the Anglophone world as humanistic and liberal arts education – one of the reasons that it has recently begun to be explored again. However, in its traditional Anglophone iteration, it has tended to be elitist, promoting both the ideals of public service yet reinforcing social stratification by emphasizing a canon of classic works of art, literature and philosophy and a selective notion of cultural heritage in the belief that children can assimilate the civilizing values these works enshrine. This leads to gold standard qualifications based on mastery of 'rich', canonized knowledge and, ideally, a place at a prestigious university, followed by entry into the upper middle-class networks within institutions and established 'old' money. The political influence of people who have 'enjoyed' this kind of education in the UK simply highlights the elitist nature of this world view.

Early history

Plato's (427–347 BCE) notion of *paideia* is one of the oldest accounts of Bildung and describes the relationship between teacher and student (in Ancient Greece, these were boys), in which he developed the notion that immature students need to have their attention directed to what is relevant and true and this can best occur through didactic means, that is, through specific tasks and particularly through questions that lead the student to understand what they need to learn.[12] Plato introduced the notion of *mimesis*, which refers to imitation and emulation, in which one person, usually less experienced and more impressionable, seeks to make themselves similar to a role model (a modern term from behaviourist psychology). Mimesis, however, is not limited to copying or reproducing but also involves the creative process of play, which is stimulated by observing others but undergoes modification, thus extending the repertoire of actions. This is very apparent in language learning. Children do not literally imitate the language they hear around them; rather, they internalize it and bring it forth in ways that reflect the child's ability to identify regularities, irregularities and communicative intentions. In a general sense, mimesis is also the process involved in participation, observing and joining in and communicative interaction. From the child's perspective, mimesis is enabling and self-forming.

Aristotle (384–322 BCE) promoted the idea of public schools in which pedagogy would be cultivated. He argued that simply showing and questioning was an insufficient basis for education and that what was needed was a systematic structure, in which the students are guided from a state of unknowing to a state of knowing within a knowledge system, and, in particular, that this process should lead from pre-knowledge based on experience to systematic knowing of the existing structures that precede the experience in the first place. The precondition for this to work is that the teachers themselves are versed in the knowledge they are pointing the learners to. Experience alone is insufficient; one must also know of the underlying structures. This is known as a teleological approach because the teaching is directed towards knowledge that is already prescribed; in other words, the goal is predetermined. For Aristotle and for many educators since, this is necessary for the good of the polis, the existing political social structures, whose reproduction is dependent on the following generation being inducted into them. Today, educational science affirms that Aristotle's method works; whether this is desirable is another matter.

Modernity

Some 2000 years after Aristotle, the Enlightenment philosopher and educator Jean-Jacques Rousseau (1712–1788) built on this basic understanding of pedagogy in his famous educational novel *Emile*, by distinguishing between three modes of educational (or *bildenden* – i.e. formative) processes: education through things, education through nature and education through people. Rousseau's new idea was that the nature of the human being at birth is disposed to being formed (i.e. it is *bildsam*) but has to learn in order to bring this forth and realize its potential. Learning through things in effect means learning through direct experiences in interaction with the world, not all of which are positive. Here we have an important distinction between *Erziehung* (which we would generally translate as education) and Bildung, since the latter can occur without pedagogical intervention. In German, *Erziehung*, differs from Bildung because the latter emphasizes the activity, agency and subjectivity of the subject, which is why it is sometimes written as *Selbstbildung* (self-formation). *Erziehung* emphasizes the intention of those responsible, such as teachers and the institutions they represent, in shaping the person. Unfortunately, today's educational discourse often conflates these terms, and they appear synonymous. The distinction, however, whatever terms we use, is important because we want to draw attention to the two basic gestures: self-formation and the intentional forming by institutions.

Rousseau gives the famous example of a stick standing in a pond, appearing to be broken. He makes the point that neither direct experience (which will not reveal the actual situation – only its superficial appearance) nor 'teaching' (an explanation beforehand that the stick only appears to be broken because of the refraction effect in the water) will activate the formative processes in the student that generate understanding. Rousseau's solution is to combine the three modes of learning. Rather than starting from the assumption that there is a necessary causal explanation, he asks the student to make accurate observations from various positions – enhancing the relationship between the student and the whole phenomenon. With the teacher's guidance, this encourages the formation of a hypothesis, which can then be practically tested.

In Benner's overview of the history of Bildung and its educational application, he draws attention to the philosopher Johann Gottlieb Fichte's (1762–1814) claim that the process of freely chosen self-activity is the basis for education and for the development of reason, and that everyone should have the opportunity to be educated in such a way that their self-activity be supported. This bodily self-activity manifests in two directions: towards the world as an active formative activity, and inwards, towards the formation of what we would call capacities or skills. This relationship to the world and to other people has two dimensions. One is a sensory experience and the other dimension is mental because these bodily experiences can also be mediated through communication, for which speech is the most important form, though images also mediate meaning. This has a social dimension because this self-activity is realized in relation to the world and other people. Education becomes a social process of exchange and interaction and as dialogue with the phenomena being studied.

Aesthetics and aisthetic education

As Christoph Wulf points out, in the Bildung tradition:

> Education is understood as a bodily-sensual process. It has a physicality and aesthetic character and thus the "sensual sensitivity and emotionality associated with [these conditions] are also important prerequisites for relationships with other people, the world, and with oneself. Education is thus both aisthetic and aesthetic, that is, it concerns human perception and theories of perception and sensual understanding, and it involves the formation of the senses, the imagination, and the body."[13]

The modern use of the term aesthetic referring to the response to art was coined by German Philosopher Alexander Baumgarten (1714–1762) in his book *Aesthetica* published in Latin in 1750, in which he sought to establish a science of sensory knowledge, which he saw as equal to logic in its significance, and of particular relevance for a human based knowledge of reality. His theory of aesthetics dealt with both perception in general but also of how art can be understood[14]. The terms aisthesis and aisthetic come from the ancient Greek term αἰσθητικός (aisthetikos), which refers to experiences through the senses, and αἰσθάνομαι (aisthanomai) means 'I perceive, feel or sense something'. It refers to "lived felt experience, knowledge obtained through the senses in contrast to eidos, knowledge derived from reason and intellection, from which we get the contemporary word idea."[15] From ancient times and through medieval and early modern times the term aisthēsis was part of theorizing about perception, epistemology and also the reception of beauty and art. Aristotle incorporated aesthesis into a comprehensive theory of perception, by it aligning disposition, activity and the production of knowledge.[16] He added the dimension of being moved by an experience, of undergoing an experience, and he linked this to catharsis in the experience of tragedy in the theatre.

The German Early-Romantic movement, starting in the 1790s, included the philosophers Kant, Fichte, Schelling and Hegel, the poets and theorists of poetry such as Novalis, Schlegel, Hölderlin, Schiller, and the biggest influence on all of them, Goethe,[17] developed important ideas about Bildung. This was a very diverse group, who did not always agree with each other but had certain core ideas in common. They did much to establish the central idea of Bildung: that the subject can come into being through engaging with the world, because the highest task of Bildung is for the individual to connect their personal embodied self with a transcendental self which is both in the world and in humanity. Thus, *Selbstbildung* (or self-formation) is a pedagogy of the self. For some this meant the study of nature (Goethe), for others the appreciation of high art (Schiller), or it meant poetry (Novalis), for still others this meant hermeneutic engagement with literary texts (Schlegel). The movement also had a wider influence through translations into English, notably through Coleridge's influence on Carlyle and Emerson in America, and into French through Germaine de Stael.

In Friedrich Schiller's[18] *Letters on the Aesthetic Education of the Human Being* (usually referred to simply *Aesthetic Letters*) we find the distinction between the drive to rationality (drive to form – *Formtrieb*) and the need for emotional expression in response to sensory experience (*Stofftrieb*), which can be read as a polarity of mind and body, which can only be resolved through the freedom of play, or artistic creativity. Schiller was moved to acknowledge the alienation of modern people from this through their increasingly mechanized and one-sided work, through cold, rational science and through developments in society, in which the promise of the French Revolution had so recently turned into terror and the military adventures of Napoleon. Civilization seemed doomed to barbarism (an idea that resonates today as we watch the news). Schiller saw in art the possibility of human transformation through Bildung, because engaging with art can lead to aesthetic experience of beauty and sublimity, not only in the contemplation of art but in learning to master its expressive possibilities and thereby awaken us from our naïve state of being embedded in nature. In self-formative creative activity (play as *Spieltrieb*), we have the possibility of attaining a moral relationship to the world. An aesthetic education in this sense, he argued, is the basis of an education towards emancipation and freedom. The precondition for this Bildung is the cultivation of the senses and the ability to extend our ability to perceive. In the 26th Letter, Schiller observes,

What we *see* through the eye is different from what we *perceive*; for the intellect leaps out over the light to the objects. The object of touch is a force which we endure; the object of the eye and the ear is a form which we create. As long as the human being is still uneducated,[19] he/she merely enjoys with the senses of feeling, to which the senses of appearance are at this stage only subservient. Either he/she does not rise to seeing or they are at any rate not satisfied with it. As soon as he/she begins to enjoy with the eye, and seeing acquires an absolute value for him/her, he/she is already aesthetically free also, and the play impulse has developed.[20]

(italics in original)

As Jörg Soetebeer[21] has shown, Schiller's programme of aesthetic education, as outlined in various texts that belong to same period as the *Aesthetic Letters*, centred on the notion of self-acting educational power (*selbsttätige Bildungskraft*). Schiller spoke of 'school knowledge' as being inert, without power or energy. When we take in such knowledge it remains alien and 'indigestible' to the person and, if retained, stays unchanged within us in a fruitless way and cannot stimulate either our feeling or our will. Schiller wrote,

> But whoever is able to communicate them in a beautiful form, not only proves that they are capable of expanding them, but also proves that they have incorporated them into their nature and is capable of expressing them in their actions. There is no other way to the will and to life than through the self-acting power of education. Nothing can come into manifestation except what is already a living act within us. It is the same with creations of the mind as with organic formations; fruit emerges only from the blossom.[22]

The term beauty in Schiller's system means any form of artistic creation that has the power to elevate both the producer and recipient. Creativity is the human form of nature's creativity, but the power of imagination requires a free will, if it is to generate realities. The creative imagination complements the power of thinking. This is supported by the teaching of material that appeals to the feelings of the learner, to which the learner can form a personal relationship, and which activates and motivates the will to self-activity. Thus, the learner's own imagination becomes a source of creativity and new ideas that are not merely unconnected flashes that simply pop up, as it were, but insights and intuitions which are deeply connected to the person's previous activities and experiences combined into a new form.

Goethe's approach to *aisthesis* also went far beyond the realm of classical aesthetics and its preoccupation with the beautiful and informed his way of studying nature. Aisthesis was on the one hand a process of awakening to self-formation, notably in the consciousness of the gap between the phenomenon prompting the experience and its significance for the person's existing understanding of the world. On the other hand it could be elevated to a scientific method. Goethe's method of observing natural phenomena was to start with the outer appearance but went deeper via the exact imagination by seeking to experience the inner processes at work within the organic phenomenon, for example in the growth of a plant or the processes of formation of bones. In the physical world, and in particular with light and colour phenomena, Goethe sought to experience the relationships starting with exact observation, going over into an inner reconstruction of the processes involved, and leading to the creation of an imaginative model as an active result of spiritual activity. In Goethe's reading, aisthetic/aesthetic experience has the following components:

- It directs attention to the primary sensory qualities of colour, sound, shape, taste, etc. Perception is accompanied by feelings (affect). This serves knowledge formation.
- The concept of gestalt (a whole living entity) combines the passive sensory and active cognitive-affective elements and is thus the basis for the self-active self-formation of the person.
- Art, understood as all human artefacts including ideas, is the medium through which people can develop their self-active self-formation.

As we shall see, Schiller and Goethe's notions of aisthetic/aesthetic experience were taken up by Rudolf Steiner, both in his theory of knowledge but also applied to pedagogy.

The idea of education as a formative process based on rationality and reason developed by the early Romantic thinkers in the German-language tradition had the implication that all individuals are theoretically in a position to understand the laws governing the world using mathematics and the scientific method, which also had radical political implications. This approach found its most systematic articulation in the philosopher Johann Friedrich Herbart's (1776–1841) book *General Pedagogy* (*Allgemeine Pädagogik*, 1806). In this influential work, Herbart described a systematic method of 'educative teaching', with the objective of enabling learners to develop the capacity to form their own judgements, out of their own insight – no longer orientating themselves to the models of Church and State. At the heart of Herbart's philosophy and practice of education, however, was his notion of aesthetics, an aspect that has often been overlooked since Herbart's ideas on education were subsequently expanded later by 'Herbartianer' (i.e. his followers) into a whole system in which classic textbook examples were designed to lead students to specific learning outcomes.

Herbart's aesthetic is of considerable interest because it offers what could be called a phenomenological approach that had much in common with John Dewey's later ideas about art and education. Whereas Schiller's *Aesthetic Letters* were aimed at the education of the self-forming (*sich bildende*) citizen, in effect – adults, and Goethe was more concerned with establishing scientific methods that avoided what he considered the mechanistic science of his times, Herbart was specifically interested in the universal education of children. An early work from 1804 has the remarkable title "Concerning the aesthetic presentation of the world as the main business of education".[23] Herbart's use of the word aesthetic went back to the original Ancient Greek word 'aisthesis', meaning perception (both sensory and in the mind) as a basis for understanding, which also has a root in the meaning 'to learn from'. Herbart's starting point was his engagement with Pestalozzi's work (he also visited Pestalozzi's institution in Switzerland) and the Swiss educational reformer's notion that encountering real things is the starting point for the formative-bildende/educative-process. Herbart went a few steps further, having met Friedrich Schiller and studied his *Letters on Aesthetic Education*[24] (1795/1965), and his reworking of aesthesis was to become the central idea in his subsequent influential works on pedagogy. However, it is his basic assumptions about the nature of experience that are important.

Herbart describes a situation in which the learner experiences something significant because the experience has been prepared by a teacher, who then directs the student's attention to it. The initial experience is of the situation as a totality, which is given as a perception, in which the *qualities* of the object (or situation) are immediately apparent – large, small, dark, light, rectangular, without boundaries etc. However, in contrast to Pestalozzi, Herbart realized that mere seeing is insufficient to make sense of the object, let alone its meaning. From a pedagogical perspective, it is not enough to simply enable the students to see the object. The object of study requires careful selection, the students need to be prepared for the encounter, and then primed to look and notice. However, perception is not the same as observation: the aesthetic pedagogical presentation is firstly enabling a perception and then subsequently revisiting the object to observe specific features in a more analytical way. The initial 'given' perception has a synthesizing function, one in which the whole rather than individual parts are experienced.

The similarity between this experience of the whole and what later became known as gestalt theory is apparent. 'Gestalt' in German means the whole form or shape of something – either a literal thing or an abstract idea. In gestalt theory, the coherent whole is more than the literal sum of the parts, and therefore involves the apprehension of what is not actually visible or immediately obvious. Herbart therefore distinguishes between the gestalt and the form, the latter being what we visually see, and he describes the whole process of perception as an interaction between gestalt and form. The knowledge we derive from the perception of the whole gestalt occurs in that we find a concept to make sense of what we perceive, and at the same time we reduce what we see to its essentials, by leaving out seemingly irrelevant details. Herbart describes the given experience as aesthetic necessity, because the image of the totality of the object and its attendant sensory qualities is 'forced' on us. The aesthetic mode of seeing (*ästhetische Anschauung*) is how we combine these synthesizing and selective/analytical elements. Aesthetic judgement is the resonance of the experience that then manifests in the learner's will.

It was this aspect that led Herbart to see this kind of aesthetic experience as the basis for ethics and morality. In aesthetic judgement, we determine what is harmonious, proportional, beautiful, coherent, meaningful and uplifting based on our perceptions, which are founded in experience. Thus, the basis for moral judgements are experiences made in real encounters with the world.

The educational significance of this theory lies in the necessity of the aesthetic judgement of the learner as subject, which is an aspect of the nature of the human being – it occurs under certain conditions because that is the way we relate to the world.

> Aesthetic 'coercion' or necessity requires a process of self-reflection that can be made accessible to the consciousness of the individual. Morality itself cannot be represented: it must be depicted and shown by means of a third party that lies outside the subject, but which, by means of contemplation of the inner event, refers to an inner disposition of the subject…In the reception and reflection of what is represented, the subject renounces itself, steps out of its immediate self-reference in the confrontation with sensual experience and enters into a relationship with its environment and with itself.[25]

In his subsequent educational works, Herbart referred to two vital new concepts in education, that of the *Bildsamkeit* of the child (and human beings generally) and the 'third thing' in the educational relationship – the subject matter that unites the experiences of teachers and students (see Chapter 8 for a detailed discussion). Herbart's understanding of Bildung includes the notion of *Bildsamkeit*, perhaps translatable as an inherent susceptibility to formation and transformation, or more simply *educability*, which implies that the subject, especially as a child or young person, possesses the core potential for formation and transformation. This capacity is inherent in the human brain's plasticity and the human species' predisposition and ability to adapt and make use of the developmental possibilities afforded by any given situation, especially in childhood.

Interestingly, the OECD project on Education for Human Flourishing explored ways of assessing the three competences of adaptive problem-solving, ethical decision-making and aesthetic judgement, and, in particular, the property of aesthetic perception of beauty in an experience that is characterized as "to behold, have a form that is memorable and invite revisiting."[26]

In the German tradition of didactics, which to a considerable extent is based on Herbart's work,[27] the educative act is not seen simply as the linear mediation of knowledge followed by the testing of whether this has been learned, but rather in the triadic relationship between the teacher, the subject and the learner. Furthermore, the learning of existing knowledge is insufficient. The learner must develop interest for the subject matter, and this can involve the social process of shared interest with others – either a teacher or other students. The teacher, in particular, has the task to awaken the interest of the student in the subject matter and having themselves genuine rather than routine interest is a vital part of the process. Though this may seem obvious today, at the time this social aspect of education was barely recognized. Thus, we see an explicit link between aesthetics (as *aisthesis*) and didactics. The 'third thing', the subject matter in question, is not only literally the object of study but also the meaning and context of that object, and the transactional relationships that arise through engagement with the text, image, idea, or natural phenomenon. The *inter-esse* (relationship between beings) cannot be reduced to a prescribed outcome but remains open to interpretation. In Hans-Georg Gadamer's sense of a fusion of horizons, the process of hermeneutic engagement with the text (or any object of study), the coming together of the different horizons, the teacher's, the students' and that of the phenomenon, can be more than the prescribed content. It is this 'more' that is 'bildend' – or formative – of the person. This process offers no position of superiority to the teacher, since the unpredictable outcome of the aesthetic Bildung process is a risk and opportunity for all concerned. Even the teacher can find their existing world view interrupted and challenged.

This insight has led to (or should have led to) a greater concern with the nature, quality and pedagogical suitability and preparation of the subject matter. One expression of this is the idea of the *Bildungsroman* (literally a novel with the purpose of educating the reader). A book is not read simply because it is deemed canonical and important as a historical cultural artefact, but because the material (and the way it is handled in lessons) is deemed to have a formative effect on the reader that contributes to their development as a person. This idea still strongly influences Waldorf education, as Philipp Kleinfercher's[28] book with the translated title of *Reading as an Art: Literature didactics in Waldorf education. The Formation of the subject through aesthetic experiences in youth*, suggests. Contemporary embodiment and resonance theory have given the idea of aesthetic education a new dimension, as Rittelmeyer's[29] work shows.

At this stage in our account, it is necessary to bring in John Dewey, whose theory of aesthetics (he spelled it esthetics) remains highly relevant. We know that Dewey was influenced in his earlier years by Schiller's *Aesthetic Letters* and was very much steeped in European notions of Bildung, which he translated into a more democratic American perspective. Dewey's basic epistemological stance was that people as living embodied beings are embedded in the world, or specifically in the organic environment. The nature of this relationship is transactional, meaning that both person and world are affected and changed by encounters, including epistemological engagements – that is, when we try to generate knowledge from experience. Each encounter leads to perturbations or disruptions in the person's existing world view, which, after processing, settles into a new state of harmonious equilibrium. In this account one can see the extent to which Dewey was influenced by Darwin.

One of the legacies of Dewey's pragmatic approach to aesthetics as a way of knowing the world through our sensory embodiment is Elliott Eisner's[30] theory of connoisseurship, which we mentioned in the Introduction. Eisner believed that educational practice requires a more subtle form of knowledge to base both its practice and its research of practice on. He coined the phrase epistemic seeing, which is very close to the iteration of aesthetic/aisthetic experience and judgement we have been presenting here. Eisner described connoisseurship as being based on epistemic seeing, which means knowing that is secured through seeing, which is a shorthand way of saying using all senses ("including the smell of chalkdust and stale milk").[31] That means it is an awareness of qualities. The richer our perception of qualities, the deeper our knowledge of the phenomenon. Specific cases are important as examples of a type of situation, "primary epistemic seeing depends upon awareness of the particular. Secondary epistemic seeing refers to seeing the particular as a member of a set."[32] By knowledge, Eisner was referring to awareness of an array of qualities, "connoisseurship is the means through which we come to know the complexities, nuances, and subtleties of aspects of the world in which we have a special interest".[33] Therefore, we propose to us the term epistemic seeing as synonymous to aisthetic experience.

Thinking, feeling and willing, and affect

Steiner introduced the distinction between thinking, feeling and willing (volition) as the primary expressions of the mind (in his terms soul) and associated these with the functional structure of the body: thinking with the nerve sense processes, willing with the metabolic and limb system and feeling in the 'middle' structures of the heart, circulation and breathing. This alignment is both intended as a correlation between body and mind, and also as the location of consciousness. This was important at the time because of the dualistic approaches that tended to dominate science (and still do, to some extent). It was also important because it enabled him to emphasize the interaction between thinking, feeling and willing in learning, and in particular the importance of addressing the students through their feelings rather than directly offering them concepts and thoughts. Ultimately, feelings activate the will and this rises to consciousness and prompts thoughts – one has to want to construct a mental image of something or remember it.

There are two primary modes of thinking that Steiner is addressing: the forming of mental images or representations of ideas and experiences, and the imagination. Mental images, Steiner says, are pale representations of reality and are based on what is already known, and mental images are 'stored' as memories. The imagination is much livelier and, in a sense, a more active cognitive activity. It can create 'images' (or other sensory modalities such as sounds or gestures) of things that we have never experienced, though the mind tends to imagine new things based on things we have experienced. In pedagogy the task is to activate the imagination and direct active thinking, so that ideas are created and recreated in the mind. Steiner devotes a whole lecture in the First Teachers' Course to the will, showing its transformation from instinct and drive to the highest form of noble intentions. Feeling is somewhat under-illustrated.

Today we can offer a more comprehensive differentiation between sensation, which is the first response to sensory stimulation, and emotion, which usually reflects body states (e.g. fear, satisfaction, anxiety, relaxation etc.) that are generally in the background of consciousness, unless they function as warning or signal emergency. Feelings require more content, have a more cognitive quality and are relational – we have feelings about something. Affect is a total bodily-mental and unconscious response to experience, akin to the process that generates pain, and provides the intensity of response that makes feeling possible in the first place. One can understand the idea[34] that affect is 'pre-personal', meaning it is not personally subjective (in the sense of liking or disliking), it is an embodied immediate response to sensory – that is aesthetic – experience, whereas as feeling is more obviously subjective and personal. Eric Shouse [35] suggests that emotions are social because they are culturally situated (for example shame). Emotions are a form of behavioural display and as such they are partly determined by cultural norms that influence whether and how we show emotion outwardly. Children communicate very successfully through emotions before they can use language effectively and all people use emotion to communicate in unconscious and semi-conscious ways, for example through mood. As Shouse writes, "affect plays an important role in determining the relationship between our bodies, our environment, and others, and the subjective experience that we feel/think as affect dissolves into experience".[36]

Postmodern bildung theory

Theories of social learning and social structuring that focus on the 'production' of the person have also responded to the socio-economic context that arises when traditional social structures disintegrate, such as clear social class structures, traditional institutions such as churches, trades unions, simple distinctions between political parties of the left and the right, stable economic conditions of unlimited growth offering jobs for life and gradually increasing prosperity over generations. Social scientists such as Zygmunt Bauman (who coined the term 'liquid modernity', in which social structures become fluid and individuals have to navigate their identities and lifestyles), Ullrich Beck and Anthony Giddens have described the precarious nature of social structures in late modernity and the implications for identity work and self-formation, which become a lifelong project. Some 15 years ago, using studies of young people in England, the sociologist Margaret Archer showed that about a quarter of them do not manage to cope with the conflicting demands in their social environment, fail to construct coherent, resilient personality structures, and therefore fail to either understand their situation or become incapable of responding in a constructive way. Today that percentage is without doubt higher.

This means that these underqualified young people are incapable of self-formation or constructing coherent and stable identities and thus they can find neither meaningful answers to their biographical questions of meaning nor work. Without any perspective of security, they become vulnerable and susceptible to right-wing and populist narratives of xenophobia, intolerance and hate. The rise of the new extreme right in Europe feeds on the alienation of young people from what they believe to be their birthright, preventing them from fulfilling their unrealistic and narcisstic dreams- what Lauren Berland calls "cruel optimism".[37] Henry Giroux recalls Hannah Arendt's[38] analysis that even in the darkest times there are voices of illumination,

> Arendt's words are especially relevant today, warning us about 'dark times' stemming from the collapse of politics, degrading of truth, and the threat of violence to public freedom. What is crucial here is her warning about the force and significance of a

repressive authoritarian educational project, one in which people are dehumanized, expelled from humanity, and that disavows their ability to think. Fascism transcends mere ideology and a set of mobilizing passions; it is also a pedagogical project that renders human beings superfluous. The far-right backlash against critical education and thinking itself is…born of the fact that…it is what connects us with ourselves and one another…[39]

Postmodern transformative Bildung theory sees education as performative. Because of the self-formative nature of Bildung and its aisthetic and aesthetic dimensions, acting, speaking (and singing), doing and making are all embodied and, combined with intentional agency, are seen as performative. Thus, education is seen as a holistic practice involving physicality, and the enactment of meaningful activities, all of which activities shape the developing human being. The term performative in this sense should not be confused with the idea of performativity (which originated with Michel Foucault), in which performance is quantified and measured and used as an instrument of coercion.

Biographical and transformative learning as bildung in late modernity

'Lifelong learning' is a term used in many debates and policies about education. In one sense, it is about economic workers being in a situation in which they continuously learn, develop new skills and adapt their identities to the rapid changes in society and the economy. Peter Alheit's term 'biographical learning' refers to the ability of the individual in any given situation, but especially in educational institutional settings, to recognize and respond to the opportunities for personal development over their life course. Guy Widderhoven expresses the importance of narrative in the process of identity formation: "the unity of a person's life is experienced in stories that express this experience".[40]

Following Hans-Christoph Koller,[41] Bildung is a process of transformation of the person in and through educational learning processes, which incorporates a synthesis of important hermeneutic philosophical ideas (e.g. Hans-Georg Gadamer, Bernhard Waldenfels and Käte Myer-Drawe) and postmodern perspectives (Jean-François Lyotard, Michel Foucault, Jacques Derrida and Judith Butler,[42] all authors one can find cited in Heiner Hastedt's book *What is Bildung?*[43]).

The German life-course researcher Peter Faulstich describes the task of Bildung as a life-history process in the course of which, and as a result of which, individuals endeavour to establish and consolidate their identity. They acquire culture by learning and in so doing, develop their personality. In this process, they develop personal identity within their biography:

> The contents of such education are not determined by a timeless canon, but historically and specifically in the face of current problems. The key issues to be addressed are constantly changing and evolving. Accordingly, education means acquiring the skills to understand specific social problems, to find one's own position in relation to them, to make appropriate decisions and to be able to act. The central educational problem, the perspective of securing identity and developing personality, is therefore tied to the acquisition of sovereignty for one's own life, of expanded agency, which also means of learning opportunities.[44]

One important humanistic Bildung approach is Dieter Benner's[45] theory of non-affirmative education. The term non-affirmative is admittedly not very helpful, probably deliberately so, but, as Benner himself explains, in the context of reflective teaching and learning processes it means that subject matter is not taught in such a way that the learners are required to accept (affirmative) what is taught, but rather learn to be reflective and critical of what they are taught. Conclusions that are arrived at in the educative process are considered preliminary, temporary, pending further application and assessment on the part of teachers and learners. This approach contradicts all dogmatic educational approaches that, for example, teach canonical knowledge, such as that listed by E.D. Hirsch,[46] which involve affirmative pedagogies.

A central idea in this version of Bildung is that education is relational. It essentially involves someone – a teacher – teaching someone (the students) something (the subject matter) with a purpose. This involves a three-way relationship, in which both the teacher and the students must have a meaningful relationship to what is being taught, which also means that both student and teacher encounter themselves in the engagement with the subject and the subject has a didactic effect on both teacher and students, whereby all three 'parties' are changed through the learning process.

This is an epistemological approach that does not start from fixed certainties and knowledge but assumes that the relationship is transactional and productive. This is perhaps easiest to understand from the perspective of the student as learner, less obvious for the teacher, who has to discover and re-discover their relationship to the subject matter each time they teach it. But the object also has to undergo a process. If the object is a natural phenomenon, a plant for example, there are various ways that knowledge of the plant can be generated. If the subject matter is a work of art or a piece of literature, or a moment in history, there are various ways in which these can be interpreted. This Bildung approach emphasizes that the subject matter itself, the phenomenon being studied, changes depending on the methodology used to access and understand it.

The teacher must form a relationship to the *subject matter*, which involves selecting material likely to provide learning opportunities that afford a meaningful encounter for the students. This involves research and developing the skills to read the effects of the teaching on the learning behaviour of the students, which John Hattie[47] identified as the most powerful process in supporting learning. We can therefore call this *teacher learning*. The students have to participate in a process involving a number of steps from initial encounter to the growth of dispositions, abilities, habits of mind and knowledge, which we can call *studying*. Thus, we get the triad shown in Figure 1.1.

In Chapter 9, we look at the pedagogy of this process in more detail.

The Danish model

Denmark, along with other Scandinavia and Baltic countries, has been seen as having a highly successful model of education based on a social consensus that government is benign and uses the considerable taxes its citizens pay to provide high-quality social care and education. Danish education has been rightly admired for its world leading and equitable approach and commitment to a lifelong learning agenda.[48] Around the turn of the Millenium, Danish education took a turn away from German-inspired Bildung, didactics and humanistic approaches to a more Anglo-American neoliberal approach. Following models in England, Canada and New Zealand, they moved to an emphasis on normative standards, New Public Management models of school governance, creating

Society or person? Different ways of seeing education 35

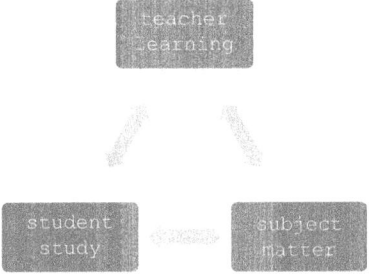

Figure 1.1 The triad between teacher learning (about the subject matter, how students learn and how to evaluate the process), student study (a multi-step process from rich experience to new abilities) and the subject matter.

market conditions for parents and students where schools compete for students, and a focus on commercialization of education and 'school effectiveness' models. The recent government of Mette Frederiksen has reversed this trend, promising to scrap 4,000 redundant learning goals, with a re-focus on so-called 'Danish' values. This includes a move away from national standardization to more local autonomy and choice and a more holistic focus on the person and the recognition of greater pluralism. The recent government green paper makes the statement, "In Denmark, it is unanimously agreed upon that education is based on a number of fundamental principles such as education for all, lifelong learning, high standards, relevance, active participation, and project work." This emphasis highlights a strong Bildung perspective. From the evidence in the media, there does not seem to be any significant challenge to this claim and most political and academic commentators affirm that these aims do indeed have consensus and are, to a high degree, achieved.

Summary

Our synthesis of these overlapping traditions of education can be summarized as follows.

- Transformative Bildung through self-activity in engaging with the world, including the student's own multicultural context and cosmopolitan perspectives and the real worlds we inhabit, remains centrally important. The main argument for this – if one is needed – is that the current world situation, which includes the crisis of truth, a world of wicked problems, the challenges of artificial intelligence, needs people who can think for themselves and make their own judgements and take responsibility for their actions and who have the skills to negotiate peaceful and creative solutions, whilst having the dispositions to stay healthy. The balance to AI is applied human intelligence.
- Following on from the above, we also recognize that the focus on Bildung needs to be balanced by a curriculum with a specific focus on key social and personal skills, the cultivation of certain habits of mind that predispose the learner to be open to the *other* (human and natural) and supports expansive life-long learning skills and biographical learning. Curriculum, therefore, needs to have a common framework yet be adaptive to changing locations over time and circumstances.

- Building on and operationalizing the ideals of 'aisthetic/aesthetic education' we suggest a curriculum approach that provides learning opportunities through rich experiences and then applies appropriate methods to arrive at a connoisseurship, which we discuss in the next chapter, and, ultimately, the capacity to form critical judgements.
- Within social learning settings with heterogenous learning groups from a wide variety of backgrounds, education needs to be fully inclusive, which means providing shared experiences for the learning groups, whilst providing learning pathways in response to individual needs and learning differences. This also requires mapping out learning descriptors as diagnostic tools (and not as norms).

Task for the reader

- From your reading of this chapter, where can you see the influence of these different perspectives on the education system of which you are a part?
- Where would you place your current educational setting on a spectrum from entirely focused on meeting the needs of society, to focused on the flourishing potential of the individual?

Notes

1 Mead, M. (1964). *Continuities and Discontinuities in Cultural Evolution*. New Haven, CT. Yale University Press.
2 Readers interested can turn to Tröhler, D. (2016). The grand narratives of modernity and the modern self: The Protestant idea of the soul and the educationalization of the world. *Education Letter.*, Spring/Summer 2016, 27–29. Tröhler, D. (2023). Curriculum theory and education history. In *International Encyclopedia of Education* (4th. edition ed., Vol. 7, pp. 117–125): Elsevier Science.
3 Steiner, R. (1985 (1919)). The Threefold Social Order and Educational Freedom (E. Bowen-Wedgewood & R. Mariott, Trans.). In *The Renewal of the Social Organism* (pp. 70–76). Anthroposophic Press. (Aufsätze über die Dreigliederung des sozialen Organismus, Volume 24 in Collected Works).
4 See Ball, S. J. (2012). *Global Education Inc. New Policy Networks and the Neo-liberal Imaginary*. Routledge. Ball, S. J. (2016). Neoliberal Education? Confronting the slouching beast. *Policy Futures in Education*, 14(8), 1046–1059.
5 See Health Behaviour in School Aged Children Report 21/22 https://hbscengland.org/hbsc-reports/.
6 See National Literacy Trust Report https://literacytrust.org.uk/research-services/research-reports/children-and-young-peoples-reading-in-2023/#:~:text=Reading%20enjoyment%3A, asked%20the%20question%20in%202005.
7 Verhaeghe, P. (2014, 29 September, 2014). Neoliberalism has brought out the worst in us: An economic system that rewards psychopathic personality traits has changed our ethics and our personalities. *The Guardian*. Verhaeghe, P. (2015). *What about Me? The Struggle for Identity in a Market-based Society*. Scribe Publications.
8 Bauman, Z. (2007). *Liquid Times: Living in an Age of Uncertainty*. Polity.
9 Humanistic approaches often cite the Americans Abraham Maslow (1908–1970), Carl Rogers (1902–1987) and Jerome Bruner (1915–2016) as primary sources, but we would add people such as Lev Vygotsky (1896–1934), the philosophers Martin Buber (1878–1965) and Hannah Arendt (1906–1975), as well as Martha Muchow (1892–1933) and Charlotte Bühler (1893–1974), Paulo Freire (1921–1997), Howard Gardiner (1943–) and Uri Bronfenbrenner (1971–2005) to this list, which just shows what a broad spectrum there is. For an overview of child development theory we recommend Shute, R. H., & Slee, P. T. (2015). *Child Development: Theories and Critical Perspectives* (2nd. ed.). Routledge.

10 Le Grange, L. (2011). Ubuntu, Ukama and the Healing of Narure, Self and Society. *Educational Philosophy and Theory*. https://doi.org/10.1111/j.1469-5812.2011.00795.x.
   Ke-Schutte, J. (2022). Ubuntu/Guanxi. In D. M. Menon (Ed.), *Changing Theory. Concepts from the Global South*. Routledge.
11 Baggini, J. (2018). *How the World Thinks. A Global History of Philosophy*. Granta Books.
12 This account follows Dietrich Benner (2020). *Umriss der allgemeinen Wissenschaftsdidaktik. Grundlagen und Orientierung für Lehrerbildung, Unterricht und Forschung. (Outline of a general scientific didactic. Basic concepts and orientation for teacher education)*. Beltz.
13 Wolf, C. (2024). Human beings and their education from an anthropological perspective: Current discourses in the field of educational science in the German-speaking world. *Educational Theory*, 74(2), 245–254, p. 249.
14 Guyer, P., "18th Century German Aesthetics", *The Stanford Encyclopedia of Philosophy* (Fall 2020 Edition), Edward N. Zalta (ed.), https://plato.stanford.edu/archives/fall2020/entries/aesthetics-18th-german/.
15 Cazeaux, C. (2011). Introduction. In *The Continental Aesthetics Reader* (2nd. edition ed., pp. xiii–xviii). Routledge. p. 5.
16 Zembylas, T. (2022). Aisthesis. In J. Siegmund (Ed.), *Handbuch Kunstphilosophie* (pp. 346–357). transcript utb, p. 346.
17 Readers who want to know more about this period are recommended to read Charles Taylor's books, (2016). *The Language Animal. The Full Shape of Human Linguistic Capacity*. Belknap Press of Harvard University Press.
18 Schiller, F. (1965). *On the Aesthetic Education of Man in a Series of Letters* (R. Snell, Trans.). Fredrick Ungar Publishing.
19 I have translated this text in a way that removes any gendered reference, including the gendered translation of the original title of the text referred to in the previous endnote. I have also re-translated the 'savage' as uneducated.
20 Schiller, F. (1965). *On the Aesthetic Education of Man in a Series of Letters* (R. Snell, Trans.). Fredrick Ungar Publishing, p. 126. We note in passing that it is ambivalent what Schiller understood by using the term savage (Wilden) here, though it seems likely that he subscribed to the widely held view am German intellectuals at the time that cultural evolution was characterized by an ascent from savagery to civilization and that the races of the earth mirrored this. Schiller's view on women in the *Aesthetic Letters*, is characterized by his gendering of aesthetic sensibility (as female), as Gayatri Chakravorty Spivak notes (2012). *An Aesthetic Education in the Era of Globalization*. Cambridge University Press, p. 32.
21 Soetebeer, J. (2010). *Selbsttätige Bildungskraft heute (Self-active formative force today)*. Edition Waldorf.
22 Schiller, 1795 Über die notwendigen Grenzen beim Gebrauch schöner Formen, quoted Soetebeeer (2010), p. 154.
23 "Über die ästhetische Darstellung der Welt als das Hauptgeschäft der Erziehung".
24 See endnote 18.
25 Markus Rassiller (2010) *Ästhetik und form- Die gestaltpsychologischen Grundlagen der Aisthesiologie Johan Friedrich Herbarts mit dem Ausblick auf die Metaphysik* (Aesthetik and form- gestalt-psychological foundations in Aisthesis-theory of Herbart with a view to metaphysics) in Prange, K. (ed.) *Herbarts Ästhetik. Studien zu Herbarts Charakterbildung*. Jena: Edition Paideia, pp. 103–126.
26 The OECD Report (2023) High Performing Systems for Tomorrow: 2023 Conceptual Framework cites (p. 15). Gardner's definition of aesthetic perception from Gardner, H. (2011) *Truth, Goodness and Beauty Reframed. Education of the Virtues for the 21st Century*. Basic Books.
27 According to Dietrich Benner (2020). *Umriss der allgemeinen Wissenschaftsdidaktik. Grundlagen udn Orientierung für Lehrerbildung, Unterricht und Forschung*. Beltz Juventa.
28 Kleinfercher, P. (2024). *lesen als Kunst: Literaturdidaktik in der Waldorfpädagogik. Subjektbildung durch ästhetische Erfahrungen im Jugendalter*. Budrich Academic Press. This is by no means only a Waldorf perspective as Christian Rittelmeyer shows. (2014). *Aisthesis. Zur Bedeutung von Körper-Resonanzen für die ästhetischer Bildung*. (Aisthesis. The significance of body resonance for aesthetic education) Kopaed, and Rittelmeyer, C. (2016). *Bildende Wirkung ästhetischer Erfahrungen*. (The educative effects of aesthetic education) Beltz Juventa.

29 See Rittelmeyer, *Bildende Wirkung ästhetischer Erfahrungen*.
30 Eisner, E. W. (2017). *The Enlightened Eye. Qualitative Inquiry and the Enhancement of Educational Practice*. Teachesr College Press.
31 Eisner, 2017, p. 68.
32 Eisner, 2017, p. 68.
33 Eisner, 2017, p. 68.
34 Shouse, E. (2005). Feeling, Emotion, Affect. *M/C A Journal of Media and Culture*, 8(6). https://doi.org/10.5204/mcj.2443 Michael Rothberg discusses this and the whole question of the 'affective turn' in Rothberg, m. (2023). Feeling Implicated: An introduction. *Parallax*, 29(3), 265–282. https://www.tandfonline.com/doi/full/10.1080/13534645.2024.2302663.
35 Shouse, E. (2005). Feeling, Emotion, Affect. *M/C A Journal of Media and Culture*, 8(6). https://doi.org/10.5204/mcj.2443 Michael Rothberg discusses this and the whole question of the 'affective turn' in Rothberg, m. (2023). Feeling Implicated: An introduction. *Parallax*, 29(3), 265–282. https://www.tandfonline.com/doi/full/10.1080/13534645.2024.2302663.
36 Shouse, E. (2005). Feeling, Emotion, Affect. *M/C A Journal of Media and Culture*, 8(6). https://doi.org/10.5204/mcj.2443 Michael Rothberg discusses this and the whole question of the 'affective turn' in Rothberg, m. (2023). Feeling Implicated: An introduction. *Parallax*, 29(3), 265–282. https://www.tandfonline.com/doi/full/10.1080/13534645.2024.2302663.
37 Berlant, L. (2011). *Cruel Optimism*. Duke University Press.
38 Arendt, H. (1970). *Men in dark Times*. Mariner Books.
39 Giroux, H. (2025). *The burden of Conscience. Educating beyond the veil of silence*. Bloomsbury Academic.
40 Widdershoffen, G.A.M. (1993). The story of life. Hermeneutic perspectives on the relationship between narrative and life history. In Josselson, R. & LA. Lieblich (Eds.), *The Narrative Study of Lives*. Newbury Park: Sage, pp. 1–20.
41 Koller, H.-C. (2003). Bildung and radical plurality: Towards a redefinition of Bildung with reference to J.-F. Lyotard. *Educational Philosophy and Theory*, 23(1), 155–165.
   Koller, H.-C. (2018). *Bildung anders denken: Einführung in die Theorie transformatorischer Bildungsprozesse* (2. aktualisierte Auflage ed.). Kohlhammer.
42 It is not our intention here simply to name-drop nor to enter wide-ranging philosophical discussions but simply to indicate the direction of travel. Koller's articles in English provide a good introduction to this kind of thinking.
43 Hastedt, H. (2012). *Was ist Bildung?* Reclam.
44 Faulstich, P. (2013). *Menschliches Lernen: ein kritisch-pragmatisches Lerntheorie (Human learning – a critical-pragmatic theory of learning)*. Transcript Verlag. p. 214 (translated by MR).
45 Benner, D. (2023). On Affirmativity and Non-Affirmativity in the Context of Theories of Education and Bildung. In M. Uljens (Ed.), *Non-affirmative Theory of Education and Bildung* (pp. 21–62). Springer Nature.
46 See for example Hirsch, E. D. (2016). *Why Knowledge Matters. Rescuing our Children from Failed Educational Theories*. Harvard Education Press.
47 Hattie, J. A. C. (2023). *Visible Learning: The Sequel. A Synthesis of Over 2,100 Meta-analyses Relating to Achievement*. Routledge.
48 We think of the contributions of social psychologist Ole Dreier, Bente Elkjaer and learning researchers Knud Illeris.

2 A (new) third way

Overview

In this chapter we propose a new third way, blending the perspectives we have identified above. This takes us to identifying the purpose of education, and recommending Biesta's three functional domains – socialization, qualification and subjectification as a heuristic to analyse the functions of education. We add to Biesta's model the further perspective of wellbeing and resilience and weave this into his three domains. We outline Steiner's idea of a threefold structuring of society with different functional principles for each of the three spheres – the economic, the political-social and the cultural domains. We offer a modification of this but retain his emphasis that education should be part of the cultural domain, governed by the principle of freedom, since the process of individuation and the development of the person should be free of economic or political interests. In conclusion, we offer a new possible structure for schooling within the social and political framework.

The need for a third way

The world is changing at such a rapid rate that it is very difficult to define what the next generation needs to know and to be able to do, and even harder to restructure education to keep up with these changes. There is broad consensus that education needs time – a lot of time if people are to lead personally satisfying, socially constructive and productive lives of well over 80 years. This process of preparing people for lifelong learning over the course of long lives clearly has to be done effectively, fairly and equitably. The paradox is that governments who are generally understood to be responsible for providing education want to improve 'standards' (measured in different ways to reflect their priorities) *and* reduce costs, but are increasingly short-term in their policies. This leads to frequent changes in educational policies and requirements, with all their attendant disruption. As a rule, modern economies in search of quick returns can only plan for the short term. Yet society is oriented toward the long term because millions of people, most of whom will live long lives have needs that include meaning, wellbeing and resilience (as well as the material securities that enable but do not guarantee wellbeing or meaning). Therefore, even though education has to prepare people to contribute to the economy and the whole process has to be politically affordable and equitable, it primarily has to meet the human need for long-term wellbeing. A humanistic approach puts the wellbeing of the human being first.

Pragmatically, we believe that the two goals are not as incompatible as might be thought. The qualities people need for long, fruitful and rewarding lives are not dissimilar from what enables them to contribute productively to society and the economy. Let us just briefly outline what we think these qualities are, though we acknowledge that these qualities will be required differently in different life situations.

The purpose of education

As we outlined in the previous chapter, educational histories and ideologies define the purpose of education. At one end of the spectrum, where education is considered to be entirely for the good of society, the purpose of education is to be 'the engine of the economy'.[1] At the other end, there are often broad generalizations such as to "prepare young people for life".[2]

We think that Gert Biesta's[3] description of the three domains of educational function offers a vital perspective, on which we would like to build. He points out that all educational models (should) have the same functions: socialization, qualification and subjectification. The differences between educational approaches lie in the weighting they give to each function, and the implications that this weighting has for educational practice. In our view, each of these functions involves self-activity on the part of the learner and the teacher and those responsible for the institutional structures in schools, because as both socio-cultural[4] and community of practice[5] theory point out, individuals learn in social contexts in relation to what that context affords and the extent to which they can respond to the opportunities that are offered.

Socialization

Socialization is about finding a dynamic balance between inner and outer realities, between what the individual brings to the learning situation and what the social context explicitly or implicitly expects. Hurrelmann's[6] theory of productive processing of external and internal realities offers one of the best accounts of socialization within the Bildung tradition. According to this theory, the individual is continuously engaged in a process of establishing coherent identities across multiple sites of biographical development, or as Ole Dreier[7] they weave a "relatively coherent sense of self across multiple contexts that are our everyday lives".[8] Learners are differently positioned in social contexts according to their cultural origin, race, gender, social background and ability both inside and outside of school and their ability to participate is enhanced or hindered by these positions. Schools therefore have an obligation to enable the participation of all, which is probably the most potent way they can support socialization because not only does the participation assist and support individuals, but the fact that the school does this, is already formative and supports the growth of dispositions towards inclusion. If the political climate is opposed to special programmes for diversity, equity and inclusion, it may be more effective if these themes are unobtrusively woven into the curriculum, without labels such as 'race theory'. The story of the 'invention' of race in European history in relation to plantation slavery and slavery's links to capitalism are, after all, just history. If there is opposition to Black History Month, just ensure that black writers are well represented across the literature curriculum. Even if some future government would legislate against the existing laws against discrimination, that doesn't mean we have to start discriminating! The point is that socialization starts in the minds and hearts of teachers and school leaders.

Education can support socialization and social integration by offering opportunities for the learning of social and cultural skills, for example in multi-cultural contexts, and also by recognizing that personal abilities and competences expressed as personal agency are not simply embodied as fixed traits. Rather, they are the personal preconditions that enable a person to participate in a social practice, though these are limited to what the practice affords. In other words, like any skill, it is dependent on there being opportunities to use the skills in authentic and meaningful ways (i.e. not in tests or exams), because personal skills are practical and contextual. Skills can also be modified through usage in contexts that afford them. It is little use merely talking about intercultural capacities; they can only be learned and expanded in situations in which they are actually called upon – just as any practical skill, such as carving wood or knitting, cannot be learned merely by hearing about or even watching it being done. The designated space of the wood workshop itself, the tools and materials, the smell of the wood and glue, the half-finished artefacts at various stages of production as well as the expert woodworker, are all aspects of the social practice that these skills belong to. This is what participation in social practice means, as the anthropologist Jean Lave describes among tailors in Goa, or Tim Ingold shows among reindeer herders in Lapland, or a cellist playing in a string quartet.[9] The same principle applies in contemporary education. Therefore students learn intercultural skills in multicultural settings through real interactions with people from different backgrounds.

As we argue below, connoisseurship and craftsmanship in the field of making things is aisthetic/aesthetic education because it applies knowledge of material qualities and processes to add value to those materials and cultivates the non-material skills of discernment, contextual thinking, and the sense that if a task is worth doing, it is worth doing well. Richard Sennett has claimed that "the craft of making physical things provides insight into the techniques of experience that can shape our dealings with others. Both the difficulties and the possibilities of making things well apply to making human relationships."[10]

Socialization is also about cultivating a relational connection to others and to the world and therefore also means fieldwork and bridging the worlds of school, the workplace and civil society by taking education out into the community and the world of work and of bringing representatives of these fields into school. This can happen through internships and projects, including those that use cultural resources, such as trades unions, non-governmental organizations (NGOs), representatives of local communities, professional associations, government agencies, cultural institutions such as theatres, art galleries, museums and so on.[11]

As we showed in our discussions of aisthetic/aesthetic education and the 'third thing', the process of forming an intimate relationship to the world through rich experience and sharing this in the triadic relation between teacher, subject matter (third thing) and student, takes all three components seriously. Therefore, the way something is taught (and selected, prepared, presented, received, engaged with, shared, conceptualized and applied – as we discuss in Chapter 9) is also a form of socialization. It teaches students how we can relate to the *other* respectfully and out of interest. The way we construct knowledge about the world, and the kind of knowledge we privilege, is also part of the socialization process. The different forms of knowledge give expression to different relationships to the world.

This becomes clearer if we somewhat polarize two different approaches.[12] The first approach treats the world 'out there' as separate from us, as something alien or *other* that can be captured, mastered, isolated from its context, analysed and instrumentalized for our use. This applies to natural phenomena or other cultures and people. It is essentially colonial in gesture. Another, opposite approach assumes that we are part of the world and we approach the object of our inquiry in a careful, respectful way, allowing the phenomenon to 'speak' for itself and in which we, as inquirers, have to learn the 'language' of the phenomenon. In this way of generating knowledge, subject and object are interlocutors, and the relationship is interactive and transactional. Through this engagement, both sides merge their respective horizons, and both are changed by the approach. The first, somewhat caricatured approach is recognizable as a positivist, empirical stance, whereas the second reflects an interpretivist paradigm that is phenomenological and hermeneutic. Teachers need to show that various forms of knowledge are considered valid and of equal value, by showing that different fields of human inquiry require different research methodologies and epistemologies, and that each has its uses.

The key thing about socialization is that it must not be too determining. We should not be training children and young people to become 'this or that' kind of person. We should provide them role models in various ways at different ages, and we should show what kinds of people there are (and have been in history and literature). We should help them feel they belong for as long as they need that, but we also shouldn't hold them back when the time comes to fly the nest, move on, have their own experiences and make their own mistakes. Teachers and adults generally have to show young people not how to be but that they can and should be someone, and that being someone needs to take account of the other 'someones' in the same social space.

Qualification

As Biesta has warned in many publications, the obvious function that schools have in facilitating children and young people to obtain the knowledge and skills they need to participate as capable citizen, often becomes burdened in the 'age of measurement' with the task of quantifying these outcomes, which inevitably influences the way these skills and this knowledge are taught and learned. Learning to the test is not necessarily the best way for young people to acquire skills and knowledge for life. In order to be able to *measure* them, outcomes have to be defined so they can be *measured* and taught so that they can be *measured*. This is the nature of standardization, which is desirable if optimizing identical functionality is the aim, as it would be in building jet engines. The assumption is that without measurement there is no accountability. Of course, teachers (and society) need to know if teaching methods are effective and lead to powerful learning, but there are other ways of demonstrating what has been learned that are in themselves useful in enhancing learning. In their book *Beyond the Tyranny of Testing*, Kenneth Gergen and Scherto Gill[13] offer a number of alternative scenarios. They also offer a poignant example of the deadening effect of learning to the text, that we would like to quote. They cite from a novel by Ted Wodicka,

> "Will this be in the examination, Mr. Hecker?", was the limit of my students' interest in any given subject. If it was going to be in the test they took notes, if it was not going to be in the test they did not take notes. Their silent, depth-less stares were unnerving. I told myself that they were not stupid – for how could the final attainment of thousands of years of human progress be stupid? [14]

Gergen and Gill claim that learning has been reduced to something merely instrumental to achieving some external goal, and has lost the idea of learning out of interest and curiosity. Klaus Holzkamp[15] made the important distinction between defensive learning, in which the motivation is entirely extrinsic accompanied by the wish to avoid stress (from parents or teachers), and expansive learning, which comes from intrinsic motivation to extend one's knowledge and skills as part of a process of self-activity and self-formation. Many politicians, aided and abetted by academics and school leaders (who, by definition, have excelled at exams), pay little attention to this aspect of education, or see awakening student interest as a means to the end of successful exam grades. The importance of social and cultural capital attached to paper qualifications is such that the notion of students' intrinsic interest is conflated with their motivation to learn. What effect does this have on learners who know from early on (as early as formal testing starts) that they are never going to get the top grades? Testing and exams are such a taboo subject in education that everything else simply accommodates it, because every action to make learning more relevant and more meaningful for students is understood by all concerned, including students, who really are not stupid, to be a means to an end, a sugar-coating of the bitter pill.

Another aspect of the drive of standardization and testing is that developmental aspects are generally ignored, especially in secondary education. Reverse engineering pedagogy from specific learning outcomes backwards leads to an 'earlier is better' perspective. The fact that complex competences are built on simpler competences does not necessarily mean that the sooner these are learned, the faster one can move onto the harder stuff. Intra-individual variation within an individual means that the different learning fields may be quite divergent; social and emotional skills may be far behind cognitive skills, motor and coordination skills may be poor, which hinders literacy within an individual. A holistic developmental approach seeks to redress these imbalances *within* individuals and *between* individuals in learning groups, thus creating richer and more inclusive learning environments. In Chapter 4 we discuss this developmental perspective in more detail.

Subjectification

Biesta[16] has paraphrased this somewhat challenging term as 'learning to be a grown-up'. The state of 'grown-up-ness' is one in which individuals step up and take responsibility out of themselves for their actions and act in ecological rather than ego-logical ways. This is about agency, including the positive decision in some situations not to do something, to stay or to go, to say yes or no, as Biesta puts it. The question is: How does education promote, assist and enable the capacity in young people to take decisions on their own? In other words, how does education promote autonomy or freedom, when it is largely compulsory? Biesta refers to Benner's[17] notion of education as a summoning to self-activity, which, as we have seen, was a key idea of Friedrich Schiller's. In Biesta's account of what self-activity means, he argues that if we address children and young people as subjects of their own lives, they will be able to become those subjects, not by telling them what to become or how to be, but by reminding them that can be someone who has the capacity to take the initiative.

Subject-ness- or grown-up-ness often gets summoned into being through resistance, or rather through overcoming resistance; not by toughing it out or fighting back, but by waking up to the opportunities that the situation affords, to ways forward that are fruitful, if possible, for all concerned. That is the work that individuals have to do themselves through their self-activity (which, as Biesta reminds us, is about bringing that self into play). So what can school do, given its obligations to socialization and qualification?

We believe that there are a number of practical answers to this, which we explore in the course of this book. At one level, it is a question of teachers being aware that whatever else they are doing in the classroom, they bear in mind that opportunities for self-activity can be offered. Sometimes it seems easier to tell students exactly what they should do and the harder way from the perspective of energy and time appears to be creating open spaces for open tasks. But a curriculum that is open to opportunities for subjectification is not about offering pseudo-choices. If the subject matter involves encounters with the world that offer authentic experiences that are rich, the question as to what we should do with this is answered by the experience itself. We discuss this in Chapter 8, but here are a couple of examples. Craft work and practical work bring their own context and options as to how to proceed, because the end result is tangible and literally useful, or in the case of performance, satisfying and even cathartic. If the task seems meaningful to the student in the first place, then the self-activity required is apparent, as indeed are the implications of the activity. (What happens if we work against the grain, or cut our cloth too short? Or how will this work fit our existing economic model? What happens if I don't know my lines?) A student who experiences how meaningful fair trade is, will have very different questions and the motivation to act. A student performing Macbeth, who is given the opportunity to interpret the role on stage, will have a very different experience than one who writes an essay analysing Macbeth's motivation based on the text alone (or more likely by asking AI).

Another aspect of subjectification is obviously the maturity of individual students when faced with potentially transformative experiences, though this is rarely addressed in discussions about the process of becoming a subject. Here Waldorf education can make a contribution, as we discuss in Chapter 4 on development, but we can briefly indicate what is presented there. Waldorf education postulates an agentic core of being, the Self, that is active throughout the person's growth and development, though initially not in a conscious way. It is the Self that engages with and 'inhabits' the body and brain, rather than being a product of the physical processes there. The Self gradually comes to expression through the process of embodiment, maturity and individuation (or incarnation as it is referred to in the Waldorf discourse) in the way the person responds to the internal, intrinsic processes and external structures and social expectations. The Self manifests in *how* development unfolds. Therefore, educational situations that prompt or afford *Self*-activity can be deemed to be preparatory to the kind of expressions of subjectification that involve decisions and actions based on insight and conscious choice.

Resilience and sense of coherence

We would like to add to Biesta's three functions of education a further dimension, which may manifest across socialization, qualification and subjectification – namely, dispositions to personal and social resilience, wellbeing, sense of coherence and to learning. Resilience and wellbeing manifest at various levels in the human being. The primary level is bodily, where our sense of interoception registers bodily well-being or distress and disease. Some aspects of resilience are embodied in the way we lead our lives, our habits and proclivities, and these may be a part of our socialization. The process of qualification involves learning about important aspects of living, which are ideally not only in the form of knowledge (What is healthy? What is good or bad for my health and wellbeing? What can I do and what should I avoid?), but in habits and daily life. Changes of lifestyle, developing mindfulness and equanimity, tolerance, patience and persistence usually involve a major effort of will and real insight, and require agency and deliberation and overcoming resistance, and thus belongs in the domain of subjectification.

We propose to include resilience and wellbeing under the heading of 'healthy' learning and development, by which we mean not only learning for healthy lifestyles but the kind of learning that strengthens rather than weakens the health-generating and -maintaining processes in the person. We take a salutogenic (the word means origins of health) approach that was first introduced by the medical sociologist Aaron Antonovsky, and which has subsequently been widely adapted to a range of fields, including education and social care.[18] The Ottawa Charter of the World Health Organization from 1986 declared that health promotion was a question of healthy lifestyles and ways of life that should be promoted through public policies that provide basic requirements of health such as peace, shelter, education, food, basic income, a sustainable ecosystem and social justice. This signalled a major shift from seeing medicine not only as treating disease, but that society can promote health by creating conditions essential to this. Antonovsky's idea of salutogenesis, which seeks to do exactly this, has profound significance for the role of education, not only in terms of educating children and young people to know about what generates health, but also in teaching them in ways that support health-creating processes. He demonstrated that people who have sense of coherence, often abbreviated to SoC, are more resilient. People who have SoC generally feel that the tasks they face in their life are comprehensible, manageable and meaningful (Figure 2.1).

We apply this model to curriculum (see Chapter 8), speaking therefore of salutogenic curricula that promote resilience and reduce the unhealthy effects of education through enhancing self-activity, aesthetic activity, and through structuring the learning process in ways that

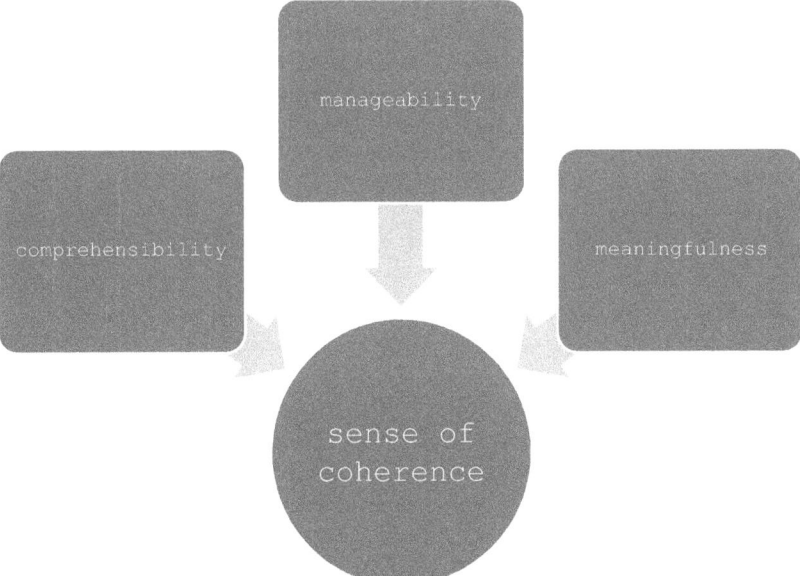

Figure 2.1 Factors contributing to a sense of coherence as a basis for resilience.

resonate with the person and are not alienating.[19] Within the function of socialization, a non-alienating education does not impose learning content and outcomes that students have little relationship to, in a school climate of competition and stress. Within the function of qualification, the learning should include healthy learning dispositions and assessment methods which take the whole person into account - not merely their academic achievements. In terms of subjectification, the agency of the person is the crucial factor in sense of coherence.

Steiner's social theory

In order to contextualize the purpose of education, we would like to explore this using the lens of Rudolf Steiner's theory of social threefolding, which we first have to briefly outline and historically contextualize.

Back in the 1990s there was an attempt by the sociologist Anthony Giddens, in a book titled *The Third Way*, to frame a political path between social democracy and neoliberalism. The third way we are suggesting draws on Rudolf Steiner's social theory, usually referred to a social threefolding.[20] Though this theory grew out of Steiner's lifelong engagement with the spiritual nature of the human being, his social theory was developed over a relatively short period of time in early 1919 in response to the crisis following the First World War in Germany. Steiner's first step was to recognize and affirm Marx's analysis that capitalism alienates the human being from the fruits of their own labour (in Marx's early writings, he also spoke of the alienation of the human spirit, the source of meaning and creativity). Steiner wrote that "Marx and Engels were right to demand a new economic order – right, but one-sided. They did not perceive that economic life can only become free when a free sphere of rights and free cultivation of the spirit are allowed to arise along-side it."[21] However, he saw dangers in utopian social models of the kind being promoted by intellectuals leading the social democratic and workers' movement. He felt that this utopian vision of equality should not be imposed on all spheres of society, and particularly not in education and the cultural sphere, in which individuality and freedom of thought were paramount, and he was against the notion that the workers in the form of a central political institution such as the party should dictate what the economy should do. A top-down imposition of 'equality' suppresses difference and is undemocratic in the sense that it denies the individuals that make up the mass of the 'people' the opportunity to express their own personal ideas based on free thinking.

Steiner was shocked by the immediate consequences of the Bolshevik Revolution in Russia of 1917 and the German Revolution in 1918, in which workers and soldiers' councils (in German these were known as *Räterepubliken*, which in Russian is *soviet*) took over a number of cities in Germany. He saw this as evidence of the negative consequences of a workers' revolution. His heavy criticism of Bolshevik educational reforms (mentioned twice in his First Teachers' Course) was perhaps based on strongly biased newspaper reports.[22] Nevertheless, his concern was that what he called the proletariat were being disempowered by utopian idealogues, in the worst case in the non-democratic one-party situations which have characterized many communist governments. He was concerned that the alternative to capitalist manipulation of the workers would simply be dictatorship of the party. In both cases, the political sphere seeks total control of economic life and cultural life.

To counter both of these tendencies, Steiner's social model recognized three separate, but interconnected spheres; the political/rights sphere, the economy, and the cultural/spiritual life. He was fully committed to a democratic political system, notably in its republican form, in which suitably qualified people are elected by the people to represent the interests of the country as a whole, the *res publica*, the matter (res) of the people (publica) as a whole, rather than only a particular interest group. The basis of a civil society was to be the rule of law under an independent judiciary. All citizens have equal rights, which it is the role of the state to protect. The function of government was to protect the rights of its citizens and defend the country from any forces that threaten the peaceful co-existence of the various social groups. The economy was to serve the needs of the common good by providing for the genuine basic needs of the population (equitable access to food, consumer products, housing, transport etc. This would require entrepreneurship and initiative, which are characteristics of a market economy, but capital formation should be re-invested and major resources including land should be in common ownership. In effect, the economy was to practice stewardship of resources and be based on associations between producers of raw materials, commodities, marketing, transport, retail and consumers. The third major sector was what Steiner called the cultural sector. This included individual thinking and creativity, science and research, spirituality and religion, people creating culture (e.g. the arts), freedom of speech, an independent press and media, as well as independent cultural and educational institutions.

The core idea was that each of these three spheres should be governed by different functional principles. The political sphere is to be democratic. Steiner said little about the forms this should take, but it is clear from his overall writings on the topic that he envisaged a participatory process, which of course only works at small-scale, local or organizational levels, in institutions for example. The Swedish scholar Bo Dahlin[23] has argued that Steiner's understanding of democratic processes is twofold: at one level, it involves participation of individuals; on the other, it means the community functions best when the talents and energies of individuals, especially the rising generation, are allowed to flow into social enterprises. Each person has the right to participate in, and contribute to, all three sectors of society. There are two sides to democratic citizenship; the first is that society should facilitate participation and the other is that individuals take responsibility for their behaviour and it is only when either these sides of the social contract are not respected that the political or rights sphere should become active.

If one thinks of the endless debates between right and left, over whether society is best served by allowing individual freedom of choice in all matters (including the right to carry and use weapons, the right to pollute the environment, to drive at high speed on public highways, and to use natural resources without constraint), or whether the state should regulate life from cradle to grave (referred to by the right as the 'nanny state'), legislating to minimize discrimination, creating equal opportunities in education and the workplace, supporting those who need care to be as independent as possible and so on- then Steiner's analysis is compelling . In the educational sphere, the choice is often polarized between expensive private education (along with social and cultural capital), and 'one-size-fits-all' public education. The question is always one of scale and of finding a dynamic balance of solutions for specific problems. At the local level, where people can better judge each other's needs and interests, it may be easier to give and take, though the evidence from places in which conflict is highly personal and located in close overlapping communities with a long history of mutual fear and hated demonstrates that this is not easy, especially when the differences are reinforced by competing ideologies (for example in Northern Ireland, Palestine and Israel, Russia and Ukraine). Usually, the more abstract and remote the 'other' becomes, the easier it is to depersonalize people and treat them generically. Real-world relationships, even among people who have done bad things to each other, still have the possibility of reconciliation because, ultimately, they know each other.[24] The generative principle of democratic participation is still the most likely route to follow, if it is lived with commitment and responsibility. Human and civil rights were to be guaranteed by law and a fair and independent justice system.

In the economic sphere, the functioning principle according to Steiner should be solidarity in creating win–win situations for all stakeholders. Steiner's idea of common ownership and stewardship of land and natural resources, was not in itself ecological at the time. Today, this aspect would be in the foreground, since the unrestricted exploitation of natural resources and, in particular, the destruction of invaluable and irreplaceable resources such as rain forests, moorland, the ocean floor and so on, has a tangible impact on human life, whatever those who deny human impact on climate change believe (and an independent science would provide the research to support this). Would an economy that used human ingenuity and entrepreneurship responsibly in the interests of all stakeholders be any less effective and innovative? Do people only have good ideas if they think they will get rich? The actual history of human enterprise suggests that the joy of successfully solving problems, adequately honoured and rewarded by fair patent laws, could be just as effective in terms of real economic growth. Those whose ideas contribute most should be rewarded and those whose work makes it possible should also be rewarded and included in profit-share. The neoliberal myth of market forces generally speaking has made a few people outrageously rich, but has not managed to provide a stable economy and secure jobs, and neither has it met actual needs nor furthered sustainability. Yet its promise of wealth for the few, even though the benefits for the majority are illusory, is an easy sell at elections, not least because the alternative, that politicians can regulate and run the economy better, is rarely successful. The American Dream and its neoliberal versions elsewhere has been aptly described by Lauren Berlant as 'cruel optimism'. Michael Rothberg describes, Berlant's perspective as a,

> contemporary moment defined by the 'fraying' of what Berlant calls 'fantasies of the good life' – fantasies that include 'upward mobility, job security, political and social equality, and lively, durable intimacy'. The 'attrition' of these fantasies leads to a paradoxical situation in which the more subjects hew to a normative vision of human flourishing, the less attainable such a vision becomes.[25]

The economy and civil society as a whole benefit from a well-educated population, a science that is genuinely objective and not manipulated to reflect either the interests of ideology or the maximizing of profit for the financial class, a lively, truly free press backed up by thoughtful discourse of ideas, and the critical reflection and stimulation of a flourishing creative world of the arts. The cultural sphere in Steiner's system is the realm of ideas, knowledge generation, of critical thinking, of spiritual activity, freedom of speech and the press, invention, innovation and unconstrained creativity - in short, its generative principle is freedom and truth.

The negative versions of Steiner's threefold functional heuristic can best be realized when one applies the wrong generative principle in the wrong sphere; unrestrained freedom in the economic sphere (as in neoliberalism) means anything goes, with all the implications for the environment and world of work. Unlimited freedom and power for the incumbents of high political office to do whatever they so desire is autocratic and totalitarian. When political leaders determine what is true, what knowledge is valid and what invalid, what people should believe, do, or not do, then individual freedom - of speech, of life choice, control over one's own body, of who one associates with - is at risk, if not non-existent. Democracy, or at least the power of democratically elected governments in the cultural sphere, can mean majoritarianism, in which minority or dissenting voices are marginalized. It may mean that politics manipulates cultural products and arts to serve its political ends.

Perhaps the weakness of Steiner's model is his commitment to a three-fold structuring. From today's perspective it might be necessary to separate the democratic sphere, with its generative principle of participation, from the legal and justice system that has civil and human rights as its generative principle. Furthermore, the nature of identity spans the spiritual-cultural realm that includes individuality and the social realm of civil society and community, making the relationship complex and ambiguous. Our major take-away from Steiner's social model, however, is the position of education.

Steiner's view of an autonomous education

It is worth citing what Steiner said about the status and function of education. Shortly before the opening of the Waldorf School he wrote,

> The real need of the present is that schools be totally grounded in a free spiritual and cultural life. What should be taught and cultivated in these schools must be drawn solely from a knowledge of the growing human being and of individual capacities. A genuine anthropology must form the basis for education and instruction.
>
> We should not ask: what does a person need to know or be able to do in order to fit into the existing social order? Instead, we should ask: what lives in each human being and what can be developed in him or her? Then it will be possible to bring ever new forces into the social order from the rising generations. The life of the social order will be what is made of it by a succession of fully developed human beings who take their places in the social order. The rising generation should not be moulded into what the existing social order chooses to make of it.
>
> A healthy relation exists between school and society only when society is kept constantly supplied with the new and individual potentials of persons whose education has allowed them to develop unhampered. This can be realized only if the schools and the whole education system are placed on a footing of self-administration within the social organism. The government and the economy must receive people educated by the independent spiritual-cultural life; they must not, however, have the power to prescribe (the education) according to their own ideas about how these people are to be educated…It is neither for the state nor the economic life to say: we need someone of this sort for a particular post; therefore test the people that we need and pay heed above all that they know and can do what we want…
>
> The development of the growing human being requires entirely different kinds of thoughts and feeling as its guide. One can only do one's work as an educator when one stands in a free, individual relationship to the pupil one teaches. One must know that, for the guidelines of one's work, one is dependent on knowledge of human nature, the principles of social life and such things…[26]

If we unpack this statement, we can identify a sequence of challenging and interesting ideas that we can update to the current educational policy context and build on:

- Firstly, education should not orientate itself *primarily* on what the economy or state are deemed to require of its new citizens alone, but that education should be based on a reading of the nature of the human being; that is, based on a pedagogical anthropology that takes human spirituality into account. We suggest this for several reasons (which

Steiner didn't outline in the text cited above) and we explain the essential aspects of this pedagogical anthropology in the subsequent chapters. These aspects essentially have to do with an education that engages the whole human being as subject and uses methods that foster a sense of coherence, as well as equipping young people to successfully navigate the uncertainties of the globalized world. As we hope to show, curriculum needs to balance the growth of health-maintaining dispositions and knowledgeable skills through a didactic approach based on themes in the form of living concepts that grow as they weave across the curriculum (rather than subjects in silos) and scaffolded learning through life experience in authentic settings. On another occasion, Steiner suggested that the 'how' of education, i.e. the methods, should be based on a pedagogical anthropology, whilst the 'what', that is, the curriculum content, should be based on analysis by educators of the current and anticipated social and economic 'necessities'.[27]

- Secondly, society as a whole will benefit most if young people are enabled to develop their full potential, even though what this comprises is unpredictable – or rather should not be prescribed. Gert Biesta[28] calls this the 'beautiful risk' of education.
- Another implication of this approach is that the new generation, if allowed to develop their potential, won't just reproduce the exiting status quo but will also bring new energies and perspectives. This is what Dahlin sees as a truly democratic element, because it relies on the new energies and ideas of the 'people' by taking them seriously, honouring what they bring, listening to them. It doesn't mean that we have to respond to their every whim and allow well-functioning structures to be dropped simply because new people don't appreciate them. But it does mean a shift in the balance of power between those in power and those whose power is needed.
- Educational institutions must be allowed to be autonomous – and, of course, accountable. This is not a license for every teacher to follow their own curriculum, or for every school leader to impose their will and ideas; but it does mean that those who take the initiative, judge new innovations, and make changes, do so within the principle of peer-review in the educational discourse, backed by free research and universities whose job it is to cultivate professional connoisseurship.[29] This is a professional skill based on an understanding of the appropriate qualities in the subtle and complex areas of pedagogical intention, organizational structure, curriculum, pedagogy and assessment. Connoisseurship is an individual quality, whereas critical reflection is aimed at developing a better perception of the field, and that requires the involvement of peers. Educational ministers, however motivated they are, are unlikely to possess either connoisseurship or the professional expertise to make judgements about education. The trend to de-professionalizing teachers also underlines missed opportunities to develop both their connoisseurship and critical expertise.
- Teachers must be researchers, creative in their lesson planning, structuring and evaluation and with a strong commitment both to the subject matter and to their students.
- The function of the state is to ensure that there is a level playing field, that all have access to quality educational provision, ensuring that education is adequately funded and that there are robust quality procedures in place. The role of the economic sphere is to signal what its needs are and to provide work experience for students (when done well, internships provide valuable learning experiences for students and companies, who benefit from and reflective educative element in the workplace).

We cite Steiner's model not because we imagine a restructuring of society along threefold lines, but to make the case that the educational approach and curriculum should ideally be in the hands of educators, particularly those directly involved. This does not mean each teacher, or each school, decides (although collaborative and distributed leadership is important). It means that there is an educational consensus in dialogue with policy makers and representatives of civil society and the economic sector. We do not believe that teachers, or even educationalists alone, can determine educational practice. There needs to be research using a range of appropriate methods and there needs to be consultation with stakeholders, including government and students. We acknowledge that it is not possible to have an educational practice without ideological influence, but a more joined-up approach based on the best science on human development and learning, within a framework of the kind of priorities we are suggesting should be possible.

A new framework for schools

We would like to suggest a new framework for contextualizing curriculum. This framework would have a Bildung focus on the development of the person and the qualities of grown-up-ness. It would build on an anthropology of learning that includes what we have described as 'aisthetic' education, and which we elaborate on in Chapter 9, including extended concepts of narrative and literacy. This element builds on practice developed in Waldorf education. The framework would also include a curriculum based on methods and didactics that prompt and support self-activity in all learners, whatever their learning differences. In effect, it would combine the best of contemporary Bildung plus a focus on learning opportunities and holistic learning outcomes that perhaps has closer affinities to anglophone curriculum practice

Such a framework would be genuinely inclusive and diverse, including allowing a high degree of pluralism – though with equitable access – within the educational landscape, because the arguments for biodiversity also apply in cultural life. Schools would have to publish their profiles and local education authorities would register and quality assure them using criteria appropriate to the school's profile. This diversity of approaches would also include a pluralism of examination models, so that student attainment can be assessed both in the specific terms of the educational profile and agreed common standards.

Parental choice on a level playing field offers an element of 'market forces'. Needing to attract parents (and therefore the state funding that goes with this) keeps schools in touch with social and cultural needs and interests. The important thing is to ensure that the 'common school'[30] is not a uniform model. Common standards can be maintained by having common teacher qualifications (though pluralism in higher education equally applies and different teacher education programmes can be aligned through common academic standards without insisting on uniformity). We believe that a level playing field of access to quality education could be achieved through diversity of school profiles – put very simply, with the same investment and funding key, different sustainable school models can emerge. This would allow both parental and teacher choice, as some countries including Ukraine currently practice.

We argue that this third way combines the best of a modern Bildung approach with the best of competence-orientated approaches. In place of the traditional competence-based curricula, we recommend a combination of themes and potentialities, dispositions, habits of mind and knowledgeable skill with purpose (which we explain in Chapter 6). What is important is that curriculum provides learning opportunities with high relevance and reality factors, within which students can learn to develop their potential across specific capacities.

We don't think Waldorf education as it is currently practiced achieves this with inclusive groups of learners. At its best it is successful with self-selecting groups (i.e. because of parental background), but in public Waldorf schools, charter schools and publicly funded independent Waldorf schools (e.g. in Germany, the Netherlands, Norway, Estonia, Australia, British Columbia etc.), it has also demonstrated that it can work very successfully with heterogenous groups in schools in which leadership and collegial capacities are able to apply a Waldorf ethos and methods. This book hopes to provide an approach in which aspects of Waldorf education can be adapted to a much wider range of school settings.

Task for the reader

The readers of this book are highly unlikely to be able to influence the way that education is organized, funded and controlled by the state. But consider:

- Do your colleagues in your school or educational setting have a shared understanding of what the purpose of education is? How do you know? How could you explore this?
- To what extent does your school have the purpose of qualification, socialization, individuation and wellbeing/resilience? Are these well balanced, or is the focus to heavily placed on, for example, qualification?

Notes

1 Gibb, N. (2015b). *The Purpose of Education*. 9 July 2015. Education Reform Summit, London. https://www.gov.uk/government/speeches/the-purpose-of-education.
2 The European Commission Eurydice website offers up to date statement of policy developments with EU member states, https://eurydice.eacea.ec.europa.eu/news/denmark-transforming-education-governments-initiative-reform-primary-and-lower-secondary.
3 Biesta, G. J. J. (2022). *World-Centred Education. A View for the Present*. Routledge. In particular, Chapter 4.
4 See Vygotsky, L. S. (1978). *Mind in Society: The Development of Higher Psychological Processes* (M. Cole, V. John-Steiner, S. Scribner, & E. Souberman, Eds.). Harvard University Press.
5 See Rogoff, B. (1995). Observing sociocultural activity in three planes: participatory appropriation, guided participation and apprenticeship. In J. V. Wertsch, P. del Rio, & A. Alvarez (Eds.), *Sociocultural Studies of Mind* (pp. 139–163). Cambridge University Press.
6 Hurrelmann, K., & Bauer, H. P. (2018). *Socialisation During the Life Course*. Routledge.
7 Dreier, O. (2011). Personality and conduct of everyday life. *Nordic Psychology*, 63(2), 4–23.
8 Here Jean Lave paraphrases Dreier: Lave, J. (2012). Changing practice. *Mind, Culture and Activity*, 19(2), 156–171, p. 165.
9 Lave, J. (1997). On learning. *Forum Kritische Psychologie. Lernen*, 38 (Holzkamp-Symposium), 120–135; Ingold, T. (2000). *The Perception of the Environment: Essays in Livelihood, Dwelling and Skill*. Routledge.
10 Sennett, R. (2008). *The Craftsman*. Penguin Books, p. 289.
11 This a practice that the XP schools have developed, see Sprakes, A. & Harri, A. G. (2019) How We XP. What happens when 2 punks from Donny decide to open a school. XP School Trust/The Edge Foundation https://www.xpschool.org/howwexp.
12 We borrow this idea from Horst Rumpf, Rumpf, H. (2010). *Was hätte Einstein gedacht, wenn er nicht Geige gespielt hätte? Gegen die Verkürzung des etablierten Lernbegriffs*. Juventa Verlag.
13 Gergen, K., & Gill, S. R. (2020). *Beyond theTyranny of Testing. Relational Evaluation in Education*. Oxford University Press.
14 Wodicka, T. (2009) *All Shall be Well; and All Shall be Well; and All Manner of Things Shall be Well*. Penguin Random House, p. 116.
15 Holzkamp, K. (1995). *Lernen: Subjektwissenschaftliche Grundlegung (Learning: a basis for a subject-scientific approach)*. Campus.
16 See Biesta, G. J. J. (2022). *World-Centred Education. A View for the Present*. Routledge.
17 Benner, D. (2020). *Umriss der allgemeinen Wissenschaftsdidaktik. Grundlagen und Orientierung für Lehrerbildung, Unterricht und Forschung* [Outline of general scientific didactics as basis and orientation for teacher education, teaching and research]. Beltz.

18 Antonovsky, A. (1996). The salutogenic model as a theory to guide health promotion. *Health Promotion International*, *11*(1), 11–18. For an overview of the applications of the construct of salutogenesis see also Mittelmark, M. B., Sagy, S., Eriksson, M., Bauer, G. F., Pelikan, J. M., Lindström, B., Espnes, G. A., et al. (2017). *The Handbook of Salutogenesis*. Springer. https://doi.org/10.1007/978-3-319-04600-6.
19 See Lave, J., & Packer, M. (2008). Towards a social ontology of learning. In K. Nielsen, S. Brinkmann, C. Elmholdt, L. Tanggaard, P. Musaeus, & G. Kraft (Eds.), *A Qualitative Stance: In Memory of Steinar Kvale, 1938–2008* (pp. 17–46). Aarhus Universitetsforlag. These authors argue that much pedagogy alienates learners from the school process and the topics that they are made to learn.
20 See Steiner, R. (2018). *Social Threefolding. Rebalancing Culture, Politicis and Economics* (C. von Arnim, Trans.). Rudolf Steiner Press. (GA338). This is a new translation of Steiner's original book from 1919.
21 Steiner, R. (1919/1985). Marxism and the Threefold Social Order in *The Renewal of the Social Organism. And What Socialist Do Not See*, Vol. 24 in *Collected Works*. Anthroposophic Press.
22 A report in a Geneva newspaper was even reported in the *New York Times* from 11 June 1919 and Steiner appears to draw on the Swiss source, since he could not have had any direct evidence from Russia. The article was lurid in its judgements "Reds are ruining children of Russia", "System of calculated moral depravity…".
23 Dahlin, B. (2010). Steiner Waldorf education, social-threefolding and civil society: Education as cultural power. *Research on Steiner Education*, *1*(1), 49–59. www.rosejourn.com.
24 The final episode of the BBC TV series *Once Upon a Time in Northern Ireland* shows the possibilities and limits of reconciliation.
25 Rothberg, M. (2023). Feeling Implicated: An introduction. *Parallax*, *29*(3), 265–282, p. 272. https://www.tandfonline.com/doi/full/10.1080/13534645.2024.2302663.
26 Steiner, R. (1985/1919) *The Threefold Social Order and Educational Freedom in The Renewal of the Social Organism*. Anthroposophic Press, pp. 71–72.
27 Steiner, R. (1996/1921) Address to Parents of the Waldorf School on 13th January 1921. In *Rudolf Steiner in the Waldorf School: Lectures and addresses to children, parents and teachers*. Anthroposophic Press.
28 Biesta, G. J. J. (2013). *The Beautiful Risk of Education*. Paradigm Publishers.
29 This term was coined by Elliot Eisner which, together with effective criticism, means focusing on qualities in education, without which criticism has no foundation. Eisner, E. W. (2017). *The Enlightened Eye. Qualitative Inquiry and the Enhancement of Educational Practice*. Teachers College Press.
30 This is a reference to Peter Moss and Michael Fielding's (2011). *Radical Education and the Common School*. Routledge.

3 What is curriculum?

Overview

We argue that the process of crafting curriculum must start with the educational aims we have, because curriculum is a means or pathway to a particular set of goals. We introduce the notion of a layered curriculum, which means that there is a common view of child and youth development, a second – meso – level of specific themes, subject content, skills and knowledge, based on what is locally required, and a micro layer of the teacher at school level. The pedagogical anthropology and notion of development that underpin this approach is taken up in subsequent chapters; pedagogical anthropology in Chapter 4, development in Chapter 5. This chapter then focusses on the meso level and explores the issues that need to be addressed to develop curriculum at the local level.

Curriculum can be a slippery concept

Readers will know that curriculum is a contested topic. National standardized curricula specify what should be taught, and what the outcomes of that teaching should be. In teacher/school-based curricula, what is taught is based on local perceptions of what is needed. The 'knowledge-rich' curriculum focuses on prescribed knowledge as a means to access the current cultural, academic and social orthodoxy. Other curricula focus on competences, which are generally understood to combine knowledge, skills and attitudes. Curriculum exists in a climate of measuring outcomes, driven by what Gert Biesta calls the 'Global Educational Measurement Industry'.[1] This creates a dilemma: knowledge is easier to assess and quantify than skills, which have to be demonstrated, and hardest of all is the assessment of learning dispositions, resilience and other so-called soft skills.

One of the rarely discussed, but important aspects of educational discourse is the fact that educational traditions, assumptions and policies reflect national (or federal state) identities. Sometimes this is explicit, as in England where, in re-writing the national curriculum, the then education minister argued that the curriculum should contain "the body of knowledge that makes up our intellectual inheritance as a society…A common stock of knowledge on which we can all draw and trade."[2] Elsewhere the influence is less obvious, but often stronger than is realized.

Language also has an impact. Key concepts in education cannot be automatically translated from one culture and language to another; even within a single language, concepts such as learning, competence, capacity, ability, methods and methodology and didactics, shift in their meaning over time.[3] As Rebekka Horlacher[4] has shown, the English term 'curriculum' is not the same as its German translation *Lehrplan*, and its

DOI: 10.4324/9781003518471-4

meaning has changed over the past hundred years. Since the 1960s, curriculum, which comes from the Latin *cursus*, meaning racecourse or the path to be followed, has become synonymous with prescribed content and outcomes. *Lehrplan*, which now has broadly the same meaning, was once the whole educational approach, often conceived as a kind of work or art, frequently the result of a single mind. *Lehrplan* in its original meaning (and still current in Scandinavian countries) is closely associated with Bildung. It is this meaning that we align with.[5]

Defining educational aims

Curriculum usually starts with subjects and what needs to be taught in those subjects, rather than starting with the aims of the educational approach or school/setting and seeing how these can be realized, including through subjects.[6] An old colleague of Martyn's often said, "we don't teach subjects, we teach students". We suggest that the aim is to teach students, and this involves subjects, but not exclusively. Often the aims are taken for granted: to educate the students, to pass exams, to equip them for the workforce. As Michael Reiss & John White put it, however, "an aims-led curriculum...starts with the needs and wants of students", unlike, for example, the structure of the National Curriculum in England. These authors recommend starting from two very general aims, to equip each child:

- to lead a life that is personally flourishing and
- to help others to do so, too.

They point out that these aims align with those of a democracy,

> An autocracy or oligarchy may want children to be brought up to serve the interests of the few in power; a utilitarian utopia, to work for the good of all; a theocracy, to carry out what is discerned as God's will. In a democracy, individuals are intrinsically important and their interests are not to be sacrificed to others...But individuals also live in a community, or more accurately, in various overlapping communities, and must be educated for this too. If democracies prize everyone's intrinsic well-being, each child should also be brought up to help protect and promote this.[7]

Furthermore, Reiss and White go on to agree that "A central aim of the school should be to prepare students for a life of autonomous, wholehearted and successful engagement in worthwhile relationships, activities, and experiences" and recommend that this should be learned as much as possible through direct experience. They make the interesting observation that teachers know best how to implement a school's aims at the local level, taking their particular students and their background context into account, but that they do not have a monopoly on determining the aims of education. We think this view is valid, although it contradicts a commonly held view within Waldorf education. Whilst Steiner said that teachers should determine the content and teaching methods, as far as we know, he did not talk about the aims, probably because he saw no further need for aims other than that of enabling each child to realize their potential, which is an idea embedded in a Bildung understanding of education. However, though we would not disagree with this 'highest endeavour',[8] the details of what specific aims the school should have probably needs a wider base of informed consensus than solely teachers.

Just as grand claims to inclusion and diversity are easier to state than to realize, having idealistic aspirations for education depends on the *how* and the *who* of actual implementation. We recommend a more pragmatic approach of exploring what the transnational policies suggest and then use this as a basis for local decisions. This way we don't have to reinvent the wheel, but we can modify the wheels on offer to include what we (i.e. those responsible for curriculum development) think is important and adapt what we disagree with.

The educational aims of a curriculum need to be formulated in a broad way, allowing multiple ways of fulfilling them. The aims should not be so extensive and detailed that basically everything is compulsory. This may seem obvious if one assumes that teachers are highly qualified professionals who are expected, and allowed, to make professional judgements. At the classroom level, teachers should be free to use their pedagogical expertise to engage in the art and craft of teaching, choosing topics, methods and materials to construct lesson plans to engage specific groups of learners.

Many contemporary frameworks highlight the importance of:

- learning as the core act in education, which should be based on the science of learning,
- learning to learn,
- adaptability and the ability to learn quickly in new work situations,
- the development of higher cognitive skills such as understanding complex concepts, creative thinking and analytical skills (recognizing that these skills are learned in the humanities subjects),
- the ability to form judgements and be discerning,
- enabling people to flourish according to their talents, with the ability to develop expertise,
- wellbeing and good mental health (and providing effective diagnostic and therapeutic tools),
- the quality of human interactions and collaboration, which can never be replaced by artificial intelligence,
- experiential learning,
- the importance of community,
- democratic capability,
- equity in access to high-quality education.

They also show that school curricula and school practice lags far behind policy intentions, and that, in some cases, national policies are also unaware of these international trends. Facts and knowledge figure little in these frameworks. Obviously knowledge is needed, but we would argue that what is more important today is knowledge about how to find useful knowledge, how to generate knowledge, how to evaluate it, how to correlate it with other knowledge, and how to apply it. The OECD report on high-performing school systems noted that "over 90% of British teachers say their role is to facilitate inquiry, yet Britain leads the world in rote learning".[9]

Reiss and White also suggest striving towards interdisciplinary cooperation and the greater use of cross-curricular themes (such as Waldorf education uses in its block system of teaching) and they suggest the use of individual student portfolios to track and monitor individual learning progression, rather than having high-stakes testing. We would also agree with the other recommendations they make regarding the role of school inspections, including the suggestion that schools be required to take all students who apply from a given geographically demarcated area. Digital portfolios would enable the integration of new students joining the school at any stage. If teachers are given the freedom to formulate how they intend to implement national aims and the pedagogical autonomy to teach in a way that meets the needs of actual students, they should also be able to integrate students with all levels of ability and backgrounds (always assuming a basic level of professional development among teachers). The price of autonomy is demonstrating high professional standards.

The aims of Waldorf education: an example of how aims shape curriculum

There are a number of different versions of the aims of Waldorf education, which just shows that this is no monolithic organization with a unified concept or policies. However, most of the formulations circle around some shared ideas. In a recent book[10] addressed to an internal Waldorf audience we formulated these aims in our own words, as follows.

Waldorf education aims to:

1 Enable each child and young person to develop and realize their potential and to flourish,
2 Enable each young person to develop the abilities to become an autonomous, well-balanced, mature citizen, capable of acting peacefully, ethically and ecologically on the basis of their own powers of judgement, discernment, connoisseurship and insight,
3 Enable each student to learn the skills, dispositions and knowledge to become lifelong learners and actively participate in and contribute to the world of work and civil society,
4 Support the students' health-creating processes and resilience,
5 Enable the participation of children from all social and cultural backgrounds,
6 Counter racism and all forms of discrimination and cultivate cosmopolitan and intercultural capabilities,
7 Encourage school communities to contribute to sustainability,
8 Encourage and enable teachers to work together in collegial ways to deepen their pedagogical understanding through reflection, study, evaluation and action research.
9 Make a significant contribution to cultural life internationally.

When describing aims, we are aware that these are aspirational and that not every school and every teacher will always be able to fulfil these aims. The important thing is that teachers are aware of the aims of their institution and align their work towards their realization. We believe these aims are realistic and meaningful as orientation.

The original layered curriculum

In the course of his work on the international development of curricula within Waldorf education, Martyn began to formulate the notion of a layered or nested curriculum. Let us briefly outline the problem that the layered curriculum was intended to solve.

When the first Waldorf School was founded in 1919, Steiner gave a few lectures on curriculum. Over the course of the five years that he was guiding the development of the school, he encouraged the teachers to develop the curriculum further, based on the following considerations.

- The teachers should orientate themselves on the nature of the developing child.
- They should consider what children and young people should learn so that they would be able to contribute to society on leaving school.
- They should consider the didactic effects of the various teaching methods and subjects.
- They should take the entire context into account.

Martyn showed, in his recent article[11] in the way curriculum in the Waldorf movement has been translated and transmitted across time and space, that most Waldorf practitioners historically believed that the curriculum they used was valid because it was original and derived from the founder Rudolf Steiner, or at least from the first Waldorf school. To use an arboreal metaphor, many assumed that their school and its curriculum had grown from an 'acorn' from the original tree, because that was important for the identity of Waldorf education. Whilst this was certainly the case in the first generations, in practice, in Waldorf schools beyond Stuttgart, and especially those in countries in which another language is spoken and there is another educational culture, teachers – and especially founding teachers – have, in fact, modified the education on the basis of their personal and cultural educational experiences. Whilst espousing their *Waldorf* identity, they have often adopted local cultural practices in a rhizomic rather than an arboreal way.

In 1925, Caroline von Heydebrand published the first Waldorf curriculum.[12] It was intentionally very minimalist, based on Steiner's advice that the less said the better with regard to the local education ministry. Von Heydebrand also pointed out that this 'ideal' curriculum would have to be adapted to suit changing circumstances. However, when Waldorf education was taken up in other countries, something which was already happening in the 1920s, it generally did not follow her guidance. Rather, the Waldorf movement tended to canonize this first curriculum, and to this day, in some places it is widely and naively reproduced on the assumption that as a totality it has the imprint of a coherent unity, which, like a work of art, cannot be substantially changed without a loss of integrity. Any innovation has generally required a legitimacy of association with the founding mythos, the narrative of the founding of the first Waldorf School in Stuttgart or by reference to Steiner, in order to maintain this legitimacy. Over recent decades, however, this adherence to the canon has gradually weakened. Instead of having to demonstrate fidelity to an almost sacred dogma, innovations have increasingly justified themselves on the basis that they meet new needs whilst remaining within the orbit of certain generative principles that are deemed to be derived from the original 'ideal curriculum'. The 'original' content of the curriculum has been modified to align with new and local perspectives.

Fortunately, the process we refer to in this book has been widely taken up around the world and Waldorf education in in the process of modifying its 'traditions' in response to changing circumstances. Martyn's 'layered' curriculum was first taken up by Waldorf UK and then by the European Council of Steiner Waldorf Education for its common core curriculum framework. The basic structure of the layered curriculum can be shown as in Figure 3.1.

These three layers of curriculum are embedded in a shared meta level comprising the generative principles of Waldorf education. If all schools share the same basic pedagogical principles and a common curriculum framework, then local variations can be

What is curriculum? 59

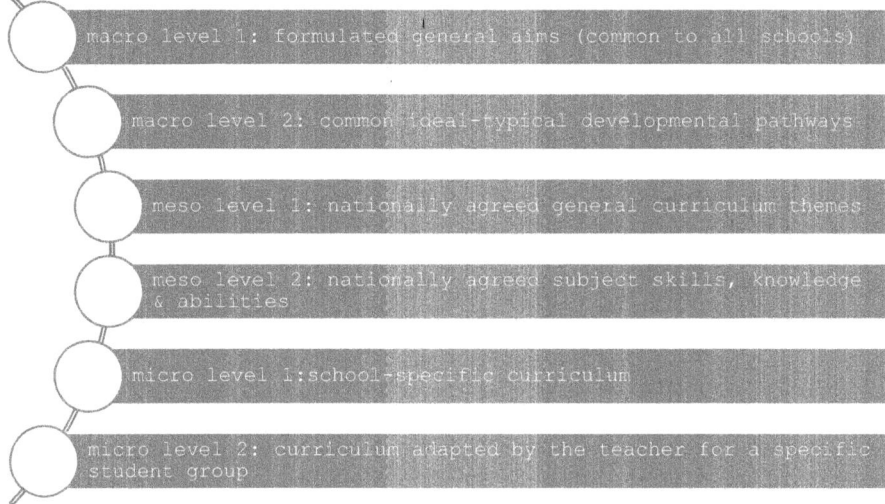

Figure 3.1 The three (double) levels of curriculum.

modified over geographical space and over time, as society changes and different demands are made on the population. At the classroom level, teachers are free to adapt their curriculum within the wider meso-macro framework according to the specific needs of their students in context.

Building on our work on the Waldorf curriculum in the UK, in Europe, as well as in Asia, we have identified generic aspects that we think may be useful for anyone crafting a curriculum in any context. We start with the meta level (meta means overall context, which is why the social media company of the same name uses the term).

Generic meta level

Education always happens in a specific social and cultural context, which includes historical, geographical, economics factors – this provides the meta-space or meta level of curriculum. All curricula depend on what the aims of the education are, and so therefore we start with a formulation of the aims of the education. This also includes referring to an underlying pedagogical anthropology, the generative principles governing teaching and learning, the school climate and learning culture that is generated by the actual lived practices in the school. It also requires that curriculum makers and implementers take account of the diverse socio-cultural context of the school.

Macro level

If, as we are suggesting here, we take a developmental, age-related view of curriculum, then we need to be aware of the developmental tasks facing children and young people at the various stages over the life course in the school context (we outline these below in Chapter 5). We are suggesting that curriculum addresses both the *how* of teaching and learning and also the *what*. Therefore, at the macro level of curriculum, we are concerned not with specific subject content but with the way in which the learning process takes account of the developmental stage.

Since our approach to curriculum builds on a developmental pedagogical anthropology (which we discuss in Chapter 4), the macro level involves an overview of the overall institutional structures and the kinds of teaching methods that belong to each developmental phase or transition – for example, the methods used in the first primary classes will be different to those in the middle school (or junior high school level). Children learn differently at different ages, and this can and should be planned, so it is not left to chance.

The macro level therefore describes developmental themes that can be taken up across the different subjects and topic fields. If the theme is, for example, the relationship between the individual and society at the basic level, then this can be taken up as a topic in story material, in lessons about food production in traditional, pre-industrial communities or how different early societies organize themselves. This topic can be used in literacy, art or life skills lessons. In other words, the developmental theme gives the subject structures another orientation than merely skills progression; it gives them a meaningful context that shapes the development of the child's understanding of their own changing relationship to the society they are embedded in and opportunities to learn how this may vary in other cultures and at other times in history.

The meso-level curriculum

At this level a curriculum specifies what should be learned, when, where and why, and what outcomes are expected. The meso-level curriculum has three dimensions:

1 The vertical curriculum. This shows the development within the individual learning fields and subjects from start (first grade) to finish (last grade), for example in maths or geography.
2 The horizontal curriculum. This shows the subjects taught in a single year group and how they relate to the overall developmental themes for this year.
3 The spiral curriculum that tracks the cultivation of key dispositions and abilities across subjects and age groups, that are not confined to any one subject. These include abilities such as social and intercultural competences or themes such as gender and identity, individual and society, sustainability, media maturity.

Since it is rare that anyone is in a position to start with an empty screen when designing curriculum, the process usually starts with reviewing the existing situation. This involves the follow issues:

- If the meso-level curriculum is to support the overall learning and development of the students, then it is necessary to establish what dispositions, habits of mind, skills and knowledge should students have and by when (e.g. at certain transitional stages or when they leave school).
- What the statutory requirements are, what room for interpretation these afford and where there is scope for shaping curriculum.
- Identifying the ways in which each subject discipline can contribute to the dispositions, skills and knowledge outlined above.
- The existing curriculum, in as much this can be modified, should be reviewed, as to whether it is still relevant on a subject by subject, or age-by-age basis. What necessity

and what scope is there for change? What criteria are relevant? Who should conduct such a review?
- Since curricula cannot be infinitely expanded and loaded with ever more content, and there is always a trade-off between quality and quantity of content, criteria need to be drawn up setting priorities and finding a balance between socialization, qualification and subjectification, between dispositions, skills and knowledge, between the wellbeing of the person and the assumption about what is considered essential.
- Curriculum work always needs to bear in mind how its tangible and intangible outcomes can be meaningfully assessed.
- Following our comprehensive approach to curriculum, we acknowledge that the way something is taught is often as important as what is taught, so consideration should be given to methods and pedagogy. This should not be prescriptive; however, some indication of the kind of methods that are suitable should be given. It is important that teachers can use their professional judgement as to how something is taught, including when and where, so the suggestions regarding methods are just that – suggestions. Their significance is that the way something is taught makes assumptions about how children and young people learn, how they do this in a healthy and effective way, what theory of knowledge informs this approach and whether the aim is to convey specific knowledge, build capacities, and establish dispositions and ways of seeing, or to provide tools for learning.

Now we will consider some of these aspects in a little more detail.

Educational aims

Since these are usually given or recommended in existing, national or transnational policy frameworks, we do not have to re-invent the wheel. What we do need to do is prioritize which aims are important for our curriculum. Since the conditions in which children and young people grow and develop can change rapidly, new priorities need to be identified and incorporated. Based on our understanding of needs, we see the following educational aims as highly relevant. Students need:

- to grow dispositions to wellbeing, resilience, personal and social skills and human flourishing.
- to develop powers of discernment and judgement across a range of literacies, including the capacity to generate knowledge,
- to develop democratic capability,
- to develop dispositions to intercultural competence, empathy and social solidarity,
- to develop the capacities to engage with others in dealing with wicked problems,
- to develop the capacity to take responsibility for one's actions.

Statutory requirements

A requirement can be general or specific and it is worth exploring in detail exactly what is required and how much leeway there is for generous (from the perspective of your curriculum intentions) interpretation. Also, one can seek to arrive at prescribed outcomes by different means and learning pathways and even through judicious renaming. A case in point some years ago was the requirement that primary school classes incorporate technology. In the UK, this included kindergarten, since the Waldorf approach prefers children to be in early childhood education up until they enter formal school at the age of six. Together with a helpful Ofsted inspector, we decided that grinding wheat in a hand mill and baking bread in an oven (and all the tools and materials required in that process) constitute 'warm' or analogue technology – which indeed it is. If children have learned to work with real tools and materials, they have a real foundation for understanding more complex, mechanical and electric tools and therefore appreciate and value the processes involved.

There is often an inflation of terminology in state curricula (the same statements are applied from secondary to PhD level – such as critical reflection), so it is helpful to be as exact as possible and give examples of what this might mean at this level.

Taking the existing curriculum into account

Before revising curriculum, it is important to take stock of what needs changing, and to consult stakeholders on this. Whilst we are arguing that teachers are the people who should be designing curriculum, it obviously helps to garner the views of students, parents, universities, and employers without committing to adopting the suggestions of any of these stakeholders.

Things to consider are new developments – the most obvious being in the digital and artificial intelligence world - but they should also be in technology more generally, updates in science and history, recent literature and art and all aspects of culture.

Subject disciplines

Within the exiting canon of subject disciplines (and potentially any new ones), it is necessary to identify the way in which each subject field contributes to the overall aims. Let us assume that you have moved beyond a curriculum based on Michael Gove's[13] version of E.D. Hirsch's 'important facts every citizen should know'; then one has to explore the didactics of disciplinary subjects, that is, how the teaching and learning within the subjects affects the student's overall learning and development. Hirsch's notion of cultural literacy, like literary literacy, is not in itself wrong; it is just a very narrow understanding of knowledge. We take the view that any form of literacy requires basic knowledgeable skills, such as knowing what literature is and how to access it, for which a limited number of exemplary experiences are needed. Once that threshold has been achieved, and this is often quite an individual matter, then literacy is unconstrained. The reader can then ask: How can I understand this literature in its socio-cultural and historical context and what does it reveal about the preoccupations, interests, mindset, and stance of people at a particular period of history, or even of the author (they may be similar or different)? We can learn how to analyse how literature has the effects it had on contemporary readers or on readers today. Students can also learn to articulate how reading affects them personally. This is called an interpretive or hermeneutic approach to literature. It also undoubtedly opens the mind to the act of reading for pleasure and edification with some degree of discernment and appreciation. Anyone who wants to write well, whether poetry, prose, journalism, non-fiction or scientific texts, needs to learn this through appreciation of existing texts and understanding the tools of the trade, the genres, the effect of stylistic devices, in short how to use language skilfully to serve whatever aims we have.

The same is true for the wider concept of cultural literacy, which includes many other expressions of culture, such as ideas, including science, religion, philosophy, the arts, the relationship of human cultures to their spiritual and physical environment, architecture, and so on. An adequate cultural literacy is a knowledgeable skill to 'read' and create cultural products. A basic amount of knowledge, together with the skills to apply and interpret this and the ability to apply these knowledgeable skills critically to other fields, is, we believe, an important aspect of curriculum, if we want our citizens to learn discernment and critical judgement, especially in the face of propaganda, nationalistic narratives, ideological perspectives and basically fake or distorted information.

Ensuring the curriculum is manageable

The main thing to avoid is adding to an already very full curriculum. Subject discipline specialists rarely consider their subject, or even aspects of it, redundant or superfluous – rather the opposite. Whoever is responsible for the curriculum review needs to listen to the subject specialists, but also to pose the question, 'Where can we do cross-curricular work (for example by offering themes across subjects, such as sustainability, democracy, gender, etc.)?'

This means that schools (or the next higher authority making the decisions) have to have a rationale for all subjects that answers the question: Why are we teaching this in this way within the overall framework of our pedagogical aims?

In the end, priorities have to be set that do not water everything down or overload the curriculum. This is why wide consultation is necessary and good arguments found for cutting anything or adding anything. It may be necessary to distinguish between core curriculum for all and options with choices, which students may make.

Micro-level curriculum

The micro level is where teachers plan their lessons, using the macro and meso descriptions for orientation. How teachers do this requires their working knowledge of the art, craft and science of pedagogy, their ability to read the needs of their actual students, and their intelligent application of methods, such as differentiation, group work, direct experience, narrative, media etc. We address this in Chapter 9 on connoisseurship in teaching.

Task for the reader

Try to identify in the curriculum you work with, or with which you are familiar, what would be the equivalents of the:

- meta level (pedagogical anthropology, aims of the education)
- macro level (developmental dimension)
- meso level (Does this include any guidance on when, where, how and why of the suggested content? If you had to expand your curriculum to include these, what examples immediately come to mind?)

Notes

1 Biesta, G. J. J. (2010). *Good Education in the Age of Measurement: Ethics, Politics and Democracy*. Paradigm Publishers.
2 Gove, M. (2009, 30 June) *What is Education For?* [Speech transcript] Royal Society of Arts. https://conservativehome.blogs.com/files/090630-gove-speech-to-rsa.pdf.

3 Nieke, W. (2012). *Kompetenz und Kultur: Beiträge zur Orientierung in der Moderne (Competence and culture: Contributions towards an orientation in modernity)*. Springer VS.
4 Horlacher, R. (2018). The same but different: the German Lehrplan and curriculum. *Journal of Curriculum Studies*, 50(1), 1–16. https://doi.org/10.1080/00220272.2017.1307458.
5 We draw on the definition of curriculum offered by Bo Dahlin (2017). *Rudolf Steiner. The Relevance of Waldorf Education*. This definition is located within the landscape of Bildung and is also specific to Waldorf education.
6 See Michael, J. Reiss and John White (2013). An Aims-Based Curriculum. The significance of human flourishing for schools. Institute of Education Press. Bedford Way Papers Series.
7 See Michael, J. Reiss and John White (2013). An Aims-Based Curriculum. The significance of human flourishing for schools. Institute of Education Press. Bedford Way Papers Series, p. 2.
8 Probably the most-quoted quote in Waldorf education is the statement, "Our highest endeavour must be to develop free human beings who are able of themselves to impart purpose and direction to their lives. The need for imagination, a sense of truth, and a feeling of responsibility – these three forces are the very nerve of education." It is not entirely clear when and where Steiner said this, and some sources name Marie Steiner, Steiner's wife and the executor of his complete works, when she edited his lectures. It certainly aligns with Steiner's thoughts.
9 OECD 2022 *High Performing Systems. Dialogues about the future of education systems in a changing world*. May 2022 OECD Publication.
10 Rawson, M., & Bransby, K. (2025). *Waldorf Education for the 21st Century. New Perspectives on Foundations, Principles and Practice*. Floris Books.
11 Rawson, M. (2024). Translating, transmitting and transforming Waldorf curricula: one hundred years after the first published curriculum in 1925. *Frontiers in Education*, 9-2024. https://doi.org/10.3389/feduc.2024.1306092.
12 Heydebrand, v. (1925/1994). *Vom Lehrplan der Freien Waldorfschule*. Verlag Freies Geistesleben. This was translated as von Heydebrand, C. (1966/1972). *Curriculum of the First Waldorf School* (E. Hutchins, Ed. & Trans.). Steiner Schools Fellowship Publications.
13 Hirsch, E. D. (1988). *Cultural Literacy. What Every American Needs to Know. Includes 5,000 Essential Names, Phrases, Dates and Concepts*. Vintage. Michael Gove was Education Secretary of the UK from 2010 to 2014. Working with Nick Gibb, he introduced a British version of a Hirsch-inspired curriculum into the English National Curriculum. The idea behind this approach is that cultural literacy is based on that idea that citizen need a certain knowledge set (of facts, ideas, literary works, history dates) to be able to function effectively and that children need to learn these facts in a highly structured way. The original ideas of Hirsch were to counter social inequality, because students from certain background lack this knowledge because of their socialization or poor education, whereas these were staples of middle-class liberal arts (notably college) education. Hirsch's ideas have been taken up by certain right-wing think tanks and it certainly was enthusiastically taken up by Michael Gove and Nick Gibb, the Schools Minister. For a discussion of the politics involved, see https://www.bbc.com/news/education-20041597.

4 A pedagogical anthropology

Overview

The chapter starts by explaining what a pedagogical anthropology is and why it is necessary for crafting curriculum, by showing that what and how we teach should take into account who learns and how this is best done. This perspective asks teachers to consider their general understanding of the nature of the human being. The anthropology that is being suggested here is also a way of studying children and young people and is located within the overall educational philosophy of Bildung. This sees the function of education as supporting the self-formation of the person in a cultural context. We then introduce the central elements in a pedagogical anthropology based on Steiner's understanding of the human being as applied in Waldorf education and show what implications this has for pedagogy. We look at several aspects of the nature of the Self as the spiritual core of the human being, the embodiment of Self, the emergence of self-awareness. This includes a discussion of the relationship between an agentic Self as core of individuality and the question of identity. We conclude by summarizing what this anthropology implies for crafting curriculum (Figure 4.1).

What is educational anthropology?

The subject of education, and thus of curriculum, is the developing young human being and therefore the way we educate has to take the nature of the human being into account. In fact, we believe it should be the starting point, from which all else follows. We start not with the individual person isolated from their context, but with the social person. Our students are embedded in social and cultural life situations that we need to take into account, and we hope that they leave their education with the capacities to contribute to society in constructive ways and make a positive contribution. We hope to educate in ways that enable them to take responsibility for their actions and for the well-being of the wider society they are part of. What they do, how they behave, their ethical actions in relation to other people and the environment are strongly influenced, but not determined by their education.

Though each person is a unique individual, we all have enough in common to consider that there are some generalities that we share. That is the meaning of the term anthropology, which is derived from the Ancient Greek *anthropos*, referring to the human being, and *logos*, which refers to knowledge and how knowledge is generated. Anthropology is therefore knowledge of and through the human being. It follows that educational anthropology is therefore the knowledge about the human being that is

66 Crafting a Curriculum of Coherence

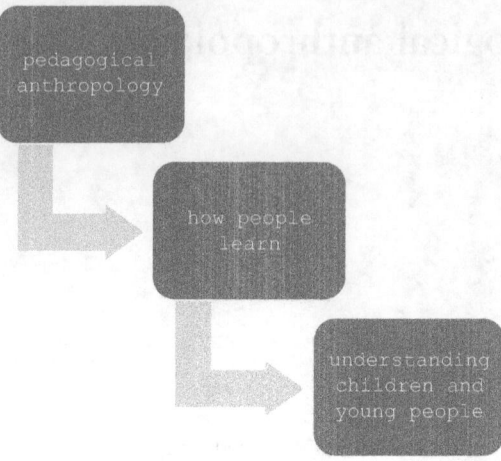

Figure 4.1 The relationship between pedagogical anthropology, learning and understanding individual students.

related to the educational process and is here used as synonymous with the term pedagogical anthropology.

As the anthropologist Tim Ingold explains, "in anthropology…we go to study *with* people. And we hope to learn *with* them."[1] This sums up the essence of the pedagogical anthropology we are recommending here. It is not a finished, complete model that we apply to judge children or young people; instead it is an attitude of inquiry, which can be characterized as a tentative approach to understanding real people, rather than matching them to exiting categorizes. The gesture is to be respectfully open to the children and young people, inviting them to show us their qualities so we can better learn how to support them in their learning process. We do have ideas about development, but these are heuristic – that is to say, they are like special lenses we can use to observe the phenomena, to help us make sense of what we observe. A heuristic model guides our attention toward certain aspects which we expect to be important, but does not determine what we actually observe or think. As Ingold puts it, referring to anthropologists who study other peoples, but which equally applies to teachers, "What we might call 'research' or even 'fieldwork' is in truth a protracted masterclass in which the novice learns to see things, and to hear and feel them too, in the way his or her mentors [i.e. the students- authors]do. It is, in short,…an education of attention." Teachers learn to attend to their field, to 'see', 'read' and understand their students.

There are interesting cultural differences relating to the discipline of pedagogical anthropology. Maria Montessori's first book in English was entitled *Pedagogical Anthropology*, but otherwise the term is rarely used in English. A recent study by three Ukrainian scholars[2] offers an interesting analysis of what they see anthropology in education as meaning. They see it firstly as a relatively independent, interdisciplinary field of knowledge at the intersection between the philosophical and pedagogical sciences, aimed at the study of the person "as a complex integrity of bio-psycho-socio-cultural nature, a subject of the educational process, an active link of interaction between the teacher and student." It explores how a person constructs their own inner life activity in interaction with nature, society and culture and what conditions are needed for this to occur in a positive way for the individual. Secondly, an anthropological approach offers theoretical, heuristic and practical orientation for educational practice, though one can identify a number of different philosophical stances within this.

Since the middle of the 20th century, pedagogical anthropology has had its most important development in Germany, Austria, Italy and Switzerland, where there was a strong desire to establish an emancipatory, democratic and civil society basis for education after the experiences of fascism in the first half of the century. The Netherlands and Scandinavia maintained a long commitment to humanistic education as part of the Bildung tradition and scientifically this has tended towards hermeneutic phenomenological or interpretive approaches, in contrast to the Anglophone world, in which positivist empirical, so-called evidence-based educational science has been dominant. In the German-speaking world, pedagogical anthropology is a well-established field of science, though one that is increasingly ignored by educational policy makers. The educational scholar Jörg Zirfas[3] points out, in fact, that there can be no pedagogy or education without an anthropology, because every approach to teaching and learning makes assumptions about how people learn and develop. The task of pedagogical anthropology is to make these assumptions explicit and interrogate them.

Thus, pedagogical anthropology is closely associated with Bildung theory, and has co-developed within this broad landscape of understandings about the nature of the human being. In practical terms, it has led to a pedagogical approach that emphasizes the development of the person and supports self-realization and wellbeing. The driving force of this development is inherent in each unique person and manifests in their learning as self-formation and in their generation of knowledge. This development occurs in social interaction and is influenced by social structures and shaped by actual biographically lived experiences and more general historical events. Thus, it promotes a student-centred learning, aimed at the growth of abilities and knowledge in the service of self-realization and capability in recognition of individual needs and interests.

Heuristic pedagogical anthropology

In contrast to the classic pedagogical anthropology in German-speaking countries, which has been strongly phenomenological and philosophical, recent developments are characterized by a significant shift to a heuristic or an historical pedagogical anthropology,[4] which avoids generalizing and essentializing terms such as *the* human being, as if it were possible to make statements that apply to all people. Rather, it takes the position that we cannot make statements about what human beings are, but one can look at specific aspects such as liminality and intersectionality, temporality (including age-relatedness), corporality and embodiment, identity and cultural aspects of subjectivity. Since this 'heuristic turn', it is recognized that such concepts are at best lenses that we can use to look at the lived experience of people; they are theoretical models that direct our attention to particular aspects. Like all the human sciences, pedagogical anthropology reflects changing interests, and we can identify narrative, biographical and affective 'turns', all of which offer multiple perspectives on developing and emerging human beings. The Bildung or humanistic framework of self-formation in socio-cultural interaction provides a basic orientation and point of reference.

The pedagogical anthropology we are recommending has a heuristic character and requires a multilayered approach. At the micro level we need to study children and young people in individual case studies in order to understand them better. Whatever criteria are chosen, they have a heuristic rather than a normative value. We are approaching the person with a tentative, open, respectful and caring attitude in the knowledge that the way we observe someone, how we feel, think and talk about them affects them at some, usually unconscious, level. The closer a person is to their spiritual connection to their environment – and like David Hay and Rebecca Nye in their famous study of children and youth spirituality,[5] we believe that includes all children and youth – the more sensitive they are to what people say and think about them. Jan Göschel[6] describes a process that he calls biographical mythos, meaning a narrative account of a person's path of individuation. This involves a phenomenological hermeneutic approach to individual case studies that not only seeks to characterize the young person's life course so far, but seeks to sense or presence the emergent future within that person's story, using Scharmer's Theory U[7] approach under ethical research conditions.

Unfortunately, we can't practice such case studies with all students, so we need a meso-level pedagogical anthropology that takes a more general view of development and learning across the life course and institutional transitions. As we show in Chapter 5 (and Chapters 6 and 7 and actually throughout the book), having a variety of anthropological and developmental tools to use as lenses is vital at all stages of curriculum work.

Self-formation in a cultural context

As we have explained, at the heart of the humanistic educational philosophy of Bildung is the notion of self-formation in a cultural context. In the 18th and 19th centuries, when the idea of Bildung as an educational philosophy was developed in its modern form, there was no real doubt as to the nature of the self implied in this idea. The self was taken to be the eternal soul, the essence of the human being, the spiritual core of the person that in the Judeo-Christian universe returns to the spiritual realm after death and is judged. Even outside of the various Christian and Hebrew faiths, the self was understood as *ideal* in character, meaning it had an essential nature that had ultimately been bequeathed to human beings by their Divine Creator, be that the Christian God, the Enlightenment idea of a divine rationality or even Nature (with a capital letter). Over the course of the 19th century, this core idea of the spirit shifted philosophically from a spiritual origin for matter and the world, including the human being, to natural origins. Spirit, if it existed at all, began to be seen as the product of nature or rather the human mind – a philosophy and ontology known as materialism. According to this view, spirit is a product of matter (i.e. physical, chemical, energetic processes), the mind a product of the brain, and individuality the outcome of genetic inheritance and social conditioning (with varying emphasis on the dominant factors, nature or nurture).

Historically, there have been a series of stages and turning points, such as the shift from an earth-centred universe, with humankind as the microcosm reflecting the order of the macrocosm, to a heliocentric solar system, in which the earth rotates around the sun (but the Divine Creator was still the cosmic watch-maker, an engineer responsible for the production and ongoing fine-tuning of the mechanism). The Copernican Revolution led gradually to the Cartesian Revolution, which saw the ascendency of the human mind at the centre of the human microcosmic universe, as expressed in Rene Descartes' famous *cogito ergo sum* – I am because I am cognitively active. At that stage even Descartes (1596–1650), or his contemporary Francis Bacon (1561–1626) and the rationalist philosophers who followed them and prepared the way for modern scientific thinking such as John Locke (1632–1704), Baruch Spinoza (1632–1677), Gottfried Leibnitz

(1646–1716), Christian Wolff (1679–1754) or David Hume (1711–1776) - none of them doubted the reality of a spiritual dimension and some kind of divine creator. Nor indeed does most of the rest of the world – its indigenous peoples, the world's major religions and world views across Asia, Africa, the Pacific region and pre-Columbian Americas – reject the idea of a spiritual dimension to life. Even in the West, many people believe in some kind of spiritual or non-material aspect of life, even some scientists. Nevertheless, the scientific orthodoxy has been overwhelmingly materialistic, particularly in the field of neurology, which maintains a strict policy of exclusion (mainly for the not unreasonable argument that they think they can account for consciousness and other higher order forms of cognition without recourse to spirit). What tipped the scales fully in the direction of a scientific account of the world without divine or spiritual intervention was Charles Darwin's *Origin of Species* published in 1859. Darwin didn't abolish God (heaven forbid!); he just made the spiritual dimension unnecessary in any account of the origins of life.

This does not mean that spirituality or belief in a divine order disappeared in the West - far from it. In fact, in the late 19th century, alongside the multiplicity of Christian denominations, and branches of Islam and Judaism, there was a flourishing of esoteric movements such as Theosophy, Freemasonry, Rosicrucianism and so on. Many combined social reform with spirituality, whilst others sought to counter the alienation of 'disenchanted'[8] and materialistic Modernity. It was only in the philosophical and scientific worlds, which has always only involved a small elite, that the spirit dropped out of favour, though the dominance of materialist and positivist science as the basis for modern technologies does tip the balance away from spiritual factors in any explanation of the world. The actual problem – and we are of the necessity of making broad generalizations here – is dualism, which polarizes spirit and matter. The alternative to dualism is monism, which argues that there is only one unified world. Scientific monism says that we don't need a concept of the spirit to explain the phenomena in the world, since physical and material causes are sufficient. Steiner's monism also claims that there is only one world, but that spirit and matter are simply different manifestations of a single reality that have evolved hand in hand, though spirit is the more permanent of the two states. The problem, according to Steiner, is that in our current state of evolution we have largely lost the capacity to experience spirit directly.[9] In Owen Barfield's account of Steiner's world view, humanity used to be in a state of original participation in the whole unified world (and young children still are, until this is educated out of them). Through developing our powers of cognition, we can overcome this separation and achieve a new 'final' participation.[10]

Towards the end of the 19th century philosophers like Wilhelm Dilthey (1833–1911) sought to distinguish the natural from the human sciences by developing interpretive or hermeneutic methods on the assumption that nature can be explored using empirical observation but that products of the human mind can only be indirectly understood through interpretation. The natural scientific method that relies on testing hypotheses through experiments in which the outcomes are expressed in measurable data and which assume an entirely mechanical, material universe with no higher meaning or purpose, has come to be known as positivist and is still widely regarded as *the* scientific method. Its success can be seen all around us when applied to mechanical, electrical or digital technologies, and in its 'greedy' reductionist world view that reduces life to chemistry, chemistry to physics and physics to quantum theory.[11] The outcomes and explanations from this kind of science tend to be seen as hard or evidence-based science and this approach has been widely adopted to the human sciences and sociology, in which quantifiable data are seen as more significant.

Since the pioneers of sociology, such as Emile Durkheim and Max Weber, sociologists have sought to establish various methods by which social and economic phenomena can use scientific methods of measurement and behavioural science has sought to find measurable causes for human behaviour. Over the past century there has to some extent been ongoing debate about the comparative validity of quantitative and qualitative scientific methods in the human sciences (e.g. psychology, sociology, anthropology, ethnology, history). Educational science has nevertheless tended to be dominated by positivist methods, though within the Continental Bildung tradition, qualitative, interpretive and phenomenological approaches have been applied, though often in ways that are highly complex. There are also strong cultural differences in the choice of scientific methodologies.

Policy makers, if they pay any attention to research at all, tend to look for metrics, for statistics and things that can be qualified.

Overall, this dominant positivist scientific climate has tended to marginalize the spiritual dimension in scientific inquiry over the past century; in terms of popular (and political) understandings of science, anything spiritual is deemed unscientific and flaky, subjective and not accessible to scientific method, and anything that can be labelled esoteric is seen as suspicious and even dangerous. There is of course a legitimate concern about religious sects and cults indoctrinating children and young people. The Christian Churches in many Western countries have traditionally had a strong influence in education, though secular states have an ambivalent relationship to this in many countries. In countries like the United States, religion and education are separated strictly by the constitution, though we also see the increasing influence of Christian fundamentalism in education policy, in an 'unholy', even illogical merging of interests with Trumpism. Other faiths are treated with less tolerance in many Western nations. In Germany, for example, which allows religious instruction by the Christian denominations in schools, this privilege is not given to other religions, such as Islam.

An example of the ambiguity about spirituality and religion can be seen in the comments of a representative of the French Ministry for Education in an online seminar hosted by the European Commission Working Group on Schools in which Martyn recently participated, when a contributor gave a talk about mindfulness classes in schools. He said that his ministry was required to ensure that education is strictly secular and that the association of mindfulness with Buddhism made this kind of approach problematic. In the ensuing discussion, Martyn suggested that rather than referring to mindfulness, if one spoke about exercises that cultivate listening, or calm alertness, there would be no problem, especially since all agree that education needs to address the so-called soft skills.

Today, we have a number of peer-reviewed academic journals, which, by definition, consider themselves scientific, devoted to aspects of spirituality[12] and the talk is very much of 'spiritual but not religious'. Lisa Miller,[13] the American neurologist, has launched a programme called Collaborative for Spirituality in Education at Teachers College Columbia University,[14] which shows the paradigm shift in education regarding the spiritual dimension. Of course, a close reading of Lisa Miller's works,[15] which are based on her neurological research, reveals that she is still ultimately talking about a neurological origin for the experience of spirituality, though this does not rule out the possibility that the brain is an organ that can perceive an objectively existent spiritual dimension, but as far as we know neither she nor other leading neurologists, who promote ideas of an embodied mind, such as Thomas Fuchs,[16] go as far as agreeing to an independently existing spiritual entity within the human mind. This is exactly what Steiner suggests.

We would like to suggest some aspects of Steiner's pedagogical anthropology sit quite easily in the current spirituality discourse and indeed, the Journal of Children's Spirituality has published occasional articles with a Waldorf context. The Waldorf and anthroposophical discourse is currently in the process of repositioning itself, from a historical assumption that Steiner was always right and that his ideas supersede most (if not all) others, to a more heuristic stance, in which his ideas are taken as possible models. The part of this process that concerns us is the repositioning of Waldorf education as an educational approach in its own right, as opposed to a field of applied anthroposophy. This move is most noticeably in the German Waldorf community, but also in the various universities around the world that offer bachelor and master level degrees and in some cases PhDs in Waldorf related themes. What follows is very much our interpretation.

An agentic self

Rudolf Steiner put forward the idea that each person has a spiritual core of being, which he called in German *das Ich*. We use the term *Self* to refer to the same thing, because translating *das Ich* as the 'I' is linguistically awkward. The idea of a spiritual Self was not unusual in 19th-century German Idealism, which was very much Steiner's intellectual starting place, and Steiner's version has its precedents in number of leading figures of the German Romantic and Idealist movements. Even as an 18-year-old Steiner was wrestling with the problem of the Self and the paradox that the Self and the activity of thinking were closely connected, as posited in Descartes' famous *cogito ergo sum* – I think therefore I am. As Christian Clement explores,[17] Steiner's engagement with this idea led to him writing his most important book *The Philosophy of Freedom*, or as it has also been translated *The Philosophy of Spiritual Activity*.[18] It is significant that Steiner locates the Self at the centre of his understanding of the human being, his anthropology, and characterizes it as the activity in the knowing process. In his philosophy and theory of knowledge, the Self is the spiritual activity in the process of generating consciousness and knowledge within the processes of cognition.

Following Steiner, the Self therefore does not have a fixed character; it is embodied and uses the brain and body as an instrument. Steiner uses the metaphor of a mirror that reflects images of the world – and, as a spiritual being, it is distributed in the world. Above all, it is emergent: it learns and develops. Because it is distributed in the world (which frankly is difficult to imagine), this means that the Self intuitively recognizes itself in the phenomena of the world in the mirror of consciousness. The human mind, Steiner wrote, is the point in the world where the world itself comes to consciousness and far from being a detached observer of cosmic events, in the knowledge process it actively co-creates reality. In the act of knowing, the human being has experiences mediated through its senses, but these are initially without meaning and context. The activity of the Self is to give these perceptions meaning in the form of ideas that can be related to other ideas.

The process of generating knowledge involves the activity of the Self directing its interest and attention to the world and then giving meaning to these, thus bringing about individualized meaning in the form of ideas or concepts. This is an iterative process, because these concepts can grow through experience and by expanding their context. Steiner referred to them, therefore, as living ideas. The fact that these ideas can grow, and that there are no limits to this growth of knowledge, is the basis for Steiner's claim that the human being can develop their powers of knowing and consciousness beyond the boundaries of knowledge that is limited to what we can perceive with our senses. In other words, this is his challenge to the positivist scientific method, which says that all claims to truth must be validated through repeatable experimentation that produces measurable, quantifiable data based on observation (or instrumental extensions of our powers to perceive). Steiner says that alongside the methods of natural science, which he in no way denigrated and declared as a significant achievement for understanding the material world, there can be a science that explores the non-material world of processes, systems, structures, relationships and qualities that cannot be physically measured but can be experienced.

Since Steiner's day, both natural science and the humanities have made significant developments. In the natural sciences, in quantum physics in particular, this has gone beyond materiality. In the life sciences, ecology has revealed the complex correlations between organisms and environments and how organisms and ecological systems regulate themselves in the process of autopoiesis. In the humanities, similarly, approaches such as hermeneutics and phenomenology have raised the process of interpretation to offer more subtle insights into complexities of lived experience and the interpretation of text and image, and social processes. Systems theory and cybernetics have revealed how natural and artificial coherent systems can be more than the sum of their parts. One could argue that Steiner's anthroposophy, his system of knowledge through and about the human being that, if practiced consistently, can lead to spiritual knowledge, should find the current intellectual climate more congenial than that of Steiner's lifetime.

Those who wish to delve more deeply into Steiner's philosophy should definitely read his book *Philosophy of Freedom* and seek orientation from some important interpreters of Steiner's philosophy who we recommend in the endnotes.[19]

There are, however, three core aspects of Steiner's idea of the Self as the spiritual core of the human being that are directly relevant to understanding his pedagogical anthropology and its connection to curriculum. These are the nature of incarnation and embodiment, the interactions between the Self and the world, the psychological function of the Self in developing a balanced inner life and the Self as learner.

Incarnation and embodiment

The first is the basic notion that the spiritual Self pre-exists the physical birth of the child and enters the body from pre-birth: it literally incarnates, meaning, as the Latin suggests, that it comes into flesh. In modern terms, the Self is embodied, and embodiment is a long process which accompanies a person throughout their early existence. The Self engages with the inherited body and metaphorically works to make itself at home in that body, eventually making it an instrument of its will, its desires and intentions. The body provides the Self with experiences through its sensorimotor organization and brain, which it processes through what we refer to as learning.

This engagement with the body does not simply occur once; it is an ongoing dynamic process, which we can imagine in the form of two streams, the first being the body - which breathes, is nourished and grows - within which gradually an inner psychological life emerges. The other stream is that of the spiritual Self which encounters the psycho-somatic dimensions of the person, meaning the combination of sentient, feeling life (psyche) and the body (soma). This encounter sets up (metaphorically) an interference, accompanied by heightened consciousness, in a series of moments we could call developmental crises. We can show this process graphically as in Figure 4.2.

The Self becomes aware of itself in such moments. When the child is still young and lacks any comprehension of this process, the crisis may be emotional: truculence,

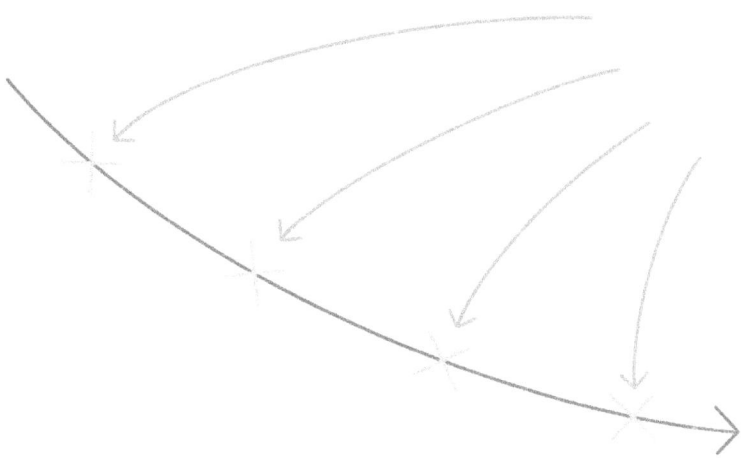

Figure 4.2 The encounter of the two streams, the bodily and the Self, as the spiritual core of being.
Credit: Aristea Klanac.

defiance, self-assertiveness or the opposite – anxiety, fear, doubt. The crisis may manifest in the physical body, through inflammatory responses, susceptibility to infection, and countless other bodily symptoms. Once the crisis has been overcome, the child is usually not only more resilient afterwards, but also often more self-aware, more present as an individual (for example, in the family, or in the peer group).

This trajectory of incarnation, or the moments of heightened embodiment, will be important for how we structure curriculum, not because they manifest as a predictable pattern, but because the process can be 'provoked'. We do this by offering students intellectual, practical, social and artistic challenges that 'pull' them into the next level of learning and competence. Curriculum can be structured so that it doesn't just follow the content logic of the subject (once you've learned C you move to D), but so that it addresses the developmental tasks in a multi-layered way (we discuss this in Chapter 5).

The interaction between self and world

The second aspect of the Self that is salient to our account is the role that it plays in processing experience and the learning process. Following Steiner, the Self has a double nature: it is the locus of consciousness in the mind, and it is distributed in the non-material environment, in the spiritual dimension of the living forces in nature. As in many traditional world views from around the globe, the human being is not merely a product of chance and natural selection but is a being in an animate world of being and mind. Mind is not the illusion of the electro-chemical processes in the brain, but a locus of a consciousness that permeates the world. Mindfulness is that state when we begin to experience that world consciousness that enables us to feel part of something bigger than just our bodily selves.

In Steiner's anthropology he distinguishes between spirit, soul and body (in German *Geist*, *Seele* and *Leib*), his version of the Aristotelian *pneuma*, *psyche* and *soma*. Since the Self as spiritual core of being is active in the psyche, he often combines them as soul-spirit element. For this combination we use the word mind. According to the Oxford English Dictionary, the word mind has an extensive etymology and use, including, as a verb to remember, to attend to, care for, look after, to be sure or certain and to heed something, with similar usage as a noun, extending to wish, desire, inclination, disposition, thinking, volition and feeling. Thus, mind as translation for Steiner's spirit-soul includes thinking, feeling (and its whole spectrum of affect, sensation and emotion) and volition (willing), and their interactions (feeling-willing, feeling-thinking etc.), and these overlap (which is important because human mental phenomena do not have distinct boundaries). The semantic field of mind includes the notion that we care (to mind something) about the things we know, feel and want.

We are not asking the reader to believe this. It is a hypothesis to explain the implications of the possibility that there is more to human beings than neurology, however complex that may be. The place where human beings can experience being part of this greater whole is our cognition. Some would argue that we know this intuitively, but that this awareness of being part of a bigger, more meaningful whole, which is what contemporary definitions of spirituality involve, is drummed out of us by what David Hay and Rebecca Nye[20] call the social destruction of spirituality – that is, adults telling children that rational explanations for what happens are truer than mythic or spiritual accounts. Most people who practice meditation or are able to feel at one with the natural world, or who experience numinous moments in their lives, have an inkling of what this state of heightened consciousness might be. Today, spirituality is discussed independently of religious experience, which may also involve spirituality. People belonging to many cultures in Asia or Africa, who are not explicitly religious, and who have enjoyed modern scientific education, take it for granted that there is a spiritual dimension to life. Steiner argued that our modern consciousness can be expanded through meditation and schooling our thinking, so that we can extend the reach of our awareness of social processes and the qualities in nature.

The primal nature of the Self is the will, a difficult concept to understand, particularly in English although it is related to willpower, force of will etc. However, if we take Steiner's description of the will forces in his introductory account of pedagogical anthropology for the teachers in the Waldorf School and his declension of the forms it can take, we can put this into words that are perhaps more accessible. The primary nature of the Self is activity, which manifests in movement, action and in reaching out to the world. This is initially channelled by what the body affords in terms of possibilities, which in an infant are still very limited: through eye movements and focusing the eyes in order to make close-range eye contact with the mother and other people physically close to the child. Once the child has mastered its hands and limbs and can, in turn, sit up, crawl and, ultimately, achieve uprightness and walking, then the world is there to be discovered using all senses. It is the Self that drives this activity and is the source of curiosity for experience. This does not rule out the possibility that genetically determined behaviour lies behind this, but this fact does not obviate the role of the Self as the source of interest and curiosity. Human babies and young children express this in what could be termed species-specific ways (i.e. as typical of human infants but different from other mammals that learn to stand up and walk), but they also do this in individual ways. Anyone who has watched the many forms of locomotion (crawling, shuffling along on their bottoms, using one foot and leg to propel them, rolling etc.) that young children discover before they learn to stand up and walk, can see that this is not a standardized process. Furthermore, part of the drive to stand up is the mimetic example (i.e. imitation or emulation) provided by people around the child, who serve as models, but each child has to achieve this through their own fascinating trial-and-error methods. That means the Self is the motor of movement, exploring the world and in the widest sense learning, which is always a process of engagement with the world and the processing of the experiences involved, which leads to a sense of self-efficacy.

The psychological self

Though thinking has a central place in Steiner's anthropology, it is not abstract, intellectual thinking that he was talking about. Steiner saw the human being as a whole integrated system that can be understood best by focusing on different aspects and taking different perspectives on the whole, and then re-integrating what has been discovered back into the bigger picture of the whole. The term thinking would actually be better translated as cognition (as indeed the philosopher Owen Barfield does, when writing about Steiner). Cognition could be described as the totality of activities of the mind (materialists would say the brain). Cognition is basically occupied with interacting with the body and with the world and processing experience and this vastly complex activity.[21] Unsurprisingly, we have a complex system of sense organs that mediate the inner states of our body to the mind (such as interoception and proprioception), as well as sense impressions of the world around us.

As Damasio[22] shows, our experiences are always coloured by feelings and emotions and thus our thoughts always contain an affective quality, which enhance the meanings we make. One of Steiner's main ideas about teaching and learning is that it is necessary to address children and young people through their feelings – they must feel something in order to form a relationship to it. Feelings are prompted by rich sensory experiences and through the imagination, and imagination is a hugely important factor in learning. Imagination is the ability to generate mental representations of things that are not immediately present, including things that we have never directly experienced. However, the imagination draws on embodied experiences and reorganizes and combines these to create images that can be modified, moved and transformed. It is therefore an active process, requiring an effort of will and the motivation to make this effort. Without imagination to visualize how things could be, to construct hypothetical what ifs, there could be no science, no art, no literature, no stories and probably no religion, which after all requires us to imagine things and powers that are not visible or even plausible.

Cognition as a whole, therefore, involves the full range of psychological experience, including memory, dispositions, habits, understanding, skills and is thus deeply woven into our bodily nature. Without the sensations from our senses, which convey experiences from within our organism (sense of balance, sense of wellbeing and vitality) and outside (sight, hearing, smell, taste, touch, temperature) and without the memory that the living body retains, the mind would be helpless. The function of the Self in this whole process is, on the one hand, to determine what is necessary, relevant and important amongst the continuous vast flow of information the body is generating about its states and the world around us, whilst on the other hand it is directing our attention to the world, directing our activities and movement and what we do. Much of this happens, as it were on autopilot, like walking, digesting, reading a text, riding a bicycle. There are also higher-order choices, however - where and when to walk or cycle, what to eat (or not), and what to read and what we do with what we read. These require executive functions, decisions, judgements and the anticipation of what options there are and how to respond intelligently to other people, to unexpected situations and so on. As the Self matures, and becomes more experienced and capable, the nature of the choices change, and moral and ethical behaviour requires inner guidance - conscience and conscientiousness and, above all, heightened consciousness.

What Steiner called in German *Freiheit* (and what we know as freedom) is based on the ethical activity of making judgements about what we do on the basis of insight rather than on embodied habits and dispositions, socialization or acquired cultural attitudes, and this can only be done by taking what the French philosopher Emmanuel Levinas called eco-logical rather than ego-logical perspectives. Eco-logical means making decisions based on insight into the possible implications of our actions for our social and natural environment. Because the Self is part of the world, rather than separated from it, we can take the perspective of the other and of the world into the process of making our choices. Even though our normal state of mind leads us to the illusion that we are on our own, observing the world from our detached position as observers, in reality we are embedded in the world, and therefore we are responsible for the other person, even the total stranger, because they are our global brothers and sisters, and we take responsibility for our actions towards them and to the world. Steiner called this ethical individualism. The term is paradoxical because ethical by definition means with and through the other person – one can't be an ethical individualist! But one can be ethical out of one's own sense of responsibility. If one acts out of self-interest, then one can't be ethical. The interest of the Self is always holistic; that is, it acts out of itself, out of its knowledge of the situation in an ethically responsible – what Gert Biesta would call a grown-up – way. This doesn't mean we get it right. We obviously don't, but the Self has the capacity to reflect on the consequences of its actions and can learn from them, which means, gradually seeing the bigger picture from multiple perspectives.

In Steiner's philosophy and anthropology, there is no single definitive way of seeing the world, no ultimate truth. It always involves multiple perspectives, looking at things from different standpoints, keeping moving. This is possible because the Self is also peripheral and eccentric; that is, it is not fixed in a position, it can move beyond its embodied position and see things from other standpoints. The Self is also dialogic; it is always in dialogue with itself and with the world. To add to this dynamic picture of the Self, the world itself is also fluid and in continuous movement. We could say that our times are especially fluid as all kinds of aspects of life change with great rapidity, older certainties are continuously being eroded whilst other parts are being built up and consolidated. The Self's most distinctive feature is that it too can change with purpose – in other words it can learn.

The learning self

The nature of the Self just described leads to the next vital role of the Self in generating knowledge about the world and learning. Following directly on from the previous point, the Self reaches out, as it were, with its consciousness to the world around it. The Self directs its attention to the objects around it and seeks to form a relationship to them. This is not just because learning about the world is useful for survival, it is also because of the dual character of the Self. As a spiritual being that gradually achieves self-consciousness through the body, the Self is also unconsciously distributed in the world: it recognizes something of itself in the world and wishes to affirm that relationship. Speaking metaphorically here, the Self experiences an affinity to beings in the world and seeks to enter into an intentional relationship with what it encounters. We see this in young children, who form attachments to things and places that have meaning for them, even though to our eyes, they are inanimate. When adults reinforce such experiences through acceptance and narrative, rather than rational explanation – "don't be silly dear, it is only a piece of…" - then children can include these objects of attachment into their world picture, at least for the time being. One can understand those accounts of Indigenous people such as Australian Aborigines, for whom the world around them is populated with beings to whom one is related, with whom one has a relationship involving mutual obligations and respect. A different perspective from those who look at the landscape and see only red earth, rocks, lizards and kangaroos in the outback (itself originally a dismissive term suggesting a lack of usefulness and therefore of meaning for white settlers).

It is unsurprising that Steiner saw a close relationship between the will and the imagination. The child has the will to reach out, connect and form a relationship, and the imagination is thus stimulated to give the experience a form and context. Furthermore, following Steiner's theory of knowledge, the simplest version of this is that the world, or at least a small portion of it, is given to us as a whole unified experience, as a gestalt. We form a mental image of this. Initially, this has no meaning to us – in effect, an impressionistic assemblage of colours, shapes, sounds and other sensory data combined with the affects that these sensations bring forth in us. The subject, in this case the child, relates what it experiences to what it already knows, because we understand things in terms of what we already know. The child, in effect, forms a spontaneous judgement about the qualities of what it perceives: whether it is big or small, dark or light, close or far, familiar or unfamiliar. Unless the child has already learned to be afraid of such an experience or something similar to it, or indeed recognizes it as something that left a positive impression in the past, the initial experience will in a sense be factual. The Self intuitively gives meaning to the perception. It can do this because it has one foot, as it were, in the sensory experience mediated by the body that it has directed attention to, and the other, because it is distributed in its environment, in the things themselves, in their qualities. The mind then makes sense of what it experiences. In young children, it does so unconsciously because they don't have the range of experiences to relate it to and lack the vocabulary to articulate the experience. Adults draw on a greater range of embodied experience but also intuit the meaning of what they are seeing, at least provisionally. With time, the mind can draw on wider resources of concepts to make sense of their perceptions and experiences.

This is how mimesis works. The child reaches out to the object of interest and already makes an unconscious connection to it 'out there' in the world. What it perceives activates its own organism. Today we know that this is the activity of mirror neurons that fire neural networks when we perceive something, that would fire if we were to perform this act or say this word. So, a double act (or probably multiple acts) of perception takes place; we already respond to the perception outside of ourselves, because that is where our Self is active. The Self is active in the object that we perceive, then we perceive the response our own body makes. If you watch young children watching a puppet show, their attention is in the puppets and their interactions, but their own mouths and even limbs are moving as if they were enacting the story. The process then leads to the internalization not only of the actions and the unfolding story as observed (heard, seen, imitated), but also the body's own responses to the experience, probably right down to the hormonal level, if the story produces a visceral response of excitement or fear. We know from trauma studies, that the body retains not only the immediate effects of the injury or the fear and the body's own response to this, but also the meaning (or lack of it) that the person made of the experience.

The point about the understandings generated through this process is that they are iterative. Because the Self has been involved in forming these understandings, they remain open and can be revisited and extended. Each time the Self revisits a similar or related experience, the understanding grows, matures, ripens, deepens and expands and this changes the way the person looks at the world. The learner becomes more experienced, and these experiences inform what the person is looking for and what they see. This, by the way, is the same as John Dewey's idea of the continuity of experience.[23] Each meaningful experience changes the way the person seeks further experiences and shapes what they can see. They are continuously engaging with the world with increasingly experienced and knowledgeable ways of seeing. The seeing becomes a skill, making it more likely that the person will notice what is salient and relevant, thus leading to expertise. The expert literally sees the same things as the novice, but is able to recognize their significance and meaning more readily and therefore understands more.

This continuity of experience and the habits of noticing and understanding dispose a person to learn more and form a personal connection to what they learn, because the drive to learn comes from the Self. It is not driven by something extrinsic, such as a prescribed structured teaching programme that tells all the learners what to attend to next. The art of teaching is to direct the learner's attention to something significant and allow the student to engage with it. Apparently, you can take a horse or camel to water, but you can't make it drink. The pedagogical trick is to make the horse thirsty and ensure that the water is sweet.

We can show in the following graphic how this process works in an iterative way. The child's attention, as an expression of both the will and the life process, flows out through our sense organs. The learner looks into the world, directs their attention to what catches their eye (or they deliberately look for something). The Self meets the world and engages with what already has meaning, which is the case in natural phenomena, or in people and other sentient beings, but also in artefacts that are also expressions of being, having been made by human beings. Having made a connection 'out there' as it were, the experience is them internalized, processed and contextualized (this may occur when the person is asleep, or their attention is elsewhere) if it is found be to be relevant. The more feelings and emotions are generated by the experience the more likely it is that the mind of the child will consider it worth retaining, and the most important things are retained as memory. What has been processed, changes to some extent what we already known and thus how we look back at the world (Figure 4.3).

The pedagogical implications of this are profound. If we want the person to learn something, then we have to replicate the natural process of learning. The Self has to direct its attention or have its attention directed towards the object and it must be able to form a meaningful relationship to it. This speaks for authentic rather than contrived experiences. It also suggests that the learning process should involve the feeling life and be affective, because the intensity of the affect, feelings and emotions makes the experience both more memorable, personal, meaningful and social (because emotions can be intentionally or unintentionally shared) at multiple levels.

Pathways of individuation

The Self has to grow into the living physical body it has inherited, and it continues to deal with this body throughout life into old age when the body stops doing what the Self wants it to. Eventually, the Self is forced to leave the body behind and continue on another type of journey, of which we know very little. Life is a journey for the Self, with challenges, trials, crises, and moments of fulfilment and peace, accompanied by the lives

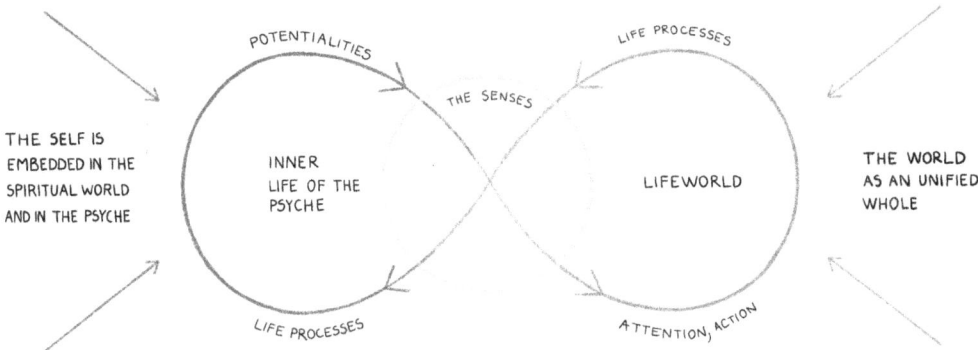

Figure 4.3 In simplified and symbolic form, this graphic shows how the will (here named potentialities) is directed through the senses into the world, where the Self makes a connection with a part of the world as a unified whole. The internalization process starts with sense organs and proceeds into the psyche or mind. Within the mind, the Self then makes sense of the experience. It can do this because of its spiritual character. Credit: Aristea Klanac.

of others with whom we become entwined in various ways. In the course of this journey the Self learns, becomes a personality, makes a small or large impact on the world and, if all goes well, becomes wise. Human life stories are always fascinating and whatever similarities and shared destinies there are, they are always unique. The journey through life, our biographical narrative involves a process of individuation. The terminology is not so important, and there are many words that describe this, but the concept is significant. The pathways of individuals, which are only really apparent in retrospect and look different when observed from the inside or the outside, are pathways of individuation because they are individual and because they lead to what the person experiences as *their* life story, their sense of who they are, where they have come from and the kind of person they think they are and that they want to become. When we study a person's life story we can generate a biographical mythos – a narrative that may give us insight into how we can support the process.

According to the anthropology of the Self that we are outlining here, throughout life the Self has to engage and come to terms with the body as it continuously grows and changes and then declines. The Self has influence over its body in terms of behaviour, but there are limits – we can hardly change the basic structure and form of the body we inherit, though we can look after it and learn to optimize it. The Self has to engage with the sex assigned to the body at birth (usually by the medical profession) and over the course of a lifetime it has to establish a gender identity and makes choices about gender expression within the context of social and cultural expectation. The Self has to engage with the community it is born into, learn its spoken and gestural languages, learn its social modes of behaviour and cultural norms and expectations, in the socio-cultural-economic situations in which it finds itself. The Self forms a relationship to the natural and cultural environments it inhabits and it forms relationships to significant others, as they are referred to in psychology. It has to deal with the challenges of education and other institutional structures as well as the demands of the world of work. Alongside all these factors are what are termed brute forces, that is external factors such as war, poverty, epidemics, accidents, and natural disasters, that have no obvious direct connection to the person.

These are the factors that the Self has to deal with in the process of individuation. We know through personal and professional experience that people respond in very different ways to these factors. The way a person responds to the various bodily, social, cultural, educational challenges also reflects what we call the Self's biographical interests, which include the dispositions and talents it was born with. In adult biography work, we talk about biographical learning, which refers to the way a person notices and responds to the opportunities their life situation or educational setting affords their personal learning and development.[24]

Long before this process can become conscious through reflection, the Self is also active in noticing opportunities to come into being, to take important developmental steps (including literal first steps), grasping opportunities, taking risks, or holding back and waiting. This is rarely conscious, but that only shows that most of what the Self does is not conscious. The Self not only acts unconsciously; it is also active *within* the unconscious, for example in sleep, when the mind sorts through the experiences of the day. We (and neurologists) say the mind does this but the stance we are taking says the Self does this.

This also shows us something about the spiritual nature of the Self. The Self is the locus of consciousness and self-consciousness, but consciousness has a variety of modes, depending on our perspective. From a certain perspective, we can say that the person is conscious, from another that they are partly or wholly unconscious. We see this for example when we direct our consciousness towards things that interest us, whilst being unconscious of the position of our body. Whilst jogging, for example, our mind may be thinking about other activities. In these cases our body continues to function even in quite intentional ways, though we are not conscious of this. However, if a wasp stings us while we are attending to something else, the pain directs our attention rapidly to the source of the pain, the surprisingly strong sensation and often our annoyance, even anger at the wasp. The nature of consciousness is the same, but the person's awareness within this varies in grades.

Perhaps consciousness is another word for the spiritual. It is definitely not physical, though we have a physical organ, the brain, in which consciousness manifests. If we leave aside the question as to the origins of consciousness, whether it is caused by brain activity, or whether it exists independently, like light, which exists whether we open our eyes or not, whether we are present or not, then we can see consciousness as a state of which we can become either more or less aware. Like consciousness, light becomes visible only when it touches a material object, even 'loose' material objects like water vapour or dust in the atmosphere. Consciousness comes to our attention under certain conditions within the brain; when this happens, the Self is active to notice it, as in pain, or vaguely, when our attention is directed elsewhere, or when we are falling asleep. Whatever its cause and origins, consciousness is a property of the Self. Some might put it the other way round, the Self is an effect of consciousness, specifically self-consciousness. This is not something we can resolve. The point is, consciousness and the Self are intimately bound up with each other.

Knowing this is important in structuring learning. In order to take in new experiences, full alert awareness is needed, and when things become habitual, less alertness is needed. Pedagogy needs to structure and control the moments of alertness and deliberately organize the habitual activities, so they remain relevant. Part of the problem of social and medial conditioning is we take in ideas and messages all the time from our virtual and actual environment, mostly in unconscious or subliminal ways. Because we do so usually not with full alert awareness but with the kind of background awareness we have of ambient temperature, we have little choice or control over the content of what we take in. When it uncomfortably hot or cold, we notice enough to make conscious decisions to put on warm clothing or seek shade. So it is with background music, the stream of impressions from advertising boards and constant background prompts from social media (influencers deserve their name).

The learning process also benefits from periods of incubation, rumination, when our awake consciousness is elsewhere or not present, as in sleep, so that the unconscious sorting and relating that goes on in the deeper layers of the mind can function when the 'noise' of wakefulness is reduced. The important aspect of this process is waking up the consciousness and retrieving the memories – as we discuss in Chapter 7 in the learning process.

The Self, individuality and identity

The Self is engaged in a continuous process of negotiating some kind of balance in the dynamic demands of intrinsic, often bodily factors, such as a changing body, and external factors such as society and education. It is in the nature of the Self that it often grows through resistance. One could say the Self accommodates itself to a given state that is stable and relatively unchanging. This is then interrupted and often disrupted by events and by life. The Self then has to reassert itself, make sense of the changes, readjust to the changed circumstances and establish a new equilibrium. Biography is often like a punctuated equilibrium in which each crisis offers opportunities for learning and growth.

Thus, the Self strives continuously to establish and maintain a coherent sense of self-identity amid these intrinsic and extrinsic demands pulling on way and another. This obviously manifests in different ways at the different stages of life. Initially, it is the body that offers the most resistance. It is clumsy, unstable, is hard to control it and make it do what the Self wants. It has overwhelmingly strong forces, such as hunger, pain and tiredness, and has powerful needs such as comfort, security, attachment, communication and so on. Furthermore, the process of individuation requires that the body adapt itself to new types of nourishment, both in the form of food and in terms of sensory impression and the Self has no way to control this flood of impressions. In the process of establishing its physical identity, establishing its autoimmune system, its self-regulatory processes of homeostasis, the body experiences discomfort through allergies, infections and teething. From a certain perspective, early childhood is characterized by long periods of sleep (parents hope), and much struggle, frustration and discomfort, interrupted by short interludes of boundless joy.

Each phase of child and youth development is characterized by the ongoing process of establishing a coherent identity within a range of social ecological structures starting with the family, siblings, the wider community, institutions and so on outwards, with increasing degrees of consciousness. During and after puberty, the process takes on a more conscious character. The sociologist Zygmunt Bauman referred to this as juggling. The young person is continuously trying balance the competing demands of social media, advertising, parents, school, awakening inner desires, fears and anxieties, whilst managing with half-finished skills and knowing only a small part of the bigger picture. The pre-teen and teenager is at a stage when the Self has still not settled on a social role, a lifestyle, a dress style, hair colour, even a gender identity, and is continuously under peer pressure, social media influence, and parental wishes to be and become something. The range of possible somethings may be narrow in some societies and contexts; in others, the choices may be bewildering. The young person needs to learn how to make choices, if necessary by trial and error. If we take a positive view of this situation, we could say that the young person can pick and mix at will. From a negative perspective, we would be more likely to say that the young person is at the mercy of external factors. School generally ignores this phase of life, treating it as the background noise in the more important process of getting grades and qualifications. Teachers – except in Waldorf schools – rarely choose to teach content in maths, chemistry or geology at this age that mirrors what is going on in the young person, for example exploring transformations of matter and explosive processes, or studying volcanic activity and geological time frames that contrast strongly with the ephemeral nature of adolescent sense of time, or awakening them to the abstract elegance and logic of geometry. Such themes engage the students by activating their embodied consciousness, their idealism and their imagination, at a time when their natural focus is much narrower. In addition, Waldorf education argues that immersing oneself in a topic over several weeks is preferable to the atomization of the school timetable, in which one subject follows the other in a random sequence of bite-sized, but incoherent chunks.

From the perspective of the individual, the Self experiences itself with increasing degrees of awareness, as a body with memories and sets of ongoing and changing relationships. Through the body, which we wake up in each morning, we have a sense of biographical continuity. We can call this the autobiographical self[25]. This is who we recognize in old photos. As the child becomes more aware of the distinction between self and world and other people, they begin to experience themselves through others who position them. The child is treated as a daughter, as the oldest sibling, as a grandchild, as a friend in a network of changing friendships, some longer-lasting than others, and as the member of a group in a kindergarten or school setting. We can call this the social self. With education, and particularly with the categorizations that come with school, children are positioned and position themselves according to their abilities or lack of them. This institutionalized self is constructed as long as people are in education or training. Overlapping the institutional self is the emergence of an adult self, which is constructed when young people start working, start being financially independent, start their own family and so on. This adult self also includes who we become through self-education. The dimensions of selfhood, the autobiographical, the social, the institutional selves go on changing, or rather the person's relationship to this self, changes (Figure 4.4).

From an anthropological perspective we can describe the overall process of individuation as an ongoing activity of establishing and maintaining a coherent identity within the constraints and opportunities of the given context and within the capacities of the child. The active, agentic driver is the Self. What emerges is a series of stages of dynamic identity work, arriving at some point (usually in adolescence) at a relatively stable self-identity and as an emergent adult, the person begins to be identifiable to others as someone with a distinct adult personality. This personality has been there all along, at least noticed by family, friends and observant teachers, but it has always been in a process of age-related transition. As an adult, this personality has become more stable, though it continues to undergo development and even significant change through crisis and experience. It is important to stress that none of these depictions of the person are fixed or the 'true self', but each represents a perspective from either within or without. We can show the overall structure as in Figure 4.5.

A pedagogical anthropology 83

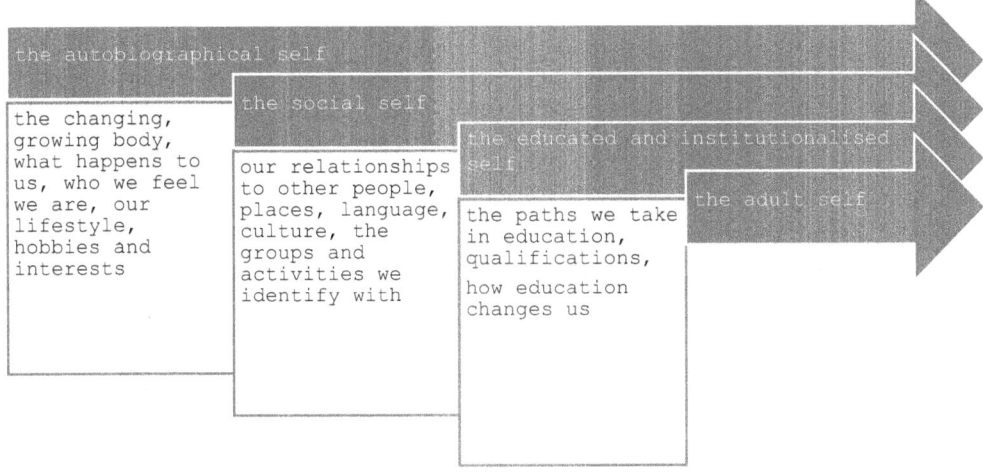

Figure 4.4 The different dimensions of Self.

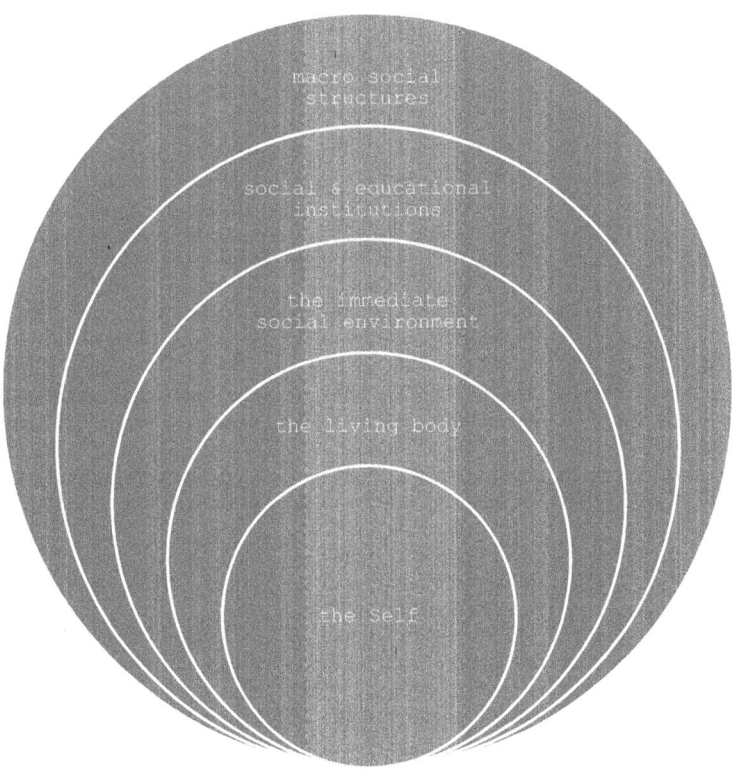

Figure 4.5 The nested ecological of the incarnating Self.

The implication of this pedagogical anthropology for curriculum design

The main implication of this pedagogical anthropology is that the Self is the subject of education. It is important not to see the Self as the object of education. If we accept that the agentic Self is the subject of the education process, that is, the Self is the one who engages with the body and interacts with the world, the one who learns and develops, then the purpose of education is to acknowledge and support the Self. By treating the Self as the object of education and trying to shape the developing human being into a certain form with sets of prescribed skills and possessing certain units of knowledge, we are denying the true nature of the human being, we are appropriating and colonizing them, which leads to alienation. Why this is the case and how it manifests will become clearer once we have explored the nature of development.

Tasks for the reader

Outline the pedagogical anthropology that informs the curriculum you currently work with or are familiar with.

- If there is no pedagogical anthropology, what is your understanding of the nature of the developing human being?
- What is your understanding of the question as to who learns?
- How would you describe (in words or pictures) your own biographical mythos/narrative?

Notes

1. Ingold, T. (2013). *Making. Anthropology, Archaeology and Architecture.* Routledge (Kindle ed., pp. 2–3).
2. Holubnycha, L., Shchokina, T. & Soroka, N. (2023). The anthropological approach to education and modern training and learning methodology. *Educational Challenges*, 28(1), 58–71. https://doi.org/10.34142/2709-7986.2023.28.1.05.
3. Zirfas, J. (2021). *Pädagogische Anthropologie.* Brill utb.
4. See Wulf, C., & Zirfas, J. (Eds.). (2014). *Handbuch Pädagogische Anthropologie.* Springer, or Zirfas, J. (2021). *Pädagogische Anthropologie.* Brill utb.
5. Hay, D., & Nye, R. (2006). *The Spirit of the Child* (revised edition). Jessica Kingsley Publishers.
6. Göschel, J. C. (2012). *Der biographische Mythos als pädagogisches Leitbild: Transdisziplinäre Förderplanung auf Grundlage der Kinderkonferenz in der anthroposophischen Heilpädagogik (Biographical myth as pedagogical leading thought: Transdisciplinary learning support on the basis of the child study process in anthroposophical curative eduction).* Verlag am Goetheanum Athena.
7. Scharmer, C. O. (2018). *The Essentials of Theory U. Core principes and applications.* Berrett-Koehler Publishers. See also the pedagogical and collegial case clinic tools on the Presencing Institute U-School website https://www.u-school.org/resources.
8. See Perry Myers' interesting discussion of Max Weber, Thomas Mann and Rudolf Steiner as intellectuals who sought to counter the trend to what Weber called disenchantment, the loss of the spiritual as a source of meaning, Myers, P. (2004). *The Double-Edged Sword. The cult of Bildung, Its downfall and the reconstitution in Fin-de-Siecle Germany (Rudolf Steiner and Max Weber).* Peter Lang.
9. Steiner explains this in his early epistemological and philosophical works, see Steiner, R. (1963). *Truth and Science* (R. Stibbing, Trans.; P. M. Allen, Ed.). Rudolf Steiner Publications. Steiner, R. (1963 (1894)). *The Philosophy of Spiritual Activity. Fundamentals of a modern view of the world. Results of introspective observations according to the method of natural science* (R. Stebbing, Trans.). Rudolf Steiner Publications. (1894 (1962)).

10 See Barfield, O. (1988). *Saving the Appearances. A Study in Idolatry*. Wesleyan University Press.
11 This expression comes from Daniel Dennett, Dennett, D. (1995). *Darwin's Dangerous Idea: Evolution and the Meanings of Life*. Penguin Books.
12 Martyn has published an article in one of these, Rawson, M. (2021). Spirituality and subjectivity in Waldorf (Steiner) education: a postmodern Bildung perspective. *International Journal of Children's Spirituality*, 26(1/2), 24–43.
13 Miller, L. (2015). *The Spiritual Child*. St. Martin's Press.
14 https://spiritualityineducation.org/about-us/.
15 Miller, L. (2021). *The Awakened Brain. The Psychology of Spirituality and Our Search for Meaning*. Penguin Allen Lane.
16 Fuchs, T. (2017). *The Ecology of the Brain*. Oxford University Press. (das Gehirn- ein Beziehungsorgan); Fuchs, T. (2023). The lived body accomplishes life. *das Goetheanum*. https://www.goetheanum-paedagogik.ch/en/publications/thomas-fuchs.
17 Clement, C. (2001). *Erkennen und Wirklichkeit. Zum Studium der "Philosophie der Freiheit" Rudolf Steiners*. Verlag Freies Geistesleben. Part 5.
18 Steiner, R. (1963 (1894)). *The Philosophy of Spiritual Activity. Fundamentals of a Modern View of the World. Results of Introspective Observations According to the Method of Natural Science* (R. Stebbing, Trans.). Rudolf Steiner Publications (1894 (1962)).
19 Examples include: Barfield, O. (1973). Rudolf Steiner and Hegel. *Anthroposophical Quarterly*, 18(2), 31–36. https://owenbarfield.org/rudolf-steiner-and-hegel/; and Barfield, O. (1988). *Saving the Appearances. A study in Idolatry*. Weslyan University Press.
20 Hay, D., & Nye, R. (2006). *The Spirit of the Child* (revised edition ed.). Jessica Kingsley Publishers. See also Nye, R. (2009). *Children's Spirituality. What it is and Why it Matters*. Church House Publishing.
21 This complex process is made particularly accessible through the work of Antonio Damasio, for example in books such as Damasio, A. (2012). *Self Comes to Mind: Constructing the Conscious Brain*. Random House.
22 Damasio, A. (2021). *Feeling and Knowing. Making Minds Conscious*. Robinson.
23 Dewey, J. (1938). *Experience and Education*. Touchstone.
24 See Alheit, P. (2018). Biographical learning- within the new lifelong learning discourse. In K. Illeris (Ed.), *Contemporary Theories of Learning. Learning Theorists…in their Own Voice* (2nd ed., pp. 153–165). Routledge.
25 See Damasio. (2010). *Self Comes to Mind: Constructing the Conscious Brain*. Random House.

5 A developmental approach

Overview

In this chapter we define what we mean by development and discuss why traditional models of stages and phases are no longer considered accurate. However, we argue that dropping a developmental approach to curriculum is equally unhelpful, since, in reality, people do experience common forms of development, albeit in individual ways. There are overall qualitative stages of development that are useful for teachers to use diagnostically, rather than as criteria for labelling or high-stakes testing. We offer a differentiated approach that is developmental at the level of the person at the macro level.

Curriculum implications

What does developmental psychology have to do with crafting curriculum?

The answer to this question has to do with the iteration we have suggested at the start of this book (Figure 5.1).

We have argued that in order to educate in a way that aligns with the nature of the developing human being yet does not conflict with it, we need a pedagogical anthropology that offers us a perspective on the whole human being, not just on their intellectual skills, and shows us a way of looking at students that enables us to recognize the processes emerging within them. That is why we spent most of the previous chapter talking about the Self and how it relates to the body, to other people and the environment and the fact that that changes over the life course. This anthropology sets out a framework for understanding development.

The central questions in theories of child development are:

- Who develops, or what is it that develops?
- How does development occur in detail? This question addresses issues such as: the respective roles of heredity and genetics and the child's environment; whether development is continuous or punctuated by crises; whether development depends on the self-activity of the child; and what the balance is between cognitive, emotional and volitional and bodily development.
- What factors influence development?

Our answer to the first question is that the whole person develops; the body, dispositions, habits, the mind, abilities, understanding, emotional skills and so on and that it is

A developmental approach 87

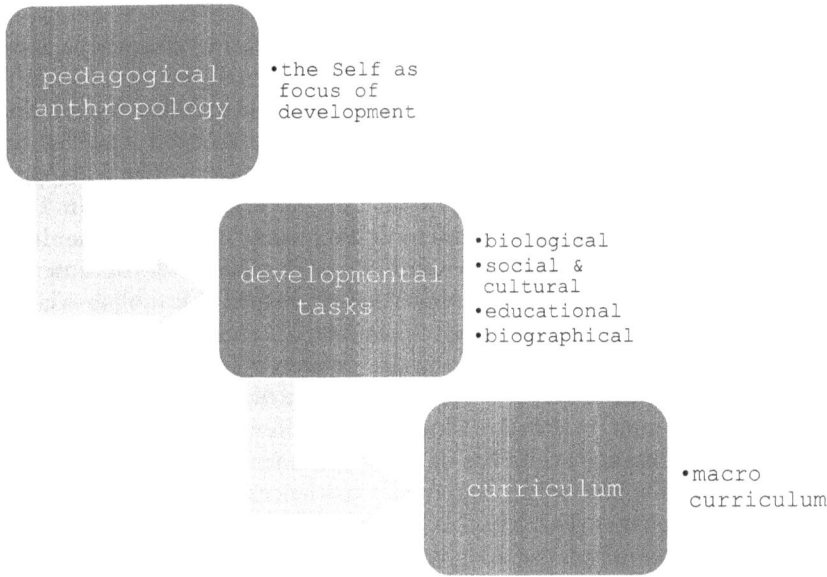

Figure 5.1 The iteration from pedagogical anthropology to developmental tasks as a basis for curriculum.

the Self that drives this process through learning. The details will follow. But first we have a few basic things to clarify.

What is development?

Development is surprisingly difficult to define, and it is often easier to describe the process of how children change as they grow and develop, the factors that influence this and the individual variations that become apparent when we observe the process in any classroom. Rosalyn Shute and Phillip Slee[1] define development, or what is also known scientifically as ontology, as:

1 Transformational or morphological (i.e. relates to form) change through which something new emerges.
2 Variational change which shows as individual differences in development (e.g. the age at which a child learns to walk).

The predominant view today is that biological development is hard-wired into our DNA and unfolds, following a predetermined timeframe in a linear, predictable way, with a natural conclusion (growth, development, decline and death), though, as Shute and Slee comment, this is a "positivist view...wholeheartedly embraced by developmental psychology [which] tends to see development as a linear unfolding of potential."[2] There are other voices that argue that epigenetic and extrinsic factors that are environmental and cultural play into the process. Systems theory adds the factor that, as complex systems, human beings have their own dynamic and not only adapt to their environments but shape them. There have been some, largely unheard, voices making the case, based on the and large numbers of children. In schools, it is considered that teachers have the main responsibility for the learning process, which obviously shapes how they go about it.

In a sense, school as an institution takes children out of everyday life in order to 'prepare' them for life, which when put like this, is odd, to say the least. Among other things, this has the effect of channelling attention away from real situations and towards abstract tasks, because children become focused on what the teacher does, says or asks them to do, rather than seeing what 'needs doing', or experiencing what the situation calls for. The example may seem extreme, but it is like young people – college students perhaps – living in a shared apartment. The sink is full of unwashed crockery and kitchen utensils, the fridge has stuff in it that has gone off, well past its 'best before' date, there is no coffee or milk. Some of the young people see what needs doing (in the interests of the community, or basic hygiene, even self-interest) whilst others don't, because they have either been socialized that someone else does it or that they only respond when someone draws their attention to it (a situation that can then escalate to reactions at another level, "who gives you the right to tell me what to do?"). In school, students basically wait to be told what to do, partly because they don't experience it as their space or task, and partly because the things that 'need doing' only need to be done because the teacher says so, not because there is an intrinsic sense of necessity. In contrast, the kindergarten and craft workshop practice of cleaning and putting away play objects, tools, putting things back in their places not only because it's the rule, but because it is a meaningful shared practice, is a good cultivation of a dwelling perspective.

Children are frequently asked to pay attention and this perpetuates the spotlight approach to attention. It takes only a little imagination to realize what difference a hummingbird mode of consciousness would mean for holistic thinking, human relations, social life and so on. By comparison, in traditional societies without formal, institutionalized education, children spend a lot of time with adults going about their work, or are free to roam around the village in mixed-age groups of children, and learning a great deal about life in the process. Jonathan Haidt,[10] in his recent bestselling book, has highlighted that these experiences are missing for today's children, which combined with extreme levels of screen time, lead to their incompetence and anxiety in real life. In traditional societies, children have multiple opportunities to learn increasingly complex skills in context by being with more competent others.

This iteration of the development of attention, which is only one key factor in development, shows how influential cultural differences can be in the development of the mind. The kind of attention that is modelled, privileged and taught is very influential in how children and adults relate to the world. The combination of spotlight attention and institutionalized schooling shapes the way people relate to young children, making teachers out of parents, who, in turn, relate to their children in didactic ways. Catherine Scott argues that this model of adult–child relationships disposes people to look to strong authorities for leadership, to the assumption that, without individualized leadership, nothing would get done if there is no one in charge. Nevertheless, the idea that we are all teachers to our younger sibling and peers, that we teach each other things is a basic aspect of being human. It just doesn't have to be hierarchical.

This is not an unrealistic or nostalgic argument for going back to living in villages or for children to play in the streets, but rather makes the point that a different kind of curriculum would be needed to enable children to cultivate both spotlight attention and hummingbird attention, in which children learn to attend to multiple things and people, and which would help in the cultivation of holistic thinking. Though Waldorf education has been largely uninfluenced by either Rogoff or Vygotsky, except in as much as Martyn has frequently referred to these scientists in his work, it does actually have much in common with both. In Waldorf early years education, environments are created in kindergartens in which some elements of traditional village life are practiced, including practical activities such as cleaning, preparing and cooking food, gardening, caring for the communal spaces, celebrating festivals, storytelling, singing while working, children's games such as hopscotch, marbles, skipping, in such a way that children can join in if they want, without the assumption of obligation. When they transition to school, there is more focus on the teacher, and often a frontal arrangement of children facing the blackboard with the assumption that all must participate, and guided participation replaces the more participatory character of the kindergarten.

In recent years, many Waldorf schools have introduced the 'moving classroom'. Multipurpose furniture facilitates greater flexible use of the space, and the classroom becomes less static, with children no longer sitting in rows facing the blackboard all the time (see Chapter 8). The Waldorf primary school still resembles the village in some respects, but has now become the village school and the children do tend to learn spotlight attention, which is essential, of course, in all forms of literacy, particularly at the stage of learning constrained skills (see Chapter 7). One of the main ways in which Waldorf education counters the negative effects of spotlight attention is structuring the school day so that the students can immerse themselves in a field of study or theme for around two hours at the start of each day for three or four weeks at a time, in lessons that involve a wide range of activities and skills.

Vygotskian ideas of development

There is more to Vygotskian approaches to learning and development than his famous dictum that all higher cognitive functions are learned twice, once in social interaction and secondly internalized as an autonomous ability, and the Zone of Proximal Development (ZPD) that maps out the theoretical space between our current horizon of capability and the next stage. As Myra Barrs[11] explains, Vygotsky's central concern was understanding the development of the personality of the person. In particular, he was interested in how the child's will develops, and how it manifests in the child's abilities of self-expression, agency, motivation to learn, what we call today self-regulation and control and the ability to direct their attention to the world around them. He was very aware of the interconnections between cognitive abilities of memory, imagination and thinking. In his studies he recognized, for example, the changes in cognition that occur in adolescence. By studying adolescents, he came to realize that there are three stages in children and young people's cognitive development that shape the person's relationship to self, others and the world. He identified an initial inter-psychological phase, in which the adult directs the child, followed by an extra-psychological phase, in which the child begins to speak for themselves and then a third phase, an intra-psychological phase, in which these processes are internalized, assimilated and individualized. This system applies to all cognitive functions. The important aspect of these processes is that each stage requires not simply a shift of location, from outside to inside, but also a remodelling and a re-integration of each system – in other words, a transformation. Vygotsky did not have access to the methods of modern neuroscience, but his observations of behaviour led him to anticipate the dynamic processes involved.

Vygotsky himself developed the new science of pedology (or paedology), which was the scientific discipline of studying children's development and behaviour and was a precursor of what became known as child psychology, though with the integration of education, it was more cross-disciplinary. Curiously, the science of pedology never established itself, being subsumed on the one hand by developmental psychology and child development studies, and on the other hand by pedagogy, which focusses mainly on teaching and learning. It is perhaps indicative of the ambivalence of the relationship between teaching and learning and development and educational/pedagogical anthropology on the other, that Waldorf education is one of the only approaches to see development as central to pedagogy.

Vygotsky, with his reputation as the Mozart of Psychology[12], has until recently been seen as a major figure in psychology but less so in terms of his pioneering educational work. Barrs' book, *Vygotsky the Teacher*, redresses the imbalance. She reports that Vygotsky started his career as, by all accounts, an outstanding and unforgettable teacher. After he was summonsed to Moscow to build up an institute, he involved teachers and children as well as psychologists and researchers. Much of his work was based on detailed case studies of individual children both in the clinic and in the classroom. His main concerns were to establish the importance of play, the imagination, emotions, the role of language and the development of the person.

In his pedology, Vygotsky advocated the study of the whole child. He became more interested in linking pedagogical practice to the development of the child and young person and sought to link teaching to the qualitative transformations in the mind, that form the basis for periodic crises, which he saw as brought about by changes in the driving forces of development during periods of transformation and re-formation, though he focused mainly on the change in the interests of adolescents. Vygotsky wrote,

> Only a decisive departure beyond the methodological limits of traditional child psychology can bring us to a study of the development of that same higher mental synthesis that, on a solid basis, must be called the personality of the child. The history of cultural development of the child brings us to the history of development of personality.[13]

In particular, he noticed that the fundamental drivers of developmental change, such as play, reflect different interests of the person at different stages of development. Whereas in young children play is very much about exploring and developing physical and sensorimotor skills and relationships, in adolescence play is about trying out social, sexual and gender roles, because these reflect the developmental interests – or, we would say, developmental tasks of the young person. Vygotsky described play in general as "self-education; what corresponds to it in adolescence is a complex and long process of transforming tendencies into human needs and interests".[14]

Thus, we can see that the phase of the young, pre-school child involves the formative forces within the child working to establish basic neurological patterns and relationships. After puberty, the will as the driver of behaviour is occupied in 'playing' with psychological structures and social roles. Hand in hand with this 'cognitive play' is the ability to form concepts and understand their significance within a wider field of inquiry. This is a qualitative change in thinking, from concrete to more abstract relationships between experience and its meaning; however, this is not the outcome of an inherent constructivist model within the child, but, rather, the emergent capacity to think conceptually, which is linked to the linguistic ability to articulate concepts, guided by teaching, which systematically introduces logical thinking in mathematics, the sciences, linguistic awareness and the attention to rules or guiding principles across different fields. In other words, this new cognitive ability doesn't just grow but also reflects the cultural expectations of the educational process, combined with an acceleration of both cultural and biological processes, in which new formations emerge and old ones die off.

The research method Vygotsky developed to track such processes was a genetic-comparative one that monitored the changing interests and abilities of the same individual child, comparing them at various key transitional stages, whilst always keeping the whole person in view. At the same time, Vygotsky was interested in the changing content of the concepts learned over time, in particular, how this shows itself in cross-disciplinary aspects. We have sought to do something similar in the development of the Waldorf UK curriculum that seeks to track evolving or living concepts vertically and also horizontally across subjects. An example is the concept of sustainability as it is developed across different fields of ecology, economics, social forms, lifestyles and so on. The third factor is how language develops to articulate the changing nature of concepts, with the idea that through thinking in words we link our thoughts to thoughts in general, a classic Bildung perspective, that Vygotsky chose deliberately by citing Humboldt's notion that thoughts have their social and cultural commonality through language. For adolescents, conceptual thinking has the double aspect of linking to universal ideas whilst linking to subjectivity, "Thus understanding reality, understanding other, and understanding oneself- this is what thinking and consciousness brings with itself. This kind of revolution in thinking and consciousness of the adolescent."[15]

Vygotsky's understanding of the phases in development provides us with an interesting perspective for our own approach. Vygotsky's approach was based on his extensive observations of individuals and on his overall understanding of holistic development as having both a biological and a cultural genesis. He rejected a periodicity based on biological changes alone, such as change of teeth and puberty, or changes based on age-related rhythms. He thought that a distinction between phases only made sense when based on the internal changes, interruptions or breaks within the overall flow of the development of the personality, such as the emergence of new formations. Development is characterized by Vygotsky as periods of stability disrupted by crises and discontinuities. At such turning points children often have difficulties with themselves, with others and with institutional forms, either because the pedagogical system does not match the child's new formation, or the child feels at odds with the institutional expectations and structures.

These crises are not by any means necessarily negative, because something new is being born, whilst something old is being overcome or rejected. What is new manifests in new interests, new perspectives, new relationships to the social and physical environment, new abilities and the reconstruction of the emerging personality. What changes through development is a general structure of consciousness as a consequence of the child's changing relationship to their environment. Vygotsky saw crises typically occurring at the ages of one, three, seven, and thirteen or puberty (whichever comes first); these were clearly not fixed chronologies.

Interestingly, talking about the crisis in the third year he doesn't talk about standardized changes, but says the diagnostic task is to identify the nature of the neo-formation that emerges. To illustrate this, Vygotsky describes four behaviours that can manifest during the third-year crisis, exploring their subtle differences in terms of what they tell us about the child's relationship to self and others. The first is a rejection of being told to do something by a particular adult. The second is stubbornness (the active assertion of the child's will). The third is obstinacy (a general revolt against family rules), and the fourth is wilfulness. The child's actions are identified by the adult world as 'difficult', the actual reasons are individual, but the overall effect is one in which the child seeks to assert their independence and has outgrown the social forms it has hitherto been embedded in. The crisis therefore takes an ideal-typical form, even though the child's individual experience may vary. In Vygotsky's words, "all the symptoms develop around the axis 'I' and the people around [the child]...In general, the symptoms taken together create the impression of emancipation of the child".[16]

This Vygotskian view has remarkable overlaps with Steiner's view of the child's (and youth's) changing consciousness, especially as this has been systematized within the Waldorf discourse, except for the perspective that Waldorf education tends to see development as driven by structures inherent to the Self, whereas Vygotsky sees a more mutually formative correlation between the emerging structures of personality and the cultural influence of education. Some will see this as fundamental. In terms of pedagogical practice, we see the difference as an interesting shift of perspective, but not as essential, which some Waldorf purists will see as a disqualification of our position.

The basic function of a diagnostic approach to development is to establish the actual level of development of the individual, which reveals the fruits of completed cycles of development so far, but also the processes of development that are incomplete. This is the task of the Zone of Proximal Development, which maps out the developmental/pedagogical space between what the child can presently do and what it can do with the help of a teacher (or competent other).

Though we obviously favour much of Vygotsky's approach to learning and development, there is an important difference, or at least a further aspect we would have loved to discuss with Vygotsky and his co-workers. That difference is the Self as spiritual core of being. Vygotsky was a Marxist and was working in the charged atmosphere in the years following the Russian Revolution, grappling with how Marx's theory was interpreted by Lenin and then Stalin. Vygotsky had been called to Moscow to found an institute and to support school reform by Nadezhda Krupskaya, Lenin's wife. He later found himself increasingly at odds with the group of scientists that were close to Stalin. So what did being a Marxist at that time mean?

It is always an interesting question in relation to dialectic materialism or Marxism, as to just what the human spirit is, not least because in his early writings Karl Marx referred to the human spirit, as that which is alienated by capitalism. In the 1840s Marx was interested in human productive activity, which he described in the following terms, "Since human nature is the true community of men (sic), by manifesting this nature, men create, produce the human community, the social entity, which is no abstract universal power opposed to the single individual, but is the essential nature of each individual, his own activity, his own life, his own spirit, his own wealth."[17] Marx began to see that the spiritually productive nature of the human being is self-formation. He wrote,

> Man (sic) makes his life activity itself the object of his will and of his consciousness...An animal's product belongs immediately to its physical body, whilst man freely brings forth what he produces...In degrading spontaneous free activity to a means, estranged labour makes man's species-life a means to his physical existence...Estranged labour thus turns *man's species-being*, both his nature and his spiritual species-property, into a being *alien* to him, into a *means* for his *individual existence*. It estranges from man his own body, as well as external nature and his spiritual aspect, his *human* aspect.[18]

Thus, the human spirit is active in 'producing' humanity, the social-cultural world and even gives meaning to nature. Work is human autopoiesis, or self-formation. Human activity is all about self-formation and self-change. In his *Theses on Feuerbach*, Marx made the statement,

> The materialist doctrine that men are products of circumstances and upbringing, and that, therefore, changed men are products of changed circumstances and changed upbringing, forgets that it is men who change circumstances, and that the educator must himself (sic) be educated. The coincidence of the changing of circumstances and of human activity or self-change (*Selbstveränderung*) can be conceived and rationally understood only as *revolutionary practice*.[19]

What Marx is saying, and what has been misunderstood, especially by Russian Leninist translations and most Marxists since, is that human activity, the activity of the human spirit, is transformative. Throughout the *Theses*, Marx uses the term *praxis*, which is understood as human relations to nature and to human relationships within society. Thinking, and the path to objective truth, occurs within and through praxis. Human nature, or the human spirit, is synonymous with praxis and with the notion of human life-activity or self-change. Human freedom lies in self-formation and emancipation through consciousness in praxis.[20] This idea certainly belongs within the Bildung spectrum of ideas on human self-formation, and this needs to be borne in mind when we draw on the work of Jean Lave and Etienne Wenger and Barbara Rogoff, among other proponents of cultural-historical understandings of communities of practice.

Vygotsky almost certainly belonged to this Bildung stream of Marxism, which is one of the reasons his work soon fell afoul of the Stalinist faction in Russia, and in many ways has been misunderstood by Western (in particular American) readings that have distanced themselves from Vygotsky's Marxist background. As Stephen Toumlin points out, one of Vygotsky's main preoccupations was transcending the division between causality and intentionality, nature and culture, nature and spirit and between free will/autonomy and determination.[21] He achieved this in terms of development by showing that autonomy and intentionality can overcome causality, and by developing scientific methods in psychology and education that are qualitative and interpretive.

What we take away from this brief digression into history is that we can locate Vygotsky within the landscape of ideas about Bildung and that the self at the heart of self-formation is neither the outcome of socio-cultural processes nor the unfolding of a genetic blueprint. The Self is an agentic reality that cannot be reduced to the mind–body, mind/brain–world dichotomies. The view we are putting forward does not claim to solve the Cartesian duality of mind and body, but rather dissolves it. To quote the pioneer child psychologist William Stern, "The irreducible fact of the world is not that there are physical substances and mental substances, but rather that there are real persons." Stern understood people generally, and children in particular, as complex and multifaceted, yet unitary beings. He also saw people as teleological beings with self-orientated purposes, primarily self-maintenance (*Selbsterhaltung*) and self-development, and that this activity does not occur in a vacuum but is also situated in time and place. Understanding this activity requires that teachers address the question as to why children act as they do, and the location and context: the person–world convergence. In school pedagogy, this means attending to how children and young people learn, what they want and need and where and how best to support this.

The life course – or biographical – turn

The life history or life course 'turn' in theories of child development, which were precursors of the widely accepted idea of life-long learning, have changed the way we think about child development.[22] The lifespan or life course approach was famously outlined by Shakespeare's character Jacques in *As You Like It* (Act 2, Scene 7, line 139), which reflected ideas from classical antiquity and the Middle Ages. It was also present in the work of Carl Jung, Charlotte Bühler and other psychotherapists. We know from history and sociology that views of childhood and youth have evolved and changed over time[23] and the construct of youth was unknown before 1900.[24]

Steiner's ideas of archetypal seven-year stages, and his detailed descriptions of the changing consciousness of the child and young person and especially his recognition that early years, primary education and education after puberty need very distinct and specific approaches, were very innovative at the time. As Martyn has discussed elsewhere,[25] whilst we have issues with the way Steiner's model of development has been received and implemented, his core approach to education was developmental, summed up by the phrase 'the child's changing consciousness'. This life course approach is at the heart of Waldorf education and has been further developed by various authors into a widely practiced biography approach and in adult education.[26]

Instead of seeing development as *nature* in the early years being replaced by *nurture* – that is, the predominance of genetics and biology being superseded by *nurture* in the form of socialization and education – life course approaches see development as ongoing change due to the inherent plasticity of the human mind and brain, in which intra-individual processes interact with changing extrinsic, social and structuring structural processes across the whole lifespan. Life course approaches are most widely applied in biography work, youth studies, and life-long learning discourses.[27]

In contrast to Euro-American epistemological traditions, African lifespan ideas include the notion of stages of selfhood: spiritual selfhood, which the child is born with; social selfhood, which lasts throughout life and has several phases; and then postmortem, the third stage of the life cycle is as an ancestor.[28] In this context, death is understood as a natural transition from this life into the next,[29] and "an integral part of their being-in-the-world".[30]

All lifespan theories of development involve some kind of contextualism. For us, the take-away idea of the lifespan or life course approach, whether continuous or punctuated, is that development across the life course is always socially and culturally interactive and mutually constituent.

Universal, general, typical and individual

Generalizing about people is always contentious, but a certain amount can be done, if it is done carefully and with no claim to being definitive. All human beings share a basic biological model, with almost endless individual variation, since no two of the 8 billion people alive today are identical to any other. Knowing how bodies in general develop enables paediatricians to treat individual children medically and teachers to work with them in support of the processes of learning and development. Knowing that sensorimotor, linguistic, cognitive, social, emotional and personal development follows broadly similar pathways from immaturity to maturity is helpful as an orientation, even when we know that every child and young person goes through this vastly complex process in individual ways. This uniqueness is why standardization is counter to emancipation.

The psychologist Robert Sternberg offered the view that, "People are probably not 'types'…but rather vary continuously and somewhat differently as a function of diverse person–situation interactions."[31]

As Remo Largo,[32] the great Swiss paediatrician, put it, what characterizes human development is variation – unique development is the norm. Or, as Hannah Arendt said, our individuality is what we have in common: "Plurality is the condition of human action because we are all the same, that is, human, in such a way that nobody is ever the same as anyone else who ever lived, lives, or will live."[33]

As Erica Burman[34] has argued, traditional models of child development with fixed stages and phases and metaphors of milestones along a pathway to well-adjusted adulthood are highly contested, not least because such models have been shown to be strongly Eurocentric, reflecting implicit notions of lower and higher development and implying (if not actually stating) a progression from savages to civilization. The education process was often seen as a kind of civilizing process in which the natural child needed to be 'tamed', socialized and educated to a higher level of moral and intellectual behaviour. Such frameworks can be applied in a discriminatory way to children who do not reach the crucial developmental milestones for all kinds of reasons, but often labelled 'behind', developmentally delayed, not meeting age related expectations, or other phrases that express a deficit in some way. Parental anxiety can be heightened when their offspring fail to reach the milestones that can be found in helpful guides for parents distributed across the internet. Furthermore, as Rosalyn Shute and Phillip Slee point out in their book on child development, for most of its history until very recently, developmental psychology has been "an overwhelmingly gendered, androcentric undertaking".[35]

The subject of child and youth development is like visiting a major art museum that spans the past and includes the present. Moving through the major 'milestones' in the development of theories of development – and Shute and Slee's book referred to above is an excellent guide – is not a march of progress from ignorance to enlightenment, but rather a complex journey, in which the various stopping-off points offer different and complementary views. We know that theories of child development over the past centuries have been strongly shaped by the images that people have had about the nature of childhood (bearing in mind that the concept of childhood is relatively recent historically, and that of adolescence or youth, very recent). These images of childhood are also reflected in various philosophical and even religious stances. Theories of child development also reflect shifting scientific paradigms, such as behaviourism, humanism, social learning, psychoanalytic, ethological, cognitive and ecological. Again, we recommend Shute and Slee's book and Laura Berk's textbook *Development Through the Lifespan*[36] as guides to what these approaches look like.

Variation is the norm

At the World Waldorf Teachers Conference at the Goetheanum in 2012, the well-known Swiss paediatrician Remo Largo held a lecture in which he emphasized that what characterizes child development is individual variation. He made this point at the beginning of his lecture, using the following example:

> A teacher of a class of twenty six-year-old children will see differences of up to three years in the children's developmental age. Some children have a developmental age of 7 to 8 years and can read at the age of six, while others have a developmental age of 4

to 5 years and have difficulty reading. Before the children reach high school, the differences between them usually increase significantly...By age 13, the developmental ages of the most and least developed children differ by at least 6 years. In addition, boys, as a group, are on average 18 months behind girls. Dealing with this 'inter-individual variability' can be challenging for parents and teachers.

(2012, p. 18; MR trans.)

The implications of this for Waldorf education, and any other approach that follows a developmental approach, can be summarized as follows. For the nature of child and youth development:

- individual variation and diversity are normal,
- heterochronous development is normal,
- learning groups are always heterogenous.

The point is, both inter-individual and intra-individual development is heterochronous. In his famous Zurich longitudinal study of child development, Largo[37] used seven different ways of measuring children's development: fine motor, gross motor, linguistic, cognitive, social, emotional and self-awareness. It is evident that children's development also varies across these aspects of development, which any teacher can confirm. If we take a holistic perspective, then we would not wish to privilege only the cognitive abilities of children and young people.

We do think, however, that it is useful to map out a pathway of development, though not as a set of milestones that have to be achieved and not as a description of what 'normal' development is, with the implication that anything outside of these parameters is 'abnormal'. We think that it is useful to have an orientation, not by setting standards or describing archetypes, but by characterizing ideal-typical steps in a developmental process that are structured to respond to different factors.

The term ideal-typical or ideal-type is used here in the technical sense first defined by the sociologist Max Weber, who was looking to establish the social and human sciences on a sound scientific basis that was equivalent to – but not the same as – the criteria used in natural science. For those interested in this idea, we recommend some literature in the endnotes.[38] The basic notion of an ideal type is that it is a heuristic tool constructed by the researcher to reflect and accentuate the aspects that are deemed relevant and important to those to whom the construct applies. In this case the ideal types are based on what teachers (and other relevant stakeholders) expect and what is useful to them in planning curriculum, and also take account of actual Waldorf practice over the past 100 years. They provide a point of reference, an Archimedean point as it were, from which to reflect on the actual development of the students, or as an orientation of what teachers think the developmental tasks in a given class should be. They are neither real nor fixed and can be modified through experience.

In other words, this approach is to map out a pathway of developmental tasks that those responsible for the curriculum and practitioners believe is desirable at a given stage. There are, however, multiple factors that play into what the developmental task is. An ideal type of developmental stages offers us a framework to compare the actual developmental situation of children and young people. The ideal-typical developmental steps are not based on the average developmental ages of a group of children or young people but offer a point from which the development of individual children or the learning group (the class) can be assessed. We can show this relationship in the form given in Figure 5.2.

A developmental approach 99

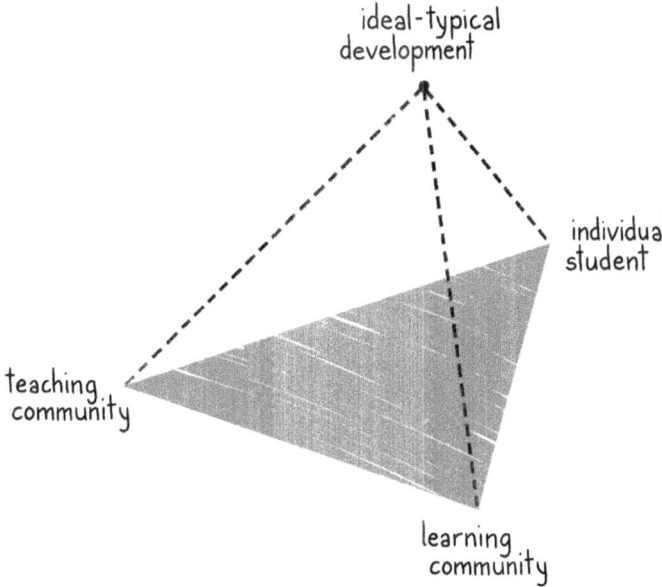

Figure 5.2 This graphic shows the role of the ideal-typical descriptor in relation to the actual development of the individual or group. Some individuals may be nearer to the ideal typical descriptor, but this does not have a normative function. Credit: Aristea Klanac.

Developmental tasks

The term 'developmental tasks' was originally coined by the American sociologist Robert Havighurst[39] and modified by the German educational sociologist Klaus Hurrelmann[40] and his colleagues. It refers to the intrinsic and extrinsic tasks that people have to successfully navigate at key transitions in the life course. We have built on this concept to match the pedagogical anthropology we have outlined.

The main developmental tasks are:

1 The growth and maturation of the body, which has genetic, epigenetic, biological, nutritional and social and cultural aspects. The emergent Self has to embody itself within the changing body. These factors lead to variation in growth and the timetable of significant changes such as the onset of puberty, which occurs much earlier than 100 years ago.
2 The social and cultural environment of language and social practices shapes development and has expectations of what the growing child should be and become.
3 The developing children and young people have to adapt to institutional transitions and structures (e.g. transition from a kindergarten to a school culture). These institutional (mostly educational) cultures also impose assumptions about behaviour, relationships to others (including authorities), nature, the world and expectations about children and young people should learn by when (and often how).
4 The biographical intentions of the person.
5 The educational aims and curriculum requirements to learn certain skills and knowledge by a given time.
6 Brute facts are things that happen to people without any obvious direct connection to them personally (e.g. through risk taking, consequences of deliberate actions etc.) such as natural disasters, collateral suffering through war, famine, poverty, epidemics, exposure to violence and accidents.

100 *Crafting a Curriculum of Coherence*

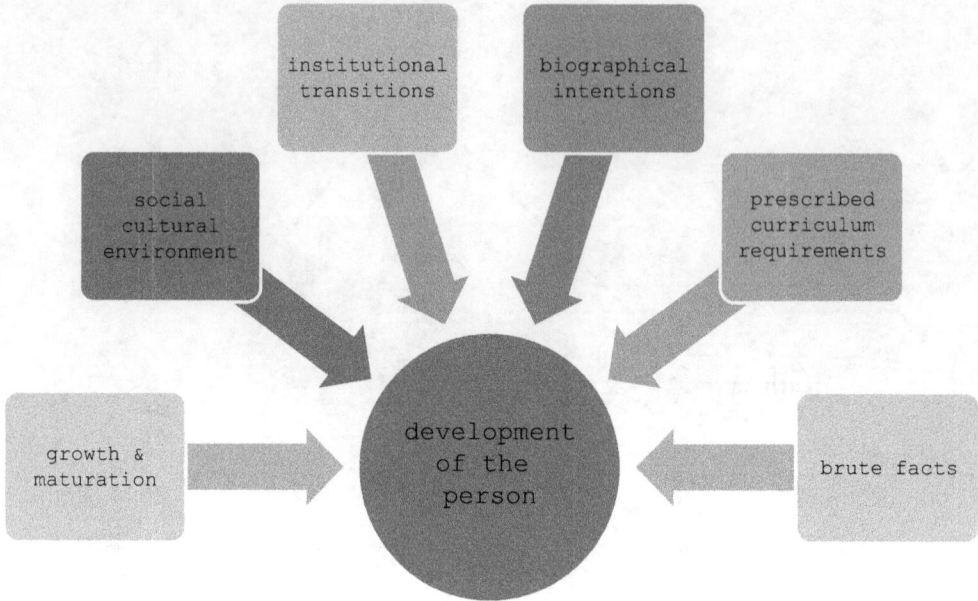

Figure 5.3 Developmental tasks: the cluster of factors that play into learning and development.

We can show these factors together in the Figure 5.3.

In order to take all these factors into account, it is necessary to address these factors in different ways within the curriculum we are crafting.

Development at the macro level of curriculum

As we introduced in Chapter 3, we recommend a multi-layered curriculum. We start our iteration at the macro-level from a pedagogical anthropology of the whole person, at the heart of which is the Self's ongoing and changing relationships to body, other people, social community and environment. One could say that these evolving relationships are a shared heritage of humanity. Over the whole course of human cultural evolution, these have always been the questions that people have had to engage with, though in vastly varying circumstances. There is a certain general correlation, though not a parallelism, between what each child and young person has to engage with and the challenges that human societies have had to engage with over the course of human history. This prehistory is within us.[41] We embody it, and it is embedded in our language and tools. Thus, our first level of curriculum is anthropological and historical and cultural. Curriculum therefore starts with archetypal human concerns of good and evil, light and dark, individual and community, life as a journey, challenges and transformations, in other words, all the themes of folktales, legends and myths from around the world and all cultures.[42] Such traditions of oracy (text versions of oral cultural artefacts) deal with central issues of being human in non-intellectual and imaginative ways that speak particularly to the young child's way of relating to the world.

If children and young people's way of thinking, their mode of consciousness changes both with maturation and through the ideas they encounter, then story material and teaching material can map out such a psychological journey and give directions to follow.

Children and young people respond to stories in individual ways that reflect their interests, experiences and thus their development. The way narrative is taken up pedagogically is therefore also important. In early years stories are simply told in an atmosphere that invites them to listen and participate. Later, the themes of stories can be discussed ('Why do you think she did that?') and later still they can be analysed in terms of the use of language, imagery, relationships, narrative voice and so on, and, of course, students can become proficient story tellers (and story writers and illustrators). This is a developmental approach, which prompts the further development of dispositions, skills and knowledge.

At the same time young children must start learning cultural techniques such as literacy and numeracy, though in ways that align with developmental processes and in ways that strengthen the child's forces and resilience rather than weaken them.

This shows how important it is to realize how the child's changing consciousness goes hand in hand with their bodily growth and the growth of the complexity of their social relationships. It is strange in a way that education, with the exception of early years, has moved away from descriptions of child development, when anyone who has accompanied children as a parent, even without special study of child psychology, can identify distinct changes and phases in the way children and young people are. Interestingly Alan Watkins and Matt Silver, in their recent book *Reinventing Education*,[43] devote a whole chapter to describing child development in twelve levels. They make the point that though the education system is based on learning it more or less ignores development: "Yet, it is development that holds the key to unlocking the vast reservoir of human potential in children, teachers, leaders and all educational stakeholders."[44] They suggest putting development at the heart of the education system and they make the interesting distinction between learning as horizontal change based on acquiring skills, whereas development is vertical development in the sense of "quantum leaps" in cognitive capacity as manifest in the emergence of a range of capabilities.

The macro-level of the curriculum that we are suggesting, therefore, is a developmental approach that takes the following aspects into account:

1 The first relationship is to the growing body. It is interesting that in human evolution the fact that childhood plays a crucial role and that human beings remain lifelong learners distinguishes us from all other creatures, and this is bound up with uprightness and its consequences.[45] Once human beings have achieved upright bipedal walking, acquired spoken language and start to imagine things not immediately present, then a certain stage of development has been achieved. In educational terms this all occurs during the period of early childhood. As we saw in the previous chapter, Waldorf education works on the assumption that during this period of early childhood the child's life processes are very active structuring and fine-tuning the brain and establishing health life rhythms with balance between sleeping and waking and a robust digestion, both in the literal sense of eating but also in the sense of processing sense impressions.
2 Once the child has made a transition to school, there are often quite different demands socially and intellectually. The peer group gains in importance as do the relationships with adults as figures of authority, both parents and teachers. These change and are often challenged.
3 Issues of identity begin early with the impact of peers, but also through the influence of advertising and social media, which present children with images of what they

should be and this often awakens prematurely – at least in comparison with previous generations – heightened self-awareness and insecurity.
4 In puberty, major changes occur in the child's relationship to their body but also to the social world and the intellect begins to turn a critical gaze towards the adult world.
5 With adolescence, the young person continues to undergo significant changes in their relationship to self, others and the world and the process of identity work begins to focus on several significant questions, that of gender identity, that of cultural belonging, that of educational orientation and possible future directions ("What do I want to become?") and that of lifestyle, ranging from bodily, appearance, style, relationships, hobbies and activities, interests. In adolescence and emergent adulthood, young people often seek to emancipate themselves from the social and cultural world they have grown up in and this can take a very idealistic form with high expectations and confidence in one's ability to be better and different from existing authorities, yet also easily disempowered by lack of opportunities, resources and self-confidence. Young people are often looking for a meaningful task and purpose that enable them to realize their potential, but this can easily be derailed by disappointment in 'the existing system' and its structures, especially when they encounter cynical self-interest, less than perfect role models, and few possibilities to develop and express their potential. Some young people in this stage are protected and cushioned by their family's care and wealth, whilst many others are exposed and vulnerable, but all are confronted by the need to take a stance, establish themselves as individuals with a purpose. This has never been easy, but it is especially challenging given the temptations and unrealistic expectations offered by consumerism and the lack of meaningful challenges. Gert Biesta[46] talks about the infantilization of the education system that regulates young people's lives in great detail, that reduces learning to the gathering of module points for delivering the desired answers to standardized questions, which, along with popular culture and the availability of everything with a click, leads to a significant degradation of intellectual capacity of the generation, or rather a stymying of potential.

This is just a very brief outline of the kind of developmental changes children and young people go through, that impact on their interests and capabilities at school. Teachers intuitively respond to their students by taking such factors into account, but this is rarely done by the curriculum, which in many cases takes a functional view of the development of skills and knowledge, beyond basic progressions from simple to complex tasks. We argue, from the experience of Waldorf education, that both the choice of topics and the methods of learning can address the developmental interests of children at a deeper, more existential level, that takes these interests seriously.

If we were to unpack this brief outline above, we can discover deeper psychological questions that should not be answered with superficial or banal responses. If we acknowledge and respect children's changing consciousness we can recognize that behind their naïve linguistic abilities and lack of cultural skills, they have a rich and complex relationship to the world. Robert MacFarlane[47] reports on an experiment with primary-aged children in Cambridgeshire, who were given the opportunity of spending one day a week in a country park, with areas of woodland, streams, meadows, a lake and so on. On the following day, they were asked to recall their experiences in pictures and narrative. The children were accompanied to ensure their safety but otherwise had no educational tasks. The project began in January and went on for six months, thereby enabling the children to experience a wide range of weather conditions. MacFarlane reports that the children journeys and encounters with other beings, perhaps with multiple crises involving transformation, finally coming to a resolution and often some new level of harmony, or at least stability. These stories can be modified to include gender and cultural diversity in ways that the traditional version often didn't have (especially in less modern collections).

Once the stories have been told or read by the students and recalled, they can be discussed in an open way, not for moral lessons that need to be drawn (as in Bible study), but in terms of their storylines, characterization, the nature of the challenges faced by the protagonists, and so on. Pedagogically, it is helpful to follow the steps in a somewhat simplified form of hermeneutic analysis. First the story is reconstructed in terms of its content (what happened to whom, when, where, how and why). In a second step the students can engage in dialogue with the text/story, perhaps contextualizing it historically (this happened in premodern times) and culturally (this story is located in Japan, which is a very mountainous island, in which the people, used to live by fishing and using the resources of the forest and had a certain religious beliefs and social structures etc.). In a third, transactional step, the students can say how they relate to the story, what it makes them think about or they can find tasks for themselves inspired by the story (writing a sequel in a different context, creating a storyboard for a short, animated film, etc.). This approach avoids (or rather minimizes) the risks of teachers moralizing or directly the students towards certain interpretations or other prescribed outcomes.

As we have seen from the previous chapter on pedagogical anthropology, activating the students' self-activity and identification is crucial to transformative learning – if that is our aim, which we strongly recommend. Sharing narratives together helps build community. When students move on to reading for pleasure, sharing what they have read, even critiquing, and recommending helps to generate discourse within the learning community.

With increasing maturity, there is a transition from a community of learning, in which everyone shares the same content (though they will respond to it in very individual ways), to a community of inquiry. This inquiry can be scientific, philosophical, artistic or practical. Individuals develop expertise in fields that reflect their interests and strengths, which can be in widely different fields (from sport to Socratic dialogue) and share and critique the fruits of their inquiries. At this stage young people can learn dispositions to craftspersonship in different fields, which means developing a sense for tools, techniques, materials, aesthetic considerations and the usefulness of what they do. Crafting is an attitude involving values, skills and knowledge in whichever field of inquiry it is applied – the craft of musical composition, writing, designing science experiments or field observations, debating politics, planning a start-up and so on.

Self-directed reading and inquiry, self-chosen projects and artistic activities enable the young people to be both self-active, thus affording their agency, and to some extent self-directed, in that students choose what they want to deepen their experience in. The art and craft of teaching in this phase is to offer guidance, methods and examples of teacher inquiry as a model and general facilitation of the learning process where needed (essential subject content is part of the meso-level described below). This phase requires reflection and an element of reflexivity.

In summary, the macro-level curriculum addresses the development of the person and general core learning dispositions and social capacities. The medium is primarily story material (either stories told or through guided reading, followed by self-directed reading) and the social processes in the learning community. The methods used will be age-appropriate and assessment essentially formative and ipsative, though projects can also be summatively assessed using criteria that are known beforehand.

The macro level in Waldorf education

In Waldorf education the macro level consists of a sequence of ideal-typical developmental descriptors that characterize the kind of developmental tasks facing the person at different stages. Because the Waldorf curriculum is structured on a year-by-year basis, with children of the same chronological age (within one year) in a class, these developmental descriptors are matched to specific classes. However, given the general variation in children's development and the importance of transitions, descriptors are given for key periods of transition. These descriptors do not offer specific content, but rather describe the developmental tasks related to the ideal-typical developmental pathway Waldorf education considers is good for the students, in the sense that it offers opportunities for self-formation.

In effect, the message the curriculum is signalling is: here is a developmental journey - like the archetypal journey of the hero in Joseph Campbell's analysis of world myths – and we invite the child and young person to accompany us on this journey. Each individual will respond in different ways and since we are not defining targets that need to be achieved but rather describing themes, that the teachers can address through whatever topics and subjects they deem appropriate, the developmental processes lie within the interests and capabilities of each student. The development of the person is not something we measure. This is a Bildung approach in which the self-formation of the individual is the primary focus.

As examples of macro-level developmental themes, we cite here the descriptions of the key transitions in development from the perspective of Waldorf education. These examples are taken from the European Council of Steiner Waldorf Education Common Core Curriculum Framework.

Key transitions

Transition: kindergarten to school Classes 1 & 2 (ages 6–7)
Following the Waldorf understanding of child development, the child's formative life forces reach a certain culmination in establishing the functioning of the organs and the bodily rhythms and processes in areas of respiration, nutrition, regeneration and so on. Growth is by no means complete, but the body has reached a stage of maturation in which the Self as spiritual core can 'feel at home' in the body. In particular, the brain-body has reached a stage of development in which basic language structures, sensory integration and motor development have reached a kind of functional stability, a basis for all subsequent learning and development. As in all aspects of development, this process is characterized by wide intra- and inter-individual variation. It may be a fact that globally, because of changed lifestyles, all children are probably more or less underdeveloped in the sensorimotor capacities. This traditional notion of school-readiness, which assumed that children were ready for the cognitive challenges of formal learning after the informal approach of early years and based on the physical evidence of the second dentition, is no longer appropriate. The cultural requirement today is that children go to school at least by the age of six (but not before – and if the state requires this, then the children need to meet a pedagogy that responds to their real needs) and the pedagogical requirement is that the school culture and the teachers are 'ready' for the children.

The transition from kindergarten to school involves an institutional cultural change, which children need time to adjust to. Ideally the transition, which is often ritualized and celebrated in many Waldorf schools, should be smooth and integrated with some elements typical of school (more task-orientated activities in which instructions are given, time structures in lessons and thematic structures between subjects and teachers, and activities such as literacy and numeracy in which individual differences become more apparent) in the final year of kindergarten and some elements of kindergarten (free play, optional participation, mixed-age groups) are carried over into the first school classes.

All children today need movement and opportunities to cultivate their coordination, fine and gross motor skills, and what they don't need is lengthy periods sitting at a desk facing in one direction. The moving classroom, which means having a flexible space with special furniture that can be quickly moved to one side, cushions to sit on rather than chairs, and structuring the school day in a more organic way (that bells ringing at regular intervals), is a highly successful model. Young school children also need to develop their senses of balance, movement and coordination, touch and establish healthy rhythms, as well as learning the rhythms of communication (when to listen and when and how to speak), along with the social skills of being in a heterogenous learning community.

One of the main characteristics of children between the seventh and ninth year [age 6–8] is their desire to learn and make sense of their experiences. Memory, imagination, enjoyment of rhythmical repetition and a desire for universal concepts presented in pictorial form, come to the fore at this stage, and a key change in their learning is to move from 'imitation' to 'listen and do', i.e. translating verbal instructions into their own actions. Children actively seek guidance from the adult world and whilst they continue to imitate what they experience, their behaviour is modelled on how significant others are, including the teachers in the school. Children start observing those around them for signs of how to be. They look to the teachers for guidance in all aspects of being in school and learning. Gesture is a powerful means of gaining their attention, words have to generate images in the minds of the children and the way the teachers act in all things great and small shows children how things can be in ways that foster wellbeing, social awareness and moral authority.

Transition: the 'Rubicon' in Classes 3, 4 & 5 (ages 9–11)
Steiner described a developmental process in middle childhood that he called the 'Rubicon'. For most children, this transition appears between the ages of eight and nine, but can occur as late as 11 years. The psychological and social challenges of the 'Rubicon' require individuals to enter a new relationship to self and community that is no longer based on uncritical family acceptance and blood ties. The emergence of a consciousness of self is also one of distance from the childhood sense of being fully embedded in the world. This is an important step in individuation and is one of the many steps in which the individual becomes aware of being different from others and therefore no longer feeling naturally part of the community and the world. The metaphor behind the notion of Rubicon is that of a transition from one state to a radically different one and crisis, in the sense of an opportunity for fundamental change. This can be an experience of a loss of inner security and identification as children turn the question of purpose and identification towards the community and the natural world, though does not have to be experienced in a negative way. Many children are ready to move on and engage with the world. Successful negotiation of the 'Rubicon' developmental tasks can lead to a new sense of belonging to the community and to the world. If this process is mirrored in narrative and myth, then the chief motives are separation, individual journeys and reunion, the need for codes and rules, human cooperation and community, and stewardship of the natural world.

Transition: Early Puberty in Classes 4, 5 & 6 (ages 10–12)
There is much evidence that the earlier onset of puberty leads to significant changes in the child's relationship to self and body, self and others and self and world. Thus, the developmental themes and tasks for Classes 4, 5 and 6 have to be taken as an overlapping continuum. This means that children are in a transition from childhood to puberty, though this is very individual, and girls tend to enter puberty before the boys. Some children are still very harmonious and fluid in their movements while others experience changes in their bodies. Many children are often strong-willed, self-reliant and creative at this age and their intellect is emerging in ways that enable them to begin to understand more abstract concepts, such as time and space.

110 *Crafting a Curriculum of Coherence*

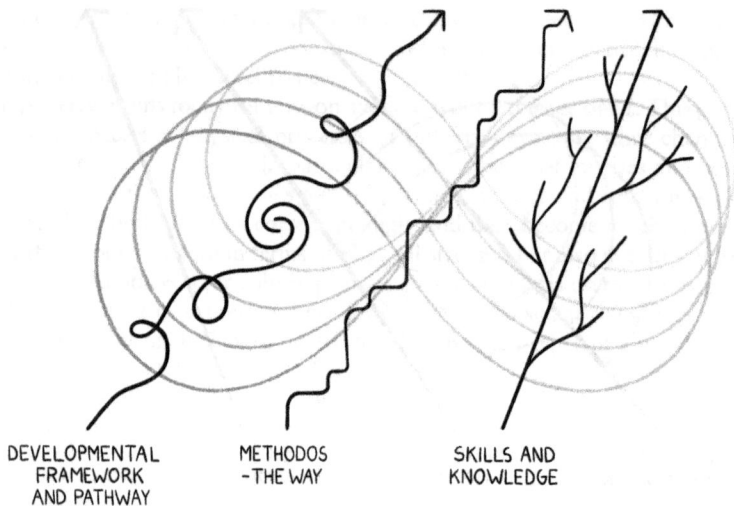

DEVELOPMENTAL FRAMEWORK AND PATHWAY   METHODOS – THE WAY   SKILLS AND KNOWLEDGE

Figure 5.6 The curriculum reality looks more like this. Credit: Aristea Klanac.

comprehensive overview of biological development. As in Figure 5.6, curriculum seeks to balance the growth of skills and knowledge in developmentally meaningful ways. The methods of teaching and learning weave a pathway between these two parameters. In reality, the task is far more complex, as the above graphic suggests. As a result, at the micro level teachers have to weave a possible pathway within this overall framework.

A pedagogical approach to teaching and learning that takes a developmental approach will,

- address the Self as agentic core of learning, which calls for self-activity and addressing the whole person, senses, bodily activity, feelings and thinking.
- use age-appropriate language (which means adapting to the language levels of the actual students and scaffold this to bridge the Zone of Proximal Development),
- frame lessons with appropriate narrative material (through storytelling, story writing and reading),
- structure the learning process in a way that involves holistic aspects of learning (which we discuss in Chapter 8) and in ways that weave new experiences into a coherent tapestry of the existing world view the students have,
- consider what is general, nationally relevant and specifically relevant for your students (i.e. take account of the macro, meso and micro levels of curriculum).

Tasks for the teacher

- Do the examples of presentations of the developmental themes above resemble your experience of students at this age?
- If this is not the case, what kind of ideal-typical descriptions would you write? Try writing an example for your educational setting.

Notes

1. Shute, R. H., & Slee, P. T. (2015). *Child Development: Theories and Critical Perspectives* (2nd. ed.). Routledge.
2. Shute, R. H., & Slee, P. T. (2015). *Child Development: Theories and Critical Perspectives* (2nd. ed.). Routledge, p. 2.
3. Muchow, M., & Muchow, H. H. (1935/1978). *The Life Space of the Urban Child*. Routledge. (*Der Lebensraum des Großstadtkindes*. Riegel Verlag).
4. Muchow, M., & Muchow, H. H. (1935/1978). *The Life Space of the Urban Child*. Routledge. (*Der Lebensraum des Großstadtkindes*. Riegel Verlag), p. 61.
5. See Ingold, T. (2000). *The Perception of the Environment: Essays in Livelihood, Dwelling and Skill*. Routledge.
6. Murray Thomas, R., & Feldmann, B. (1996). *Comparing Theories of Child Development*. Wadsworth Publishing Company.
7. Scott, C. (2015). *Learn to Teach. Teach to Learn*. Cambridge University Press. Kindle edition-.
8. Rogoff, B. (2003). *The Cultural Nature of Human Development*. Oxford University Press.
9. Rogoff, B. (2003). *The Cultural Nature of Human Development*. Oxford University Press, p. 49.
10. Haidt, J. (2024). *The Anxious Generation: How the Great Rewiring of Childhood is Causing an Epidemic of Mental Illness*. Penguin Press.
11. Barrs, Myra. (2022)*Vygotsky the Teacher: A Companion to his Psychology for Teachers and Other Practitioners*. Routledge. Kindle Edition.
12. Toumlin, S. (1978/2021). The Mozart of Psychology. *The New York Review of Books*, 25(15). https://archive.org/details/toulmin-vygotsky-the-mozart-of-psychology-1978/page/2/mode/2up.
13. Barrs, 2022, p. 105.
14. Vygotsky, L.S (1998/1931) Pedology of the adolescent in Vygotsky, L.S. The collected works of L.S. Vygotsky. Volume 5, Child Psychology pp. 3–184. Rieber, R.W. (ed.) New York, Plenum Press.
15. Vygotsky, L.S (1998/1931) Pedology of the adolescent in Vygotsky, L.S. The collected works of L.S. Vygotsky. Volume 5, Child Psychology pp. 3–184. Rieber, R.W. (ed.) New York, Plenum Press, p. 49.
16. Vygotsky, L.S. (1998/1932) The crisis at age 3, in Vygotsky, L.S. The collected works of L.S. Vygotsky Volume 5, Child Psychology, pp. 283–288. Rieber, R.W. (ed) New York, Plenum Press.
17. Marx, K. (1970/1843)). *Critique of Hegel's Philosophy of Right* (A. Jolin & J. O"Malley, Trans.; J. O"Malley, Ed.). Cambridge University Press, p. 217.
18. Marx, K. (1970/1843)). *Critique of Hegel's Philosophy of Right* (A. Jolin & J. O"Malley, Trans.; J. O"Malley, Ed.). Cambridge University Press, pp. 276–277.
19. Marx, K. (2008 (1845)). Thesen über Feuerbach. In J. R. a. P. H. Breitenstein (Ed.), *Philosophische und ökonomische Schriften* (pp. 46–49). Reclam. Martyn's translation.
20. Readers who are interested in these ideas are advised to read Cyril Smith (2004) Karl Marx and Human Self-Creation. Lexington Books https://www.marxists.org/reference/archive/smith-cyril/works/alteration/index.htm.
21. Toumlin, S. (1978/2021). *Vygotsky: The Mozart of Psychology*. Harvard University Press. pp. 8–-9.
22. Among the important early texts were Havighurst, R. J. (1948). *Developmental Tasks and Education*. David McKay; Erikson, E. (1968). *Identity, Youth and Crisis*. Norton; and Levinson, D. (1978). *Seasons of a man's life*. New York.
23. See Cunningham, H. (2006). *The Invention of Childhood*. BBC Books. Frijhoff, W. (2012). Historian's Discovery of Childhood. *Paedagogica Historica*, 48(1), 11–29. https://doi.org/10.1080/00309230.2011.644568.
24. Hurrelmann, K., & Quenzel, G. (2012). *Lebensphase Jugend: Eine Einführung in die sozialwissenschaftliche Jugendforschung (Life phase youth: an introduction into social science research into youth)* (11th revised edition ed.). Beltz Juventa.
25. Rawson, M. (2024). A holistic theory of child development for Waldorf education. *WaldorfWorkingPapers*. https://e-learningwaldorf.de/wp-content/uploads/2024/12/No.-12-A-holistic-theory-of-child-and-youth-development-for-Waldorf-education.pdf.

26 For example Lievegoed, B. C. J. (2005). *Phases of Childhood: Growing in Body, Soul and Spirit* (T. L. a. P. Peters, Trans.; revised edition ed.). Floris Books; and van Houten, C. (1995). *Awakening the Will. Principles and Processes in Adult Learning*. New Adult Learning Network; Pannitschka, S. (2019). Im Modus des Lernens über Kindheit und Jugend hinaus: von den Lebens- zu den Lernprozessen in Erwachsenenalter. (In the mode of learning beyond childhood and adolescence: from life processes to learning processes in adulthood), in A. Wiehl (Ed.), *Studienbuch Waldorfschulpädagogik* (pp. 223–238). Klinkhardt.

27 See Illeris, K. (2018). *Contemporary Theories of Learning: Learning theorists...in their own words* (2nd. Edition ed.). Routledge. Biesta, G. J. J., Field, J., Hodkinson, P., Macleod, F. J., & Goodson, I. (2011). *Improving Learning through the Lifecourse*. Routledge.

28 This is cited in Shute and Slee (2015), p. 153.

29 Mariette, G. C. (2013). International healing and collaboration structures. *Journal of Black Psychology*, 39, 261–268.

30 Baloyi, L., & Makobe-Rabothata, M. (2014). The African conception of death: A cultural implication. Papers from the International Association for Cross-Cultural Psychology Conferences.

31 Robert Sternberg and Elena Grigorenko (1997). Are cognitive styles still in style? *American Psychologist*, 52, pp. 700–712. Cited in Claxton, 2006, p. 6.

32 Largo, R. (2012). As a social and learning being each child is unique. *Journal of the Pedagogical Section at the Goetheanum, Special edition World Teachers' Conference 2012*, 18–31.

33 Arendt, H. (1958). *The Human Condition*. University of Chicago Press. p. 8.

34 Burman, E. (2017). *Deconstructing Developmental Psychology* (3rd ed.). Routledge.

35 Shute, R. H., & Slee, P. T. (2015). *Child Development: Theories and critical perspectives* (2nd ed.). Routledge.

36 Berk, L. (2013). *Development Through the Lifespan* (6th ed.). Pearson.

37 Largo, R. (2019). *The Right Life. Human Individuality and its Role in Development, Health and Happiness*. Allen Lane.

38 Weber, M. (1949). Objectivity in the social sciences and social policy. In E. A. Shils & H. A. Sinch (Eds.), *The Methodology of the Social Sciences*. Free Press; Rosenberg, M. M. (2015). The conceptual articulation of the reality of life: Max Weber's theoretical constitution of sociological ideal types. *Journal of Classical Sociology*, 16(1), 1–18; Crotty, M. (1998). *The Foundations of Social Research: Meaning and Perspective in the Research Process*. SAGE.

39 Havighurst, R. J. (1948). *Developmental Tasks and Education*. David McKay.

40 Hurrelmann, K., & Bauer, H. P. (2018). *Socialisation during the Life Course*. Routledge.

41 The archaeologist Chris Gosden points out that we all carry our prehistory in our bodies and unconscious as a substate of our being, Gosden, C. (2003). *Prehistory: A Very Short Introduction*. Oxford University Press.

42 See Campbell, J. (2008 (1949)). *The Hero with a Thousand Faces*. New World Library; Shah, I. (1991/2003). *World Tales*. The Octogon Press; Zipes, J. (2011). *Fairy Tales and the Art of Subversion*. Routledge,

43 Watkins, A., & Silver, M. (2025). *Reinventing Education. Beyond the Knowledge Economy*. Routledge.

44 Watkins, A., & Silver, M. (2025). *Reinventing Education. Beyond the Knowledge Economy*. Routledge, p. 75.

45 See Gamble, C., Gowlett, J., & Dunbar, R. (2014). *Thinking Big: How the Evolution of Social Life Shaped the Human Mind*. Thames & Hudson. See also Kingdon, J. (1996). *Self-Made Man. Human evolution from Eden to extinction?* Wiley.

46 Biesta, G. J. J. (2020). Have we been paying attention? Educational anaesthetics in a time of crisis. *Educational Philosophy and Theory*. https://doi.org/10.1080/00131857.2020.1792612.

47 Macfarlane, R. (2016). *Landmarks*. Penguin.

48 Kingdon, J. (1996). *Self-Made Man. Human Evolution from Eden to Extinction?* Wiley.

49 Rogoff, B. (2014). Learning by observing and pitching in to family and community endeavours: an orientation. *Human development*, 57, 69–81; Rogoff, B., Paradise, R., Arauz, R. M., Correa-Chavez, M., & Angelillo, C. (2003). Firsthand learning through intent participation. *Annual Review of Psychology*, 54, 175–203.

50 Rogoff, B. (1995). Observing sociocultural activity in three planes: participatory appropriation, guided participation and apprenticeship. In J. V. Wertsch, P. del Rio, & A. Alvarez (Eds.), *Sociocultural Studies of Mind* (pp. 139–163). Cambridge University Press.
51 Martyn used this model to evaluate three communities working with people with severe intellectual and physical disabilities in Vietnam, Kyrgyzstan and Lebanon being funded by the German Ministry of International Cooperation and Development. See Rawson, M. (2017). *Lernen als Partizipation in Gemeinschaften der Praxis: Ein Bericht für das Ministerium für wirtschaftliche Zusammenarbeit und Kooperation und Freunde der Erziehungskunst Rudolf Steiners (Learning as participation in communities of practice. A report for the German Ministry of Economic Cooperation and the Friends of Waldorf Education)*.
52 See Rawson & Bransby. (2025). *Waldorf Education for the 21st Century: New Perspectives on the Foundations, Principles and Practice*. Floris Books.
53 Rawson, M. (2025). A holistic theory of child and youth development for Waldorf education. *Waldorf Working Papers, 12*.
54 Berk, L. (2013). *Development through the Lifespan* (6th ed.). Pearson.

6 Potentialities as a basis for dispositions and skills

Overview

In this chapter we take a wider view of learning than just the acquisition of knowledge and we apply our pedagogical anthropology to develop a differentiated approach to understanding the different modes of learning dispositions, habits, constrained skills and unconstrained skills. The key to this is the notion of potentialities. Building on Steiner's account of the transformation of the life processes into learning processes, we show that learning is a process analogous to digestion. Each child comes into the world with a set of potentialities that express the primary drive to engage with, and communicate with, the world. These manifest in a series of modalities, which we explore in detail, looking at their relevance to crafting curriculum. Figure 6.1 shows the role of potentialities in development.

Digesting the world

One of Rudolf Steiner's amazing insights was his recognition of multiple life processes acting within the human organism and their transformation into learning processes. The relationship of any living organism to its environment is one of interaction. From the perspective of the organism, this involves being embedded in rhythmical ecological processes and taking in light, warmth, water and substances, which are reduced, assimilated and transformed, leading to regeneration, growth and ultimately reproduction. Steiner[1] identified a sequence of seven non-material life processes or activities, which apply to the digestive and metabolic processes in human beings.

1. Breathing/taking in (air, light, warmth, liquids and foodstuffs)
2. Warming (what is taken in is identified, reduced, modified so it can be processed)
3. Digesting (the forces and qualities of what has been ingested are released for the body to use)
4. Separating out/selecting (the organism selects what it needs, excreting the rest)
5. Maintaining (the forces and qualities selected are used to activate self-processes of regeneration)
6. Growing (when appropriate, this process takes the form of growth)
7. Reproducing (all organisms invest energy in reproduction).

The idea underlying Steiner's somewhat unusual account of the digestive processes is that the human being does not convert the physical matter in foodstuffs into bodily substance,

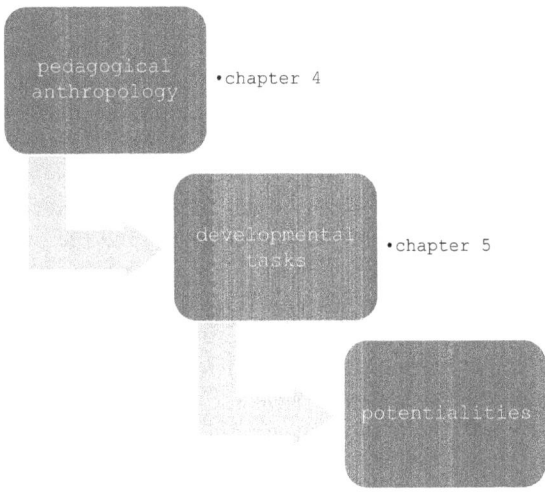

Figure 6.1 The relationship between the pedagogical anthropology, developmental tasks and potentialities.

but rather allows the life processes within the foodstuffs we take in, whether it be plant, animal or mineral in origin, to activate the body's own processes in specific ways – for example, the magnesium in a fruit like the banana stimulates the magnesium processes in the body.[2] One of the insights of the functional medicine approach is activating the body's own restorative activities, for example, by restoring healthy bacteria in the intestines. This perspective focuses on transformative processes and takes in the bigger picture that all living organisms transform the energy of the sun and draw on the formative forces of the minerals in the earth, either directly or indirectly. The same processes occur in human beings, and one of the arguments for organic and biodynamic food is that the life processes are more natural than industrially processed foodstuffs and genetically modified plants. Approaches like functional medicine[3] and anthroposophic medicine[4] are integrative and holistic, and some practitioners combine them.

Anthroposophic medicine builds on the same anthropology as Waldorf education. Both not only start from the assumption of a spiritual core of the human being but also apply a differentiated lens to understanding the formative processes at work in the human organism. This starts with the physical formative processes at the genetic, cellular and molecular levels (which education does not take into account). The second level is that of the formative life processes that form and regulate our bodily rhythms and processes and that we have in common with the living organic world in general. The third field of processes within the whole system are psychological, which function at the interface between the living body and the mind and, in particular, in the processing of motoric and sensory data. The fourth dimension of formative forces are the activity of the Self in the mind, as manifested in our cognitive, reflective life and consciousness.

Furthermore, the body is interpenetrated by three major functional systems; a polarity between the neural, nerve and sensory processes and the metabolic, energetic and motor activities; mediating between these is the rhythmic breathing system and the circulatory systems. These three functional systems correlate with different psychological activities and also different states of consciousness: the nerve-sense system is the basis for our consciousness and mental activity, the metabolic-limb system involves movement, and the production of energy through nutrition and is the least conscious. Between the two polarities, the rhythmic system is connected to an inner life of feeling and affect[5], which is not fully conscious. When the body is at ease, the motor and metabolic processes are usually fully unconscious, and only become conscious in pain, discomfort or feeling unwell.

Within the Waldorf discourse,[6] the life processes have been interpreted pedagogically by applying a developmental perspective. This is based on Steiner's idea that in the first phase of life (i.e. up to between 5 and 7 years of age), the life processes are primarily occupied in the formation and structuring of the brain and the regulation of the major bodily organs. Making cognitive processes conscious and being able to form concepts at will, as well as understanding and combining abstract symbols such as letters and numbers, requires high levels of energy in the brain. Even standard textbooks on child development, such as Laura Berk's comprehensive *Development Through the Lifespan*,[7] demarcate early childhood (2 to 6 years) from middle childhood (from 6 to 11 years) on the basis that this transition marks a significant change in potential cognitive ability. Berk notes that there are always two factors at play here – biological maturation processes and cultural practices – for example the fact that most countries in the world start formal education at the age of 6. Waldorf education has long argued that delaying early formal learning of literacy and numeracy using abstract symbols is better for children, enabling them to establish their basic organic, sensory and cognitive systems. Given the lifestyle of many young children with relatively little fine and gross motor activity, underdeveloped senses, remoteness from nature and massive overload of digital images, a strong case could probably be made for even later delay or a shift of life practice to one in which children are given opportunities to develop all their senses through natural movements and real and meaningful activities. This is unfortunately unlikely to be accepted (and in fact Steiner had to make compromises in 1919 – he did so by insisting that the introduction of abstract symbols like letters and numerals be done artistically in the transition phase, using images and movement).

In Chapter 8 on learning we go into more detail about the learning processes. The point here is that through the life processes the developing human being is in a close, formative relationship to the environment, both natural and cultural. The life processes that permeate nature but also in a transformed way, the cultural world, flow into the human being through the different modalities of the various sense organs. Each organ system has a different qualitative relationship to the world – visual, auditory, tactile, form and movement, scent and so on – and sense processes are two-way. Unlike simple models of the senses merely as receptors, Steiner argued that the sense system is integrated with the movement system and that we actively engage with the world through the same senses that we receive sense impressions[8].

It would take us too far here to go into the theory of the senses that underpins Waldorf education[9] but Table 6.1 shows the ways in which the human being perceives the interior and external worlds.

Once the primary organic rhythms and architecture of the brain have reached a certain level of maturation with the acquisition of language, high levels of capability in movement and the establishment of a more robust digestive system, with corresponding levels of basic emotional stability (i.e. children can leave the intimate family or care environment and spend their days in school), a part of the life processes becomes freed up to be transformed into learning processes – a process that reveals itself most visibly in the change of teeth but in a whole range of other symptoms.

Table 6.1 The 12 sensory modalities (after Rudolf Steiner) with modern terminology

Senses that primarily mediate internal states of the body (interoception)	Senses that mediate the outer world (exteroception)	senses that mediate our experiences of other people
Touch (tactile sense)	Smell (olfactory sense)	Hearing (auditory sense)
Interoception (sense of life orvitality, visceroception)	Taste (sense of gustation)	Sense of word, speech or gesture of the other person, linguistic-kinesic sense
Proprioception (sense of movement)	Sight (visual sense)	Sense of thought of the other person, sense of concept
Balance (vestibular sense)	Temperature (thermoception)	Sense the other person as a self

Table 6.2 The correlation between the life processes (with modern terminology) at the biological level (digestion and sensory processes) and transformed to the psychological level

Life processes at the biological level	Life processes at the psychological level
Breathing, ingestion, taking in (nutrition, respiration, sensory activity)	Attending to, perceiving
Assimilating, converting to digestible form, converting sense impressions into neurological forms	Assimilation/forgetting/processing
Absorption (analysing and reducing)	Recalling, ruminating on, sharing, clarifying
Separating out/selecting	Making meaning, connecting, understanding, generating concepts
Maintenance and regeneration	Practicing/applying
Growth	Developing habits, dispositions, abilities
Reproduction	Transformative learning, creativity

The steps in the life processes at the biological level follow the typical stages of the digestive process: ingestion, digestion, absorption, assimilation, and egestion, or in the processing of sensory data, with one significant difference. In Steiner's model there is a turning point, or rather a point of no return. At the stage of separating out, the Self as agentic core within the body, makes a choice and selects the energy and processes that it deems good for the body, or in the case of sense perceptions, what is relevant, what is deemed 'useful' to retain, based on existing values and criteria. The body strives to achieve homeostasis by continuously applying biological values to regulate itself, through body-to-brain signalling, through interoception of the interior state of our bodily processes and through exteroception of the world around us, and through our perception of other people[10].

The Waldorf theory, based on Steiner's suggestions, is that there is a correspondence between body states and psychological states – in both cases, this can be influenced by our behaviour and through incidental and intentional experience, such as education. The correlation between bodily and psychological processes is as shown in Table 6.2.

This anthropology goes a step further and translates the 'language' of sensory modalities into internal experiences that shape both our cognitive processes and how we understand the world and also flow into our actions, what we do, and how we act to shape both our thoughts but also what we do with our hands and bodies, what we make and how we express ourselves. What flows back into the world, speaking figuratively, takes two primary forms, moving and communicating. This brings us to our potentialities.

What are potentialities?

The human being comes into the world with the potential and the will to enter into relationships with the world, starting with their own body and with the people closest to them. This potentiality has its origins in the human will to engage with the world, influence and shape it and learn from it. The will is the most direct expression of the spiritual core of the human being – the Self – and it manifests as movement. The first environment the infant engages with is their own body and the sensations this body generates through the sense of warmth, touch, movement and sound (the senses for which are even present in the womb). The first major transition and crisis is birth, which apart from the experience of massive forces and often accompanied by distress, soon leads to a kaleidoscopic world of light, multiple sounds, smells, tastes, the body's own changing states of comfort and discomfort, gravity and movement and other people and living beings. In other words, the human infant is a total sensory being.

This is a very unfamiliar idea, but when one considers it, the ability to recognize patterns, and distinguish between regularities and irregularities that underpins all learning processes,[11] must come from somewhere. One could say that they are hard-wired, that means genetically predetermined, which would mean we have genes that dispose us to recognizing patterns, regularities and contrasts. If this is the case, then this genetic trait must have been selected for at some point in human evolution. Since human beings have a very deep evolutionary history and 99% of it was lived embedded in nature, it would not be surprising if humans are genetically predisposed to recognize natural patterns, rhythms, shapes and processes. Everything we know about people who live close to nature suggests that they are excellent observers of natural processes, cycles and rhythms. Furthermore, human beings share internalized processes of digestion, processing and transformation with all other animals, sensory processing with all those animals with a central nervous system. Plants have different life processes, being dependent on photosynthesis, which involve a different constellation of life processes, and these are partly external to the plant.

Some animals have more highly developed sensorimotor systems – one needs only to observe large birds in flight in high winds and strong thermals to see how their processing of sensory data and ability to respond must be highly sophisticated. Some mammals are highly alert to their environments – social animals have the ability to monitor complex social behaviour among the members of their group – whilst other animals have powerful and complex digestive systems, such as ruminants. Human beings are unique in having both complex and balanced abilities – we are very mobile, omnivorous, have highly developed senses (e.g. full-colour, bifocal vision, the ability to identify dozens, if not hundreds of different wines by smell and taste, etc.) but humans have the added abilities of complex language and the associated ability for abstract thought and they can apply their cognitive powers to creating artefacts and tools. These abilities are the outcome of a very long evolution, which, to repeat the often-overlooked fact, has involved being embedded in the natural world. Though modern people have separated themselves from the natural world, our primary faculties, however, are bound up with nature. It is the tragedy of modern humanity that it has lost this understanding. The answer is not a back-to-nature rejection of modernity, but a better understanding of the life processes in relation to the learning processes.

The child is embedded in a rich and multisensory social world, including subtle senses for shared communicative intentions and meanings. As we have seen above, in the anthropology we are drawing on, the physical body is animated by life processes that are the same as the forces in nature. The life processes flow from the natural world into the child's senses. Even harder to understand is the idea that the creative processes that people put into creating artefacts such as tools, fabrics, buildings, colours, are also perceived by the child's unconscious will. The more these objects have been shaped by hand the more these creative forces are present, whereas machine-made, mass-produced materials and forms, or digitalized images have far less correspondence. Writing this sentence (on a laptop) in an old house full of handmade furniture and objects has a distinctive aesthetic valence that we are normally unaware of, but the young child cannot filter out.

The shapes and processes of both the natural and the social world enter into the child through her sense organs, thus animating her own bodily process. These sensory impressions, and the rhythms that many of these impressions transport, shape and structure how the child processes her experiences, and how she retains these as memory. Memory takes the form of muscle or body memory through learned movements and patterns of behaviour, but also as habits of mind and dispositions. These rhythms and shapes that the child assimilates provide structures that enable the child to recognize patterns, similarities and differences, both as spatial relations (e.g. distance, mapping our environment, recognizing shapes) and as temporal sequences. Among other things, these embodied structures enable the child to understand and produce spoken language and thus imitate and later produce structures of meanings.

The term potentiality refers to "a power or a quality that exists and is capable of being developed" (Oxford Learners' Dictionary) and "the ability to develop or come into existence" (Merriam-Webster Dictionary). Thus, potentialities are at the heart of learning and development as an emergent process of coming into being. When these potentialities are in a dynamic state of balance, we call this a state of health, and imbalance, ill health. When the human being is in balance with her social world, a state of social health can occur and when the person's interactions with the natural world are in balance, we call this sustainability. This global potential manifests in a wide range of modalities that subsequently become skills and abilities that build the core structure of our being and self-identity.

One could say that at birth, the child is involved in two basic core activities:

1 reaching out and interacting with the world, and
2 internally processing what comes through the senses, respiration and nutrition.

These two primary activities are complemented by intentional movement and its coordination in the development of skills and the will to communicate and acquire language. Thus, we arrive at the four primary potentialities:

1 sensory integration of the senses directed to what comes from outside,
2 sensory integration of senses that mediate experiences within our body,
3 movement and coordination,
4 communication and language (initially oral and subsequently literate).

These primary potentialities differentiate further into a range of secondary potentialities (see Figure 6.2), which is not exclusive and could be extended.

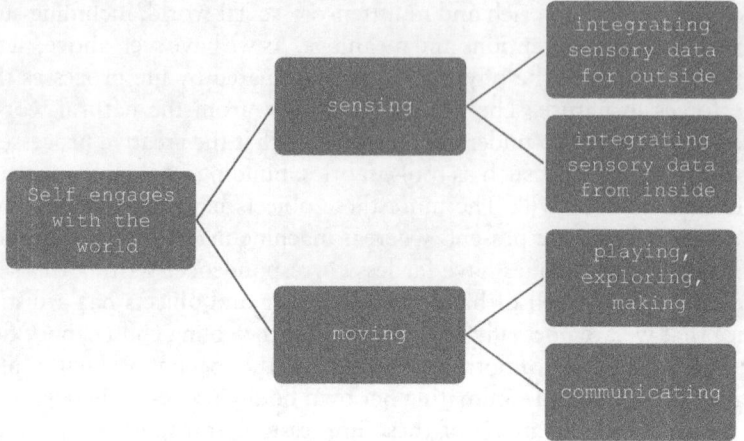

Figure 6.2 Primary potentialities differentiating into secondary potentialities.

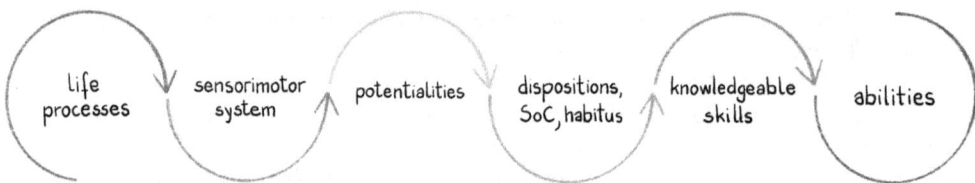

Figure 6.3 The transition of life processes through the sensorimotor system into potentialities, which form the basis for knowledgeable skills and abilities. Credit: Aristea Klanac.

Through these potentialities, the human being meets and engages with the world. They are the basis for self-formation and for transformative learning leading to the integrated development of the whole person, body, soul and spirit. Potentialities grow over time, becoming dispositions, habits, habits of mind, skills, abilities and capabilities, professional expertise and practical wisdom over the life course. With the growth of potentialities, the person as a whole grows in her development and understanding. In Figure 6.3, we can see a depiction of the iteration from the life processes, sensorimotor processes through potentialities to dispositions (including sense of coherence and habitus), skills and abilities.

Because the potentialities are the basis for dispositions, skills and abilities, it is important to understand them in order to craft curriculum and plan learning. Each school subject and activity involves specific potentialities leading to dispositions and skills, which, when practiced, can lead to abilities. As one can see, the range of activities associated with each potentiality is extensive and incremental. They start out simple and basic, for example, mobility starts with the basic function of moving, but through learning develops into making using technical skills, specific modes of movement such as sports and artistic expression through movement. Through our innate potential and will to move, we can develop upright walking and manual skills, and the powers of gesture and speaking, which are also based on movement. As these skills become more internalized, we develop the ability of thought and the inner mobility in our cognition. There are clearly elementary potentialities and secondary potentialities that grow out of these

(Table 6.3). In Table 6.3, the second column shows the movement from basic, constrained skills to more complex development.

There are many overlaps between the different potentialities and separating them out in this way is only a heuristic tool to enable us to focus more on their relevance for crafting curriculum. It is simply a way of looking at the potentialities, and we should bear in mind that this is only one way of conceptualizing the different ways the human being engages with the environment. This perspective belongs to our overall pedagogical anthropology and epistemology of learning and development. It assumes that the embodied agentic Self's basic gesture is to engage with the world, starting with its own body. Potentialities in this sense are an expression of the will of the Self. The will directs our attention through the senses. This is perhaps most easily understood if we think of the visual sense. We actively look into the world and because of the dual nature

Table 6.3 The list of potentialities and their associated activities

Potentiality	How does the potential show itself?
Mobility/embodied learning	Willing, moving, doing, participating, making, acting, enacting, technical skills, expression through movement, sport, social and political participation, dispositions, habitus, behavioural habits, habits of mind, ways of being, ways of relating
Sensing, noticing,	Directing attention, focusing, sense perception, listening, recognition of patterns, structures, sequences, differences, irregularities, incidental and informal learning, inquiry
Orality/communication	Speaking and listening, expressing, gesturing, enacting, speaking, singing, storytelling, narrative, poetry, drama, dialogue, competence in other languages
Literacies	Text literacy, linguistic literacy, visual literacy, spatial literacy, media & digital literacy, audio literacy, numeracy, scientific literacy, intercultural literacy
Empathy	Imitating, emulating, mimesis, participating, openness, understanding the biographies of others, biographical learning
Resilience & wellbeing	Maintaining bodily, psychosocial wellbeing, sense of coherence, self-control/inhibition, ability to construct coherent identities
Cognition, holistic thinking, spirituality	Mental imaging, memory, recognizing patterns, spatial and temporal awareness, executive functions of working memory, cognitive flexibility, planning
Imagination	Visualizing, conceptualizing, executive functions of working memory, cognitive flexibility, planning, problem solving
Intuiting, subtle sensing	Tact, subtle sensing, intuition, mindfulness, spirituality
Creating knowledge	Forming concepts, combining concepts, deduction, using data, reflection
Forming judgements	Aesthetic judgements, sense of proportion, estimation, discernment, sense of beauty and harmony, logical judgements, personal judgements, moral judgements, critical judgements
Creativity	Play, inventiveness, artistic creativity, creative solutions, engaging with wicked problems

Note: Readers of some of our other works will find slightly different lists of potentialities. This idea is new and we continue to work on it to refine their constellation. The idea of potentialities was influenced by Howard Gardiner's idea of multiple intelligences, Martha Nussbaum's capability approach, the capacities described in the UNESCO/Learning for Wellbeing What Makes Us concept (which Martyn was involved in researching) and the European Commission Competencies Framework. All these ideas and approaches are helpful, each taking a somewhat different perspective.

of the Self as embodied and as distributed in our environment, we encounter being in the world, that is, we encounter the meaningful relationships that are either the results of natural processes – the changing wind strength and direction driving the waves at a certain angle and with a certain energy towards the beach, the pull of the moon on the tide, the ocean currents and so on in vast complex, interrelated, natural phenomenon located where the Baltic Sea merges with the North Atlantic. The cool orange of the early morning horizon and the waning gibbous moon on the opposite horizon. I see a windsurfer astride her board wearing a neoprene suit against the mid-March chill of the wind, steering her kite and tacking at exhilarating speed across the choppy bay. I notice the simple, yet high-tech equipment, and admire the skill of the wind surfer, imagining the buzz she must be having mastery such skill and braving the cold. While we are watching the surfer our consciousness, and with it our Self, is outside in the world at the focus of our attention. At the same time, what we see prompts an emotional response and at deeper unconscious levels of our consciousness, our muscles mimic the muscle power and skill of the windsurfer, our embodied knowledge analyses what we know of materials (neoprene, nylon, aluminium – materials we might not know the names of but we can imagine their properties), activates our knowledge of wind and wave, sun and moon, prompts perhaps further questions and identifications ("looks exciting but not for me").

The message of this tale is to highlight a number of points central to our theme of crafting curriculum.

1 The spiritual core of the human being participates in the world. This view offers a counterbalance to the idea that we are spectators constructing knowledge 'in here' about what is 'out there', an attitude that underpins an ego-centric view of knowledge and our relationship to the world. This may seem very philosophical, but it is highly relevant for the status of the knowledge process we build into the curriculum.
2 Should curriculum simply mediate existing knowledge about the world, or should it engage students in a process of co-construction of knowledge? We take the view that the latter not only reflects the reality of human nature but also leads to a more eco-logical relationship to the world.
3 Potentialities as various modes of relating to the world have, as the name suggests, the potential to grow as life-long learning and development.
4 The growth of potentialities is developmental in character. The mimetic character of participation in the world enables us to embody qualities and processes. By raising these progressively to consciousness, we can move from immersion and imitation to reflexive and critical awareness.

We can show this process in graphic form, as shown in Figure 6.4.

In this image we see the life process in the human being manifesting as potentialities, streaming through the senses into world directed by our Self, which takes interest in the world around us and reaches out, as it were to meet and engage with the world around us. Because the Self as a spiritual being is distributed in the world, it recognizes being in the world. Our personal Self reaches out and meets being in the world and our consciousness is therefore momentarily out there in the world. This stream flows back through our sense organs into the inner life, where cognitive processes of perception and mental processing are activated. The Self in the mind takes up what it finds 'memorable' from these experiences and retains this as memory within the living processes of the brain.

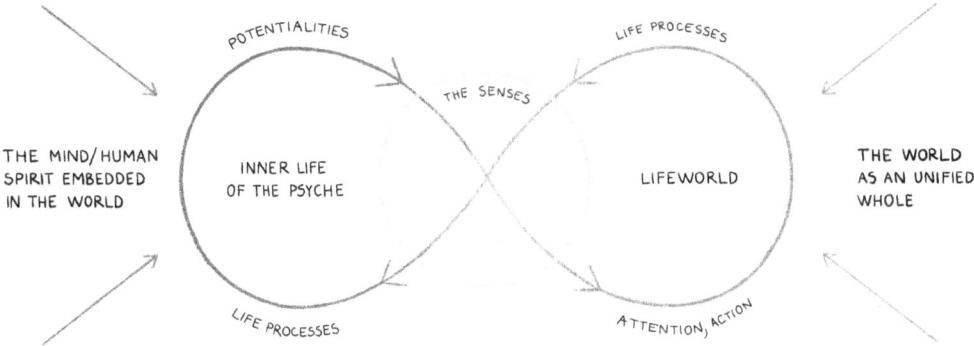

Figure 6.4 The cycle of the life processes connecting the Self to the world. Credit: Aristea Klanac.

Over time, as we have seen these, these embodied memories are transformed into dispositions, habits of mind and abilities. In the course of development over the lifespan, the inner, psychological life of the person grows and matures.

Potentialities and learning

When teachers plan their lessons, they orientate themselves on the curriculum and on the intended learning outcomes. Having an awareness of potentialities enables teachers to look at their lesson planning and explore ways in which these can not only be interdisciplinary but also provide multiple opportunities for potentialities to develop.

Learning involves changes in the way people relate to their own changing body, to themselves, to other people and to the cultural and natural worlds. The ability to relate to the world starts with innate potential that manifests in different domains. Through these potentialities the human being meets and engages with the world: they are the basis for self-formation and for transformative learning, leading to the integrated development of the whole person, body, soul and spirit. Potentialities grow over time, becoming bodily habits, habits of mind, dispositions, skills, abilities and capabilities, professional expertise and practical wisdom over the life course. With the growth of potentialities, the person as a whole grows in her development and understanding. Thus, it is important to understand potentialities in order to understand and plan learning. Each subject and activity involve specific potentialities, dispositions and skills.

Potentialities manifest when the child engages with the world. Through being enacted and repeated, potentialities become skills, which range from simple to complex and span a spectrum between general and specific. A very early example of this is when young children engage with the things around them in a process of experiential learning – seeing, hearing, reaching out, touching, tasting, smelling, moving objects, moving in relation to objects and gradually learning to hold and manipulate them. Thus, they become more skilled in manual dexterity and, whilst learning about the properties of these things, they match their experiences with the behaviour and practices of others and learn the language that accompanies these activities. A more complex skill is learning to read. A specific skill is knitting, a general skill is designing and making something useful.

Learning is a hugely complex process and involves a number of loops involving the learning of knowledge and skills and the development of dispositions. Knowledge and skills evolve through experience, retrieval and practice and this process depends on the kind of learning dispositions we learn and develop. Dispositions such as resilience and reciprocity are examples of positive dispositions that have been learned.

Dispositions are habits of mind (and body) that are learned through the formative experiences we have. They are not innate or inherited but are learned, albeit often unconsciously through the way people around us behave, the expectations they have of us, the way social situations are structured. If, for example, people tell you continuously that you are stupid and always make a mess of things, this is unlikely to lead to a resilient learning disposition, but if people around us cheerfully put things right that didn't turn out well, or show interest in mistakes as something we can always learn from, this is more likely to lead to a resilient learning disposition that shows itself in persistence - the willingness and ability to learn from mistakes. Such dispositions influence how children and students learn and enhance the skills they have and, of course, this is also strongly influenced by the role of teachers and the learning culture in the class. Once skills have been mastered, they become abilities or enhanced capacities and provide a basis for a new level or phase of learning and development.

The ways a potentiality manifests vary depending on the nature of a person's relationship to the world and the opportunities the specific environment offers. Different cultures at different times in history have probably expressed these potentialities in different ways, giving rise to distinctive cultural forms, philosophies, religions and ways of being in the world. If we go far back into human cultural history people expressed their potentialities in the things they did and the artefacts they made, which – from the archaeological perspective – makes it possible to identify certain cultures through the assemblages of artefacts and behaviour.

As we discuss in greater detail in Chapter 7, the learning process as a whole follows an iteration that starts with *immersion* and participation in activities, is followed by an *emergence* in which the experiences are raised to consciousness and then through subsequent phases of skills growth to reflection and transformation. This trajectory shows the transformation of potentialities into abilities.

It is important to take a holistic, ecological perspective on these processes. The way potentialities function is always a mutually formative process; our potentialities shape the relationships we have and the cultures these create and these, in turn, shape how we express our potentialities. Thus, the age and consciousness of the individual will also influence the way they express their potentialities, some of which already assume a degree of maturity.

Though described here separately, in reality these potentialities function together in intermeshed clusters. We can distinguish between primary potentialities that develop first and are the basis for many early skills, such as learning language and motor coordination, secondary potentialities that develop later and tertiary potentialities that require relatively high levels of maturity and learning. In their transformed mode in adults, potentialities can change the conditions under which children grow up and how society is shaped.

Whilst potentialities are innate as potential, they are also emergent and can thus be enhanced through nurture, education and self-development. They arise out of bodily, psychological and spiritual human needs and can be transformed through learning. They inform the ongoing ability to construct coherent narratives of self and stable identities across different social settings and thus the ability to bring about the conditions that enable human growth and development. They shape the structures they are embedded in. Thus, potentialities are not static but emergent and evolving and, as such, lead over time to social and cultural change.

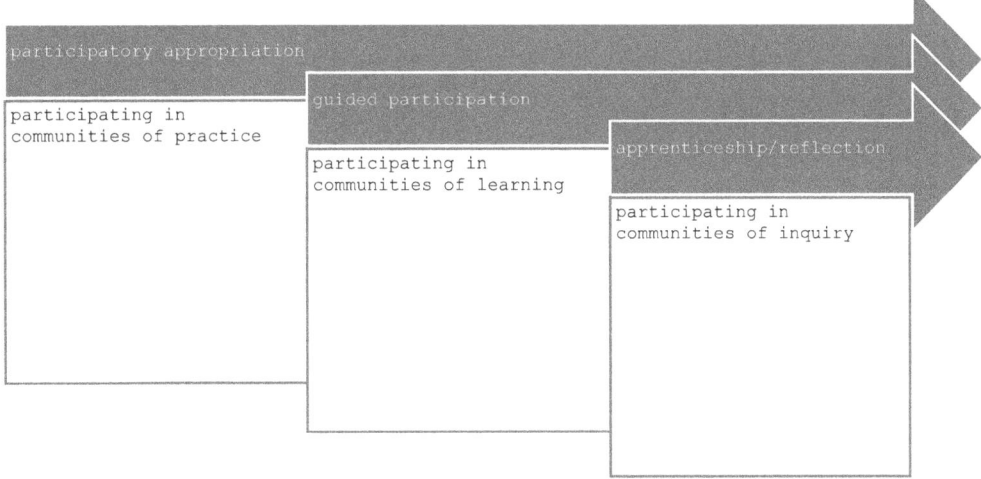

Figure 6.5 The three modes of learning. They are not successive, and each new modality adds a new dimension, whilst the existing modes are modified and developed.

It should be clear from this brief summary that potentialities are vital to our relationships, to our wellbeing, to our learning and development and thus to healthy social processes, peaceful co-existence and sustainability.

We believe that potentialities develop into dispositions and skills in three basic stages, which are also three different modes of learning that correspond to the three stages of participation mentioned above: participatory appropriation, guided participation and apprenticeship. Dispositions are not usually taught directly but are 'caught' through participation in practices in which the skills are embedded and contextualized. In educational terms, this means the modes of learning shown in Figure 6.5.

From participation to reflection – considerations for curriculum design

The curriculum for younger children should, in our view, be based in a community of practice: a group of people who share activities, ways of being and talking that give the community meaning and identity. When new members join the community, for example a kindergarten group or school class, they are allowed to watch and join in when they feel able and the other members, including adults, try to make the newcomers welcome and enable them to participate in whatever way it takes. The practices convey a set of values and have a 'cultivating' effect. The community also conveys understandings and ways of doing things that are generally implicit in the way people act with one another. The main purpose of the community of practice is to cultivate the practices that are important to the community. For example, in a kindergarten class or school class, this will include how the day starts and finishes, certain routines and rituals, the celebration of festivals and birthdays, the singing of songs and telling of stories, or exchanging news – it depends on the age of the community.

In middle childhood, a community of learning, many of the same qualities pertain as in a community of practice, except that the main function is learning. The community cultivates practices that enable, support and foster learning. The experts in the community, the teachers but also students who have been there from the beginning, take the lead in showing the others how to learn. This often involves more direct guidance and instruction.

In an adolescent (or adult) community of inquiry, all members – both students and teachers – are inquirers and the main function of the community is to cultivate practices of knowledge making, research (in groups or individually) and reflection. The teachers too are involved in deepening and expanding their specific subject knowledge and keeping abreast of developments in their field. Though these three stages have an age-related component, they are also qualitative and overlap. We apply this structure to each of the potentialities.

The potentialities in detail

Mobility and embodied learning

This potentiality is very comprehensive, which is unsurprising when one considers that movement and making are primary human activities. Like all potentialities, it has unlimited potential for development, starting with grasping, holding, manipulating with the hands, moving the body in space from crawling, to ballet or Olympic gymnastics, making things and because we are embodied being, expressing ourselves through gesture. It is the basic for all performative activities in education, the arts or any other field that involves using the body and movement. Mobility includes inner mobility in thinking, in being able to be flexible and change positions, just as much as it is in taking a stance, finding a position, and holding it. The point about potentialities is that they start out bodily and physical and then transform into higher-level capacities. In any curriculum activity, teachers, if they want to engage the whole person, need to think about how movement, doing and making are involved in any curriculum activity, which, as the word suggests, involves acting and moving.

Movement that leads to successful and useful outcomes is consolidated as neural pathways and the more frequently these pathways are used, the more permanent they become, creating what we know as habits and habitual dispositions, and what in Aristotelean terms are virtues (hexeis),[12] which are habits not only of movement and gesture but of attitude, behaviour and intention. In educational discourse today these are often referred to as competences, which are generally deemed to include knowledge, skills and attitudes. Virtues in Aristotelean terms do not simply grow through repetition of actions like habits, but they have to be done consciously and deliberately enacted and it is this, that transforms dispositions into higher abilities and habits of mind or virtues, in the sense of being able to make wise judgements (thus linking to the 'higher' potentiality of making judgements below) (Figure 6.6).

Key questions for crafting curriculum: what are we asking the students to physically do? What learning opportunities afford embodied learning that can become dispositions and ultimately virtues across the various age groups and subjects?

Language and communication

The ability to use and understand languages and the relationships between languages is a vital capacity. This includes all forms of orality and language literacy, symbolism and the

Potentialities as a basis for dispositions and skills 127

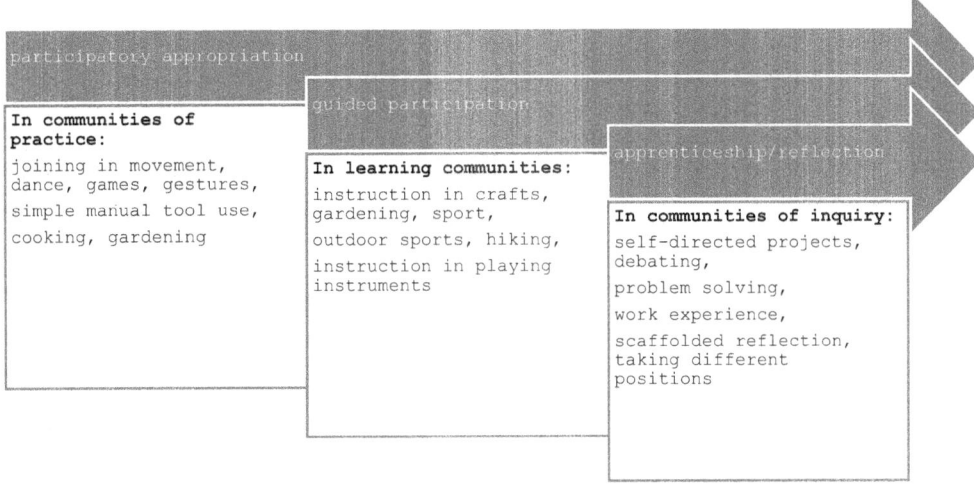

Figure 6.6 The three primary modes of learning in the fields of mobility and embodied learning.

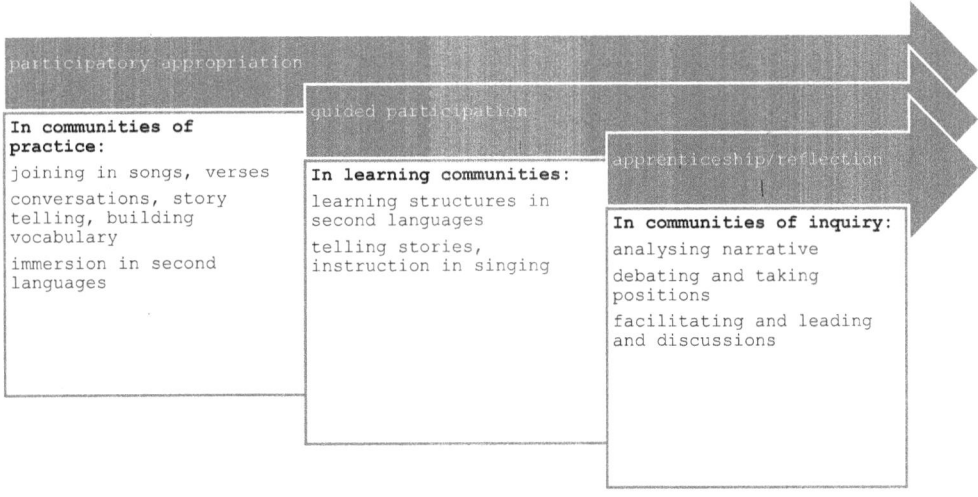

Figure 6.7 The three modes of learning in language and communication.

use of signs and logos. Language literacy includes digital and media literacy. Being able to speak and have some levels of literacy in at least two other languages is important not only for understanding people from other cultures but also for understanding the relationship between words in different languages to pre-linguistic concepts, many of which are general, and some may even be even universal (e.g. life/death, inside/outside, light/dark). Each language expresses these concepts in different ways, and even individuals can use words in unique ways (e.g. in poetry). Language in all its forms gives each person and each community voice. In Figure 6.7, we can apply see the different stages in language learning.

Key question for crafting curriculum: what opportunities does a curriculum activity offer for self-expression?

128 Crafting a Curriculum of Coherence

The senses, noticing

Highly developed senses and, in particular, the capacity to integrate a number of sensory modalities are important for our relationship to the world and our understanding of it. In order to perceive and understand other people, their communications and artefacts we need to be sensitive to a variety of sense impressions and know how to process these meaningfully. Being able to direct our senses towards the world through noticing, attending and focusing on what is salient is a skill that requires time and opportunity to develop. One of the most important senses is the ability to listen and sense what comes to expression when people communicate, in social settings and spaces – hearing what the world has to say (which has been described as resonance[13]). Figure 6.8 depicts the development of the potentialities inherent in the senses and in particular in noticing and directing attention.

Key question for crafting curriculum: what opportunities does the curriculum offer for the optimum use of multi-sensory experience?

Literacies

The term literacy has come to mean more that knowing how to read and write. Today, to be literate in a field means having unconstrained skills (see Chapter 7), understanding how to use the techniques of that field, and how to reflect critically on their significance. Therefore, the term literacy can apply to any field that requires constrained and then unconstrained skills, mastery of certain techniques, and critical understanding of the related discourse. Today the main literacies include reading and writing and linguistic skills in more than one language, media literacy, IT literacy, numeracy, scientific literacy, historical literacy, geographical literacy, visual literacy (being able to 'read' and understand the language and effects of images), emotional literacy, civic and democratic literacy, intercultural literacy, and spatial literacy (the ability to apply spatial thinking in daily life in three dimensions and across life space,

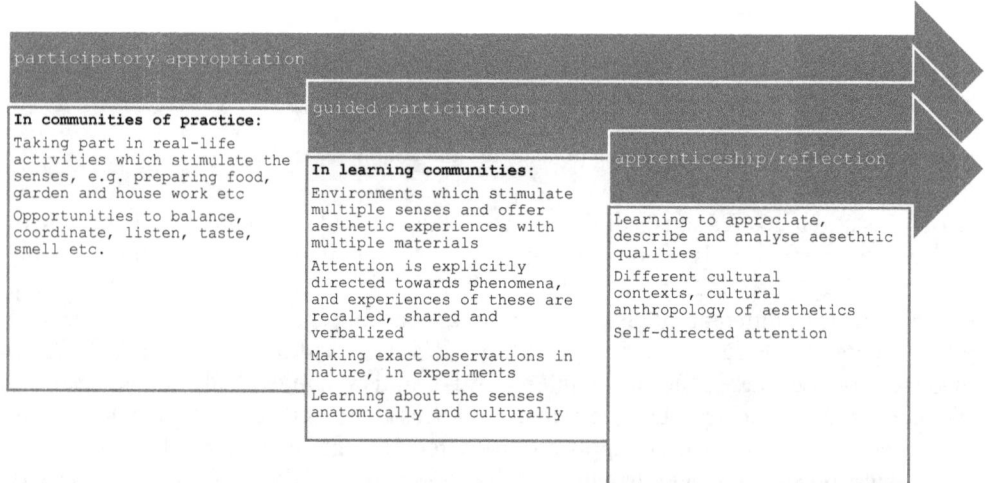

Figure 6.8 The three modes of learning in the fields of sensing.

Potentialities as a basis for dispositions and skills 129

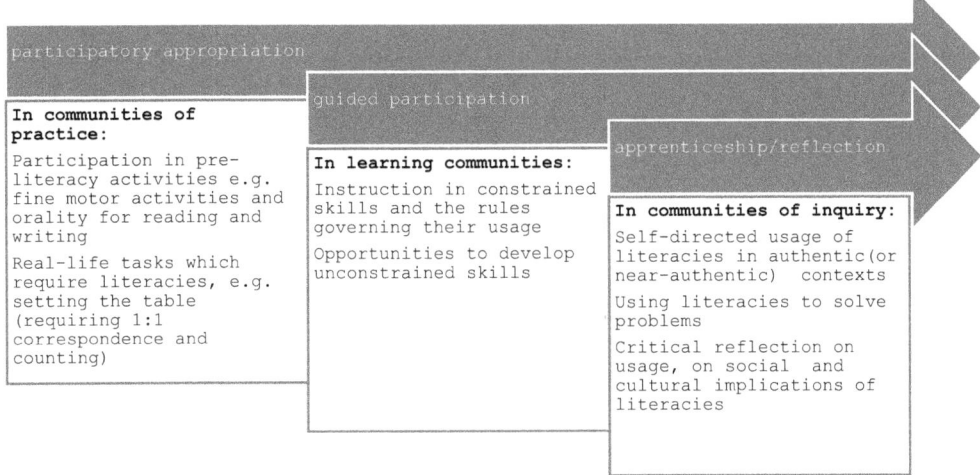

Figure 6.9 The three modes of learning in the various literacies.

physical space and intellectual space). In Figure 6.9, we see the three modes of learning literacies across the curriculum.

All literacies start with the equivalence of orality, that the practical, un-reflected usage of the skill (e.g. moving in space, using pictures and images) and participation in practices in which these skills are used.

Key question for crafting curriculum: where are the opportunities for cross-curricular literacies?

Empathy (social and emotional competence)

Empathy is the basis for sociality. It takes embodied form in the direct bodily, intersubjective perception of the other person, their emotional state and intentions and thus forms the basis for understanding others. This perception of the other is given to us in an unreflected, direct way and is the basis for imitation, mimetic learning and perception of language. As a basis for social skills, empathy is necessary for being able to work with people with diverse backgrounds, which is essential in a multicultural society and to counter all forms of discrimination. Just as empathy is an essential social skill, having empathy for oneself is also key to emotional self-regulation and being relaxed. Emotions and feelings are an essential part of life and being in the world, they are only a problem when they get the better of us, when we can't regulate or control our emotional life and this has to do with lacking self-compassion. Thus, empathy is the basis for consciously perceiving and recognizing the other person as a sentient, agentic and integral being with the same needs and rights that we have and the ability to act out of this insight. Empathy expresses itself in the ability to work with diverse others on "wicked problems". Empathy is also the basis for knowing about the world in a phenomenological and participatory way. In Figure 6.10, we show the development of empathy developmentally across the curriculum.

Key question for crafting curriculum: Is empathy expressed in the assessment procedures used and is it valued in people's behaviour?

130 *Crafting a Curriculum of Coherence*

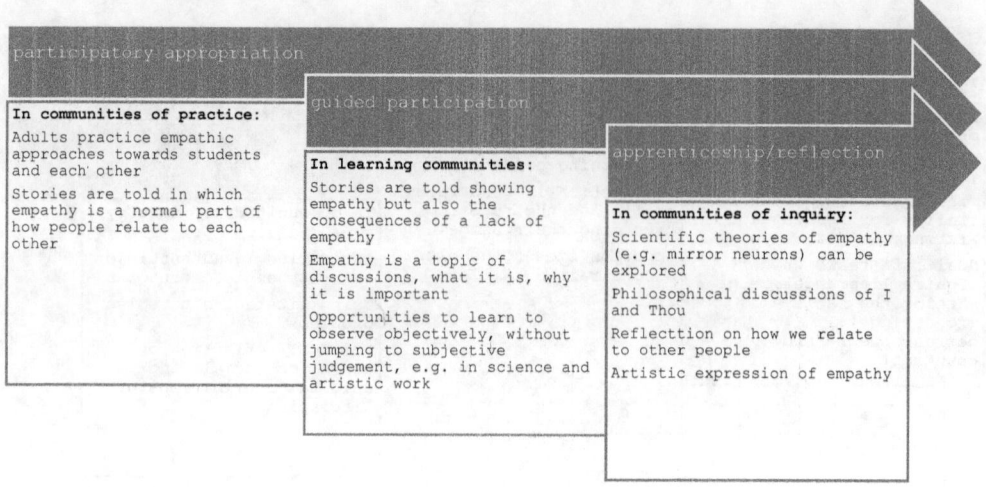

Figure 6.10 Examples of empathy in the three primary modes of learning in communities.

Health, wellbeing and resilience

This refers to a person's potential for health, wellbeing and bodily integrity. This depends on children and young people feeling at home in their body, having their basic nutritional, emotional and sexual needs met. Health means being able to generate the health-creating salutogenic processes that orientate the person towards balance in mind and body by establishing sense of coherence.[14] This is the basis for self-efficacy and self-assurance. Wellbeing ultimately depends on a healthy and dynamic balance in the interactions between all processes of bodily, psychological, emotional and spiritual development. Steiner referred to this as a process of 'breathing', which regulates the exchange between the inner and outer life of the human being and the transformations that this involves. Children and young people feel safe, secure, seen, heard, recognised and understood and they feel that they have the opportunities they need to learn and develop. This includes the ability to have meaningful, trusting relationships and attachments based on having experienced such in childhood and youth. Bodily integrity means that people are able to relax and have control over their bodies, are free from violence and manipulation and that they respect the integrity of other people's bodies. In Figure 6.11, we show the development of health and wellbeing across the curriculum.

Key questions for crafting curriculum: How does the structure and content of the curriculum (or any particular part of it) create learning environments that foster rather than hinder the health-creating forces in the students and teachers?

Cognition/thinking, holistic and ecological thinking, spirituality

This may seem a very broad potentiality, but thinking is an essential precondition for holistic thinking. Conscious thinking starts with intentionally constructing mental images of things, such as mathematical quantities or values, or geometrical shapes. Therefore, in teaching thinking, it is necessary to start with tangible experiences and then visualize them through recall. Children can recall and visualize things that are not present, they can start intentional thinking, which is more than associative thinking, which is strongly

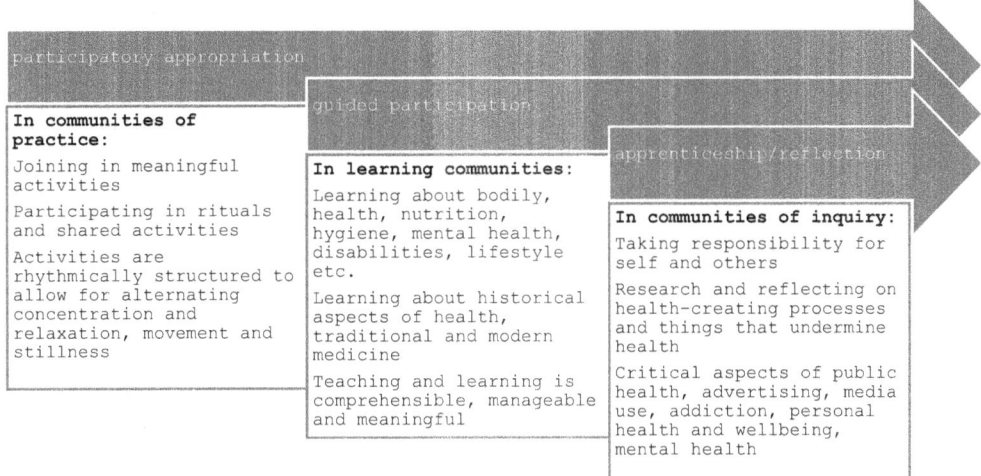

Figure 6.11 Examples of health and wellbeing in the three primary modes of learning in communities.

situational. Generally, this capacity becomes available once the life processes become free to construct shapes, forms, sequences, and images in the mind, without external reference. Anything that requires an abstract representation requires an act of thinking, such as visualizing a landscape as a map and using a scale, or analysing the structure of a sentence: what belongs to the verb, what to the subject, whether a clause is essential or subsidiary. Holistic thinking involves bring different thoughts together into relationship with each, thinking in three spatial dimensions or working out cause and effect. Planning, for example, requires sequential thinking. Generalizing is another achievement of thinking, as is summarizing. Thinking/cognition is never just dry, logical thinking. It is always filled with feeling (and feelings always have a content – we have feelings *about* something) and it requires considerable will to focus on complex ideas and turn them around in our mind, hold one thing, while developing another.

The capacity for holistic, living, joined-up thinking manifests in systemic and ecological thinking and enables us to recognize patterns and understand complexity and multi-dimensional phenomena, such as processes over time involving a multiplicity of factors. It means being able to make coherent wholes out of separate parts and understand correlations and mutual interactions. An important aspect of holistic thinking, feeling and willing is spirituality, the transcendent experience that we are part of something larger and intangible, which gives meaning to the whole, and from which we can gain ethical orientation in our actions.

In ecology, we must hold a number of different complex processes in mind and be able to combine them in a bigger context and concept. For most children, this kind of thinking does not come from teaching alone but needs to be built up gradually and systematically. We usually think of spirituality as something intuitive that happens to us – which of course it can and does – but the step from holistic and ecological thinking is also one that prepares the mind for the intuition that we are part of something bigger. In Figure 6.12, we show the different modes of learning and practicing thinking across the stages of the curriculum.

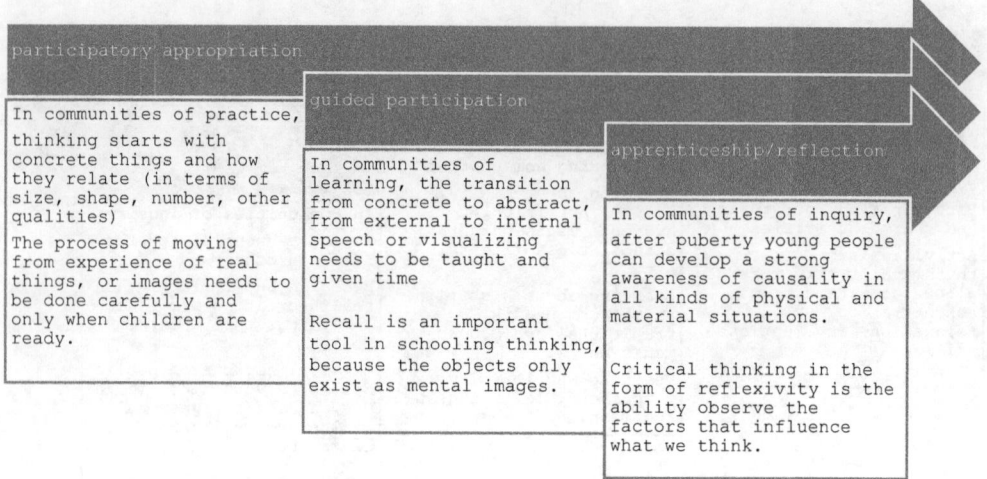

Figure 6.12 The three modes of learning applied to thinking cognition, holistic, ecological thinking and spirituality.

Key question for crafting curriculum: Are we giving the student challenging tasks they have to think about, or are we just expecting them to think what we tell them, which is really reproduction and not cognition?

Imagination, intuition, subtle sensing

Imagination follows closely on mental imaging and is sometimes impossible to distinguish, except that mental imagining has a more direct relationship to concrete facts and is therefore also more logical. Logical thinking occurs more in steps, like a mathematical proof, or a causal explanation. Imagination is part of thinking, but is freer to visualize things which are not facts. The capacity for imagination is an essential aspect of knowledge, particularly when it is based on direct experiences of the world. It makes it possible to visualize other worlds, in history, in literature, or as scientific hypothesis, and enables us to generate visions of a possible future or solutions to complex problems and processes, as well as being the basis for artistic activity.

Play and creativity express the application of the imagination to different situations to bring about novel, unexpected and meaningful outcomes. In free, non-instrumental play, spirit/ideas and matter can be combined to produce novel forms of action, artefacts and knowledge. Intuition needs to be valued as a legitimate form of knowledge, that – like all forms of knowledge – needs to be critical reflected on. Intuition, like tact and fast thinking, is the ability to grasp the meaning of a whole complex situation is the moment and be able to act meaningfully in the basis of this insight. By allowing time for experiences and ideas to germinate and gestate before being recalled and reconstructed, we offer the unconscious mind time to ruminate and make connections in the unconscious, before becoming accessible in the situation. Intuition or subtle sensing is often based on dispositions that have been previously internalized and embodied and which become available as ways of seeing in the situation. Rehearsing moves in practice enables people in sports to respond intuitively in the situation on the field in the middle of a game, just as

Potentialities as a basis for dispositions and skills 133

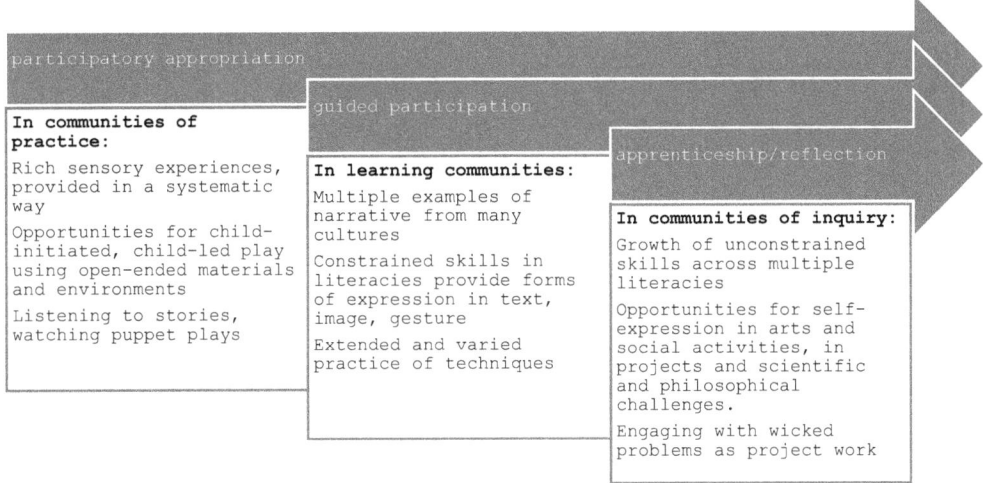

Figure 6.13 Examples of imagination and intuition in the three primary modes of learning in communities.

embodied knowledge of forms and sequences enables a musician to improvise. Neither of these abilities just literally appear from nowhere. In Figure 6.13, we show how imagination is cultivated across the stages of the curriculum.

Key questions for crafting curriculum: In what ways does the curriculum cultivate imagination and in what ways does it stymy it?

Democratic participation and social capacities

Human learning and development are located in social practices that have a history, indeed also a history of interactions with other communities of practices. Each person has both the need and the right to participate in practices and not be excluded, and each community ideally enables the participation of each new member. Thus, social practices not only reproduce themselves but are also modified through the participation of new members and through the changing participation of existing members of the community of practice. This is the basis of democratic participation. The capacity for democratic participation has to be learned through the experience of democratic behaviour in all its diversity as well as through understandings of different kinds of societies over historical time and cultural space. The ability to recognize what hinders, manipulates and perverts democracy also belongs to this capacity. Learning about governance in different settings and self-management are also aspects of democratic capacities. In Figure 6.14, we see the way democratic learning can be introduced across the curriculum.

Key questions for crafting curriculum: How do the structure and the aims of the curriculum influence democratic behaviour?

Creating knowledge, inquiry

Being able to ask questions out of curiosity in ways that open situations up and generate knowledge is important to agency. It is the basis for scientific methods and understandings as well as interpretive, hermeneutic approaches, symptomatology, artistic activity

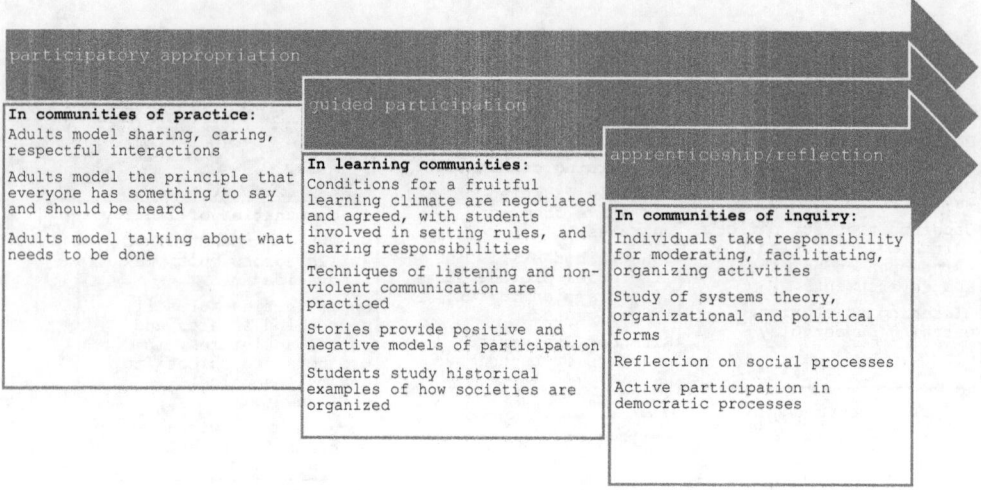

Figure 6.14 The three modes of learning in the fields of democratic participation and social capacities.

and research of all kinds. The process of generating knowledge starts with curiosity and wonder, which can be modelled if the teachers themselves have genuine questions and interest in everything the children meet, they can create a mood of curiosity and appreciation, rather than explanation. If the teaching and learning process at school involves moving from rich experience to understanding, as opposed to starting with theory and fact, the students will learn how to generate knowledge. At a later stage, the various methods of inquiry in the different subject disciplines can be learned and applied to generate, contextualize and assess knowledge. It is important that different forms of knowledge as symbolic systems are valued, and not limited to certain types of scientific knowledge. Students should learn the different processes in generating knowledge, observation, data collection, analysis, forming concepts and constructing theory through deduction, induction or abduction, and the different forms that knowledge can take, such as operational and procedural (know how), propositional, conceptual, personal and participatory (the knowledge of what role we play in our environment and relationships). In Figure 6.15, we the different modes of knowledge generation across the curriculum.

Key questions for crafting curriculum: Does the curriculum stimulate students to ask questions, and does it offer them ways of generating knowledge?

Forming judgements, cultivating discernment

One of the most important educational tasks of today is learning how to form judgements and be discerning. This is the antidote to political and commercial influencing and fake news. There are many types of judgements: practical, aesthetic, social, biographical, political, scientific and philosophical; but all are based on the basic process of giving meaning to experience and cultivating the dual ability of mindfulness and practical wisdom, the ability to read the situation. Judging means weighing up possibilities and then making a decision, so it is quite close to the process of making aisthetic judgements based

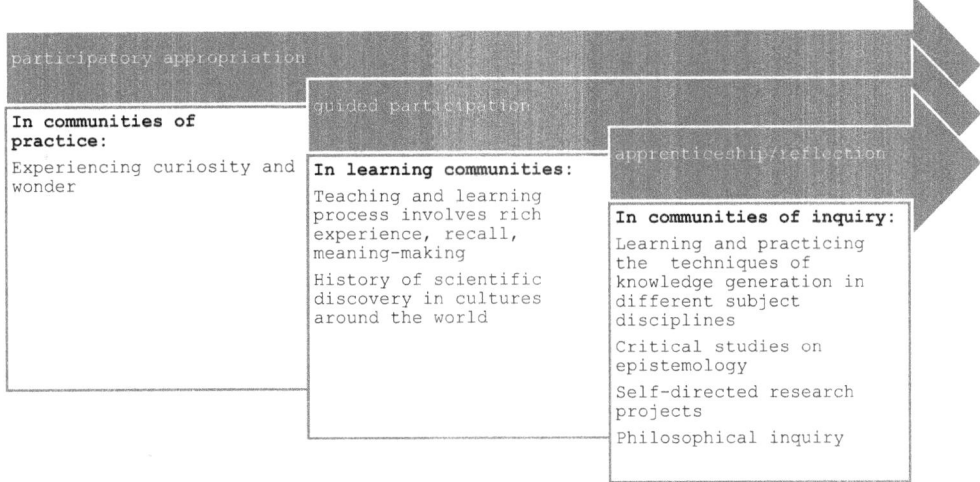

Figure 6.15 The three modes of learning in the field of knowledge creation.

on epistemic seeing, in which the value of qualities are identified, 'weighed' and balanced. An education that cultivates aisthetic experience through the senses and learning to appreciate qualities in nature, in materials, in arts and language, in our subjective experience, is laying a foundation for the different forms of making judgements. A sense for aesthetics means being able to experience and appreciate the inherent qualities of things and beings in the world, such as colours, shapes, forms, textures, sounds, movement and so on and being able to respond to and engage with these in an artistic way. Art is a way of understanding the world. Everyone is capable of aesthetic sensibility and can be moved, uplifted and sustained through aesthetic experiences. Aesthetic values support identity and meaning-making and are at the heart of each culture.

Appreciation of the aesthetics of other cultures can be a liberating experience for all concerned. Aesthetics also includes engaging with materials, recognizing their qualities and transforming them into artefacts of all kinds through designing, shaping and making. Judgement means developing a sense of proportion and being able to estimate. This is learned, above all, in practical work. Moral judgments are learned in real-life situations, through narrative, and perhaps practiced in theoretical problems. Many subjects contribute to the various techniques of forming judgements, some based on causality, some based on holistic thinking and correlations, some based on doing the right thing at the right time. Being able to form autonomous judgements in various fields, such as logic, rights, aesthetics and ethics, based on insight and on the weighing up of numerous factors, is also the basis for managing one's own life, including constructing coherent biographical narratives. Practical reason or wisdom is the ability to do the right thing for the common good in a given situation. Sound, autonomous judgement is the basis of ethics and being able to take up positions and the justify and explain them. In Figure 6.16, we show the possible ways in which making judgements can be practiced across the curriculum.

Key question for crafting curriculum: Do students have the opportunities and techniques to form judgements across the different subjects and how can we assess the quality of the judgements they make?

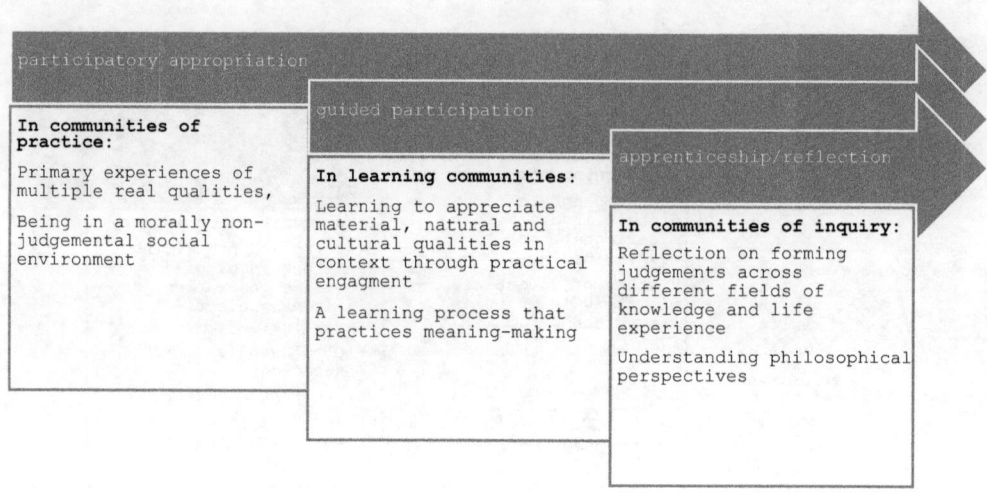

Figure 6.16 The three modes of learning in the field of making judgements.

Summary of the implications of potentialities for crafting curriculum

- Potentialities are the foundation for dispositions, skills and knowledge.
- One can use the lens of the descriptors of potentialities to ask critical questions about aspects of the curriculum.
- The perspective of potentialities gives us a more holistic view of overall learning and the kinds of learning opportunities that need to be created.

Tasks for the reader

- Does this account of potentialities make sense to you?
- Does it in any way help you to imagine how curriculum could take these aspects into account?
- Are there potentialities you think are missing here? Could you describe them?

Notes

1 Steiner, R. (1996). *Anthroposophy (A fragment)*. Anthroposophic Press.
2 This idea also comes to expression in the traditional saying "It is not the bread that feeds us, what feeds in the bread is God's eternal light and love", or the song "No bread with out sun, no sun without God, no soul without life, no life without love".
3 For an introduction to functional medicine see the website of the Institute of Functional Medicine https://www.ifm.org/.
4 Here is a scientific account of anthroposophical medicine Kienle, G.S., Albonico, H.U., Baars, E., Hamre, H.J., Zimmermann, P., Kiene, H. (2013 Nov.) Anthroposophic medicine: an integrative medical system originating in europe. *Global Advances in Integrative Medicine and Health* 2(6), 20–31. https://doi.org/10.7453/gahmj.2012.087. PMID: 24416705; PMCID: PMC3865373.
5 Reader who wish a more comprehensive account are recommended to read Heusser, P. (2016). *Anthroposophy and Science. An Introduction*. Peer Lang Edition; Soldner, G., & Stellmann, H.M. (2014). *Individual PAEDIATRICS: Physical, Emotional and Spiritual Aspects of Diagnosos and Counseling - Anthroposophic-homeopathic Therapy*. 4th edition. Medpharm;

Evans, M, & Rodger, I. (2017). *Healing for Body, Soul and Spirit: An introduction to Anthroposophic Medicine*. Floris Books.
6 Martyn has summed up the backstory on the correlation between the life processes and learning processes in this article, Rawson, M. (2018). Life processes and learning in Waldorf pedagogy. *Research Bulletin for Waldorf Education*, *XV111*(2).
7 Berk, L. (2013). *Development Through the Lifespan* (6th ed.). Pearson.
8 A revolution is taking place in relation to the senses in the human sciences, see Howes, H. E. (2018). Medieval drama and the mystery plays. *British Library: Discovering Literature: Medieval*. https://www.bl.uk/medieval-literature/articles/medieval-drama-and-the-mystery-plays.
9 See Rawson, M. (2021). *Steiner Waldorf Pedagogy in Schools. A Critical Introduction*. Routledge.
10 For a detailed account of the neurological processes see Damasio, A. (2012). *Self Comes to Mind: Constructing the Conscious Brain*. Random House.
11 For a scientific account of this see Marton, F. (2015). *Necessary Conditions of Learning*. Routledge.
12 Aristotle. (2009). *The Nicomachean Ethics* (D.Ross, Trans.; L.Brown, Ed.). Oxford University Press.
13 Rosa, H. (2019). *Resonance. A Sociology of Our Relationship to the World* (J. C. Wagner, Trans.). Polity.
14 Antonovsky, A. (1996). The salutogenic model as a theory to guide health promotion. *Health Promotion International*, *11*(1), 11–18; Mittelmark, M. B., Sagy, S., Eriksson, M., Bauer, G. F., Pelikan, J. M., Lindström, B., Espnes, G. A., et al. (2017). *The Handbook of Salutogenesis*. Springer. https://doi.org/10.1007/978-3-319-04600-6.

7 Skills and dispositions

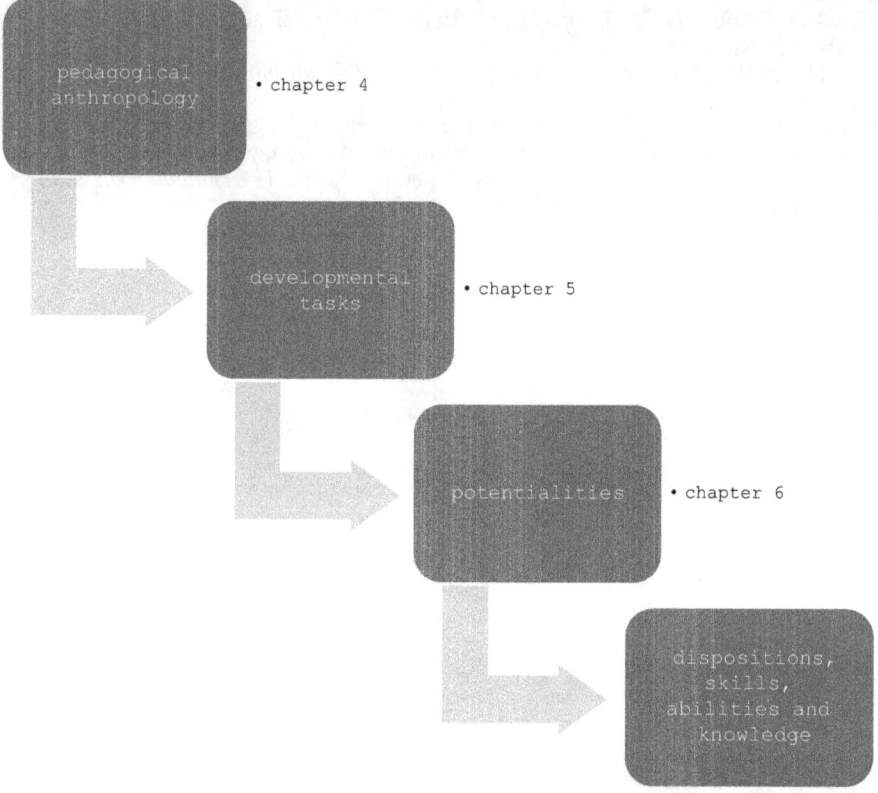

Figure 7.1 The iteration from pedagogical anthropology to dispositions, skills and knowledge as described in this chapter.

Overview

In this chapter, we start our discussion of dispositions with a brief look at Steiner's account of how skills develop, as the action of the Self on embodied experiences. Since the terms dispositions, skills, capacities, capabilities and competences have a complex set of meanings across different discourses, we offer our definition in the context of this approach. We elaborate on the way that Waldorf education interprets the well-known

DOI: 10.4324/9781003518471-8

call to engage head, heart and hands. We outline an interpretation of skills that derives from the pedagogical anthropology we are advocating and, in particular, we develop the notion of dispositions that Guy Claxton has introduced into educational discourse. We also introduce two new constructs, firstly that of skills as knowledgeable action with purpose, showing how skills and knowledge can interact in meaningful ways. Then we outline the transition from constrained to unconstrained skills.

A Waldorf anthropology of abilities

There are many theories about learning, about skills and knowledge but very few holistic accounts that actually offer an explanation of how all these belong together. Waldorf education has implicitly drawn on its own understanding of the nature of abilities, which are ultimately drawn from Steiner's use of the term. Over recent years, Martyn has tried to delve deeper into the origins of this perspective on abilities and how they grow (the choice of an organic metaphor is deliberate), in order to provide teachers with a better understanding of the learning theory that informs Waldorf education.[1] This is also important in terms of the dialogue between Waldorf and other educational theories, not least in the context of the view expressed by some educationalists, that whilst Waldorf is an interesting and successful practice, its theory is unscientific[2].

In order to ground the Waldorf understanding of learning it is necessary to go back to Steiner's original anthropology. In a book Steiner published in 1904, with the German title *Theosophie*,[3] he carefully outlined his view of the "essential nature of the human being" from the perspective of his spiritual science. There were numerous editions of this book during Steiner's lifetime, many of which were revised in a process we can interpret as Steiner wrestling with the challenge of finding ever better ways to explain spiritual processes for which there was no clear or established terminology. In such books one can see the extraordinary care he took to make sure his descriptions of the processes and their interrelationships that *he* could experience were comprehensible to the open-minded reader. One early biography of Steiner was entitled *Scientist of the Invisible*, which is a very appropriate way of describing the way Steiner tried to find concepts to describe a world that was 'invisible' to our normal perception, but for him was as real as any uncharted geographical location for a scientific explorer.

In contrast to his lectures, in which Steiner sought to narrate his experiences to specific audiences, this book was carefully written and revised for a wider critical public. This makes parts of it a standard reference for Waldorf education's understanding of Steiner's pedagogical anthropology because his later lectures on education drew closely on these basic ideas. In this book Steiner gave an account of the growth of abilities, which we paraphrase here. He provides a detailed phenomenology of the functional physiological and pschological structures of the human being, differentiating between the physical body, the formative life processes, the sentient body, which is organized to process sensory data, and a sentient soul, which experiences the qualities mediated by the senses (the redness of the colour red, for example), provides us with a rich experience of the world, and is the basis of our thinking.

Thought forces permeate the sentient experiences and give them meaning and context: "It is thought-power that has built ships, railways, telegraphs and telephones, and by far the greatest proportion of these conveniences serves only to satisfy the needs of sentient souls." In Steiner's terminology the sentient soul emerges as an immediate response to the sensations mediated by our sense organs. These impressions (the sensations literally make an impression on the sentient soul, leaving a temporary pattern or 'footprint') are coloured by subjective responses of pleasure or displeasure, satisfaction or dissatisfaction (or in Buddhist terms, grasping and aversion), which reflect affects, embodied drives, desires, fears or acquired attitudes. The evolved or educated (or in Bildung terms *gebildete*) form of the sentient soul is the intellectual or mind soul, which bears the values and insights that culture develops. Within this mind soul, the Self combines with the intellect to produce a more comprehensive form of consciousness, which Steiner called the soul within the soul, or the consciousness soul. The Self, which Steiner referred to in German as *das Ich*, lives within these distinct structures of the whole human being.

Steiner then describes the process by which skills and abilities develop. He starts by explaining that the soul retains the experiences of the day as memories – each time we recall our experiences, we change them, though the Self retains continuity. We quote this somewhat longer passage from Steiner, to give the reader an impression of the style and context, and then we interpret it.

> Recollection consists in the fact, not that a visualization can be revived, but that we can present to ourselves again and again what has been perceived. What reappears is something different from the original visualization… I remember; that is, I experience something that is itself no longer present. I unite a past experience with my present life… Who, then, conjures up yesterday's picture in my soul? It is conjured up by the same being in me that was present during my experience yesterday, and that is also present today…Were it not for this faithful preserver of the past, each external impression would always be new to us. It is certain that the soul imprints upon the body, as though by means of a sign, the process through which something becomes a recollection. Yet it is the soul itself that must make this impression and then perceive what it has made, just as it perceives something external. Thus, the soul is the preserver of memory…
>
> As the keeper of the past, the soul continually gathers treasures for the spirit…These treasures by no means remain unchanged in the mind. The impressions that a person gains from experiences gradually fade from memory. But not their fruits. One does not remember all the experiences one went through in childhood while acquiring the art of reading and writing. But you could not read and write if you had not had these experiences and their fruits had not been preserved in the form of skills and abilities. And that is the transformation that the mind carries out with the memory treasures. The spirit consigns to its fate whatever can lead to pictures of the separate experiences and extracts therefrom only the force necessary for enhancing its abilities. Thus, not a single experience passes by unutilized. The soul preserves each one as memory, and from each the spirit draws forth all that can enrich its abilities and the whole content of its life. The human spirit grows through assimilated experiences, and although one cannot find past experiences in the spirit as if in a storeroom, one nevertheless finds their effects in the abilities that man [sic] has acquired.[4]

We can interpret Steiner's term *soul* as being mind and with *spirit* he means what we here refer to as the Self, the spiritual core of the human being. This account starts with the fact of autobiographic memory, which enables us to recall who we are when we wake up each day and which accumulates the experiences that give us a bodily identity ('the imprints upon the body') and provides us with a sense of continuity, in which we recognize the things we have seen before and relate them to our growing understanding of the world. It is the mind, however, rather than the body, in the form of the neurological structures of the brain, that 'reads' the signs or patterns it has imprinted in the brain. When people refer to muscle memory, this means the embodied patterns of behaviour and movement retained, in Steiner's terms, in the life processes active in the muscles. So, it is the mind (which includes the learned structures of the life processes) rather than the brain/body that retains memories and makes these available to the spirit, the Self. Memory, as we know from experience, but also from the neurosciences, is not a storage and retrieval system like a computer, because the 'docs' or images we retrieve do not stay exactly as we last remembered and 'saved' them as they do in a computer; they change and modify over time. In the process of change, a kind of distillation occurs, in which only the essential parts - the 'treasures' - are retained.

The Self takes up the fruits of experience retained in our memory, by which we should not understand single remembered episodes but repeated experiences that yield fruits in the form of habits and simple forms of learning, especially bodily learning (as we discussed in Chapter 6). The key point is that the Self extracts "only the force necessary for enhancing its abilities" from the clusters of memories related to learning, *not* all the steps taken and the practicing one has done. Somehow, the Self takes up the generative structures that underly many actual experiences of practicing something and makes these into an ability, or enhances an existing ability out of this, discarding what is not needed. This process is akin to the selection process we referred to in Chapter 6 in connection with the life processes; the Self selects what it needs to develop a new ability.

This tells us that the Self, as the agentic core of the human being, acts to select and extract from the mass of embodied experiences, general tendencies that further the Self's own development and transforms these into permanent abilities. What is interesting is that in Steiner's account of the life of the Self after the end of earthly existence, the only thing that remains, he tells us on the basis of his spiritual research, are the dispositions and abilities that have been developed in the course of a lifetime. These new abilities substantially change the Self and are retained in a non-bodily existence in the spiritual dimension. Whether one holds Steiner's ideas on reincarnation to be serious or not, this perspective offers an account that explains why some children appear to have individual dispositions from birth onwards that cannot be easily explained by inheritance nor by nurture, just as identical twins are not as identical in how they relate to the world as they are in the physical appearance. We call these spiritual dispositions (spiritual because they are not *caused* by the physical body but are embodied in the body as attributes of the Self, if we assume the Self pre-exists the current body) or biographical intentions. This account would mean that Lionel Messi is not a great footballer *because* of his body (or its DNA), though his body evidently has the capacity to realize his intentions to be a great master of the game, nor *because* he had the right coaches at the right time. No doubt Richard Dawkins would object to this account, but his explanation – a lottery of random determinants – is in our view equally speculative.

Steiner's original interest in questions of education and child development started long before he was involved in founding a school. He was looking for ways to show that his spiritual scientific approach could contribute something to understanding the important social issues of the day, but he was also looking for evidence of the spiritual dimension in human life. His thoughts about individual talents, gifts, tendencies that are observable in people who are exceptional in childhood, such as Mozart, led him to consider how the spiritual core of the human being, which he experienced as real, could be so individual and unique from such an early age, even taking all other factors into account. The outcome of these considerations was the recognition that the Self has a unique relationship to the body it has inherited, and the environment it grows up in. His explanation is that the Self must have been somehow pre-formed, and that it must learn from incarnation to incarnation, that the macrocosmic dimension of multiple earthly lives at different times and in different places predisposes the Self to ways of being in and through a new body.

Our understanding is that Steiner did not envisage this as any kind of conscious memory, but just like the body remembers trauma, for example, and this disposes a person to ways of relating to the world subsequently within one life, the 'body' or structures of the Self retain the 'fruits' of the transformation that occurs through learning abilities. The child is not born disposed to becoming a great soccer player, but rather the relationship to the world and one's own body that these innate abilities enable, are retained (such as, for example, balance, extreme powers of bodily coordination, uncanny and rapid awareness of spatial relationships, anticipation of the movements of others, a heightened sense of rhythm and flow, a desire for perfection, micro-learning skills, the powerful ability to focus on what is salient…whatever it takes to become a Messi!). Once a person starts applying these skills in the right situation, they develop at an astonishing rate (Messi, unlike Ronaldo, is not known for his intense commitment to training, and appears to thrive in certain constellations of other players, which suggests that even his talent has some situated element).

In this way we can imagine that learning an ability, such as writing or reading, transforms us. We do not need to retain a memory of the long, difficult efforts involved in acquiring the constrained skills, because once we can write and read, we are significantly changed, our biographical opportunities expand because reading, for example, opens us to new ideas and worlds. The same is true of any learned ability – we are changed and become more capable and, in certain given situations, more competent. The more capable we are, and especially if these capabilities (or intelligences) are multiple, the more we can do, experience, understand and also enjoy. One doesn't need to follow Steiner's ideas about reincarnation, but his insight into the transformative power of skills and abilities certainly offers a fruitful dimension to the question of transformative learning.

What are dispositions, skills, abilities and competences?

Based on this perspective, and what we have developed so far in the book, we would like to offer a tentative definition of dispositions, skills, abilities, capabilities and competences. Each of these terms has a historical and etymological meaning, but mostly these have been instrumentalized more recently to serve particular functions. Some curricula list outcomes in terms of students' dispositions, intelligences (in the sense of multiple), sensibilities and life skills. Skills are often considered preliminary to capability. The makers of each curriculum will have to define for themselves which terminology to use and relate it to a coherent theory of the human being or a pedagogical anthropology.[5]

Skills (knowledgeable action with purpose)

Conventional curricula are usually framed in terms of skills and knowledge – often in the form of competences – that have to be learned and can be tested. We take the view that being able to apply skills always requires knowledge of the context and the relevant tools and materials, and that knowledge is of less value if it isn't applied, even in thinking, i.e. theoretically. Acquiring knowledge per se is not a meaningful academic aim in school. Being skilled means "the ability to use one's knowledge effectively and readily in…performance" (Merriam-Webster Dictionary). As the same dictionary definition goes on to say, it also refers to dexterity and coordination in the execution of physical tasks and a "learned power of doing something competently". We suggest, instead of treating skills and knowledge separately, it is more useful to think in terms of skills as knowledgeable action with purpose. The consequence of this way of thinking is that it is only really meaningful to assess skills when they are applied in authentic (as opposed to artificial or contrived) situations.

Skills always have a function and a purpose, and one cannot really speak of potential skills, since skill only manifests when an act is performed. Skills involve applying knowledge and, in the course of regular use, such knowledge can be applied more skilfully. Having knowledgeable skills means that learners can perform cultural techniques, such as reading and writing, which are embedded in different contexts that afford and support the performance of the skills (i.e. a range of appropriate reading materials are available and time for reading is provided). Being skilled also means being able to apply knowledge of materials, resources and tools in different and changing settings, and being able to relate units of knowledge to larger contexts. Through observation, imitation and practice the learner gets a 'feel' for the way things need to be done "by introducing novices into contexts which afford selected opportunities for perception and action, and by providing the scaffolding that enables them to make use of these affordances"; (Ingold, 2000, 354). This requires a schooling of attention.

How and when are skills learned?

Children learn and develop skills through repeated meaningful engagement with their environment. In an educational environment these skills are intentionally cultivated, though many skills are also learned incidentally outside of formal education.

In order to learn skills children and students need to have opportunities to explore and use their existing skills, but also to develop a sense of purpose and the usefulness of the skill (e.g. why we need to be able to do this). Thus, being skilled constitutes knowing with purpose in knowledgeable engagement with the changing world, because skills are bound up with our whole knowledgeable relationship to the world we live in, which involves body and mind and the whole field or relations each person is embedded in. This is why it is less helpful to look at skills solely as properties of individuals. We also need skills to gather, generate and apply knowledge across different fields, such as society, nature and human life. We need different skills in different ways of knowing, for example in natural science, social science, art, religion, language, maths and practical life.

In order to monitor the growth and development of skills across school subjects and in different learning situations, it is useful to have a loose taxonomy of skills – loose because there are many overlaps, and the same skill may be performed in different contexts (Table 7.1).

Constrained and unconstrained skills: from taught to caught

It is helpful to place skills on a spectrum from constrained to unconstrained.[6] Highly constrained skills are those which it is possible to master entirely, contingent on various factors including maturation and the learning environment. Some children may individually take longer than others to become proficient in certain specific skills, but most achieve mastery. The timeframe for learning such skills can depend on the onset of instruction but the time required is broadly compatible across most children. Constrained skills are learned through explicit teaching and are the basis upon which knowledgeable action with purpose can be developed. Highly unconstrained skills are far more variable in their scope and in people's mastery of them, taking longer to acquire and requiring a more nuanced, complex, exploratory pedagogical approach.

Table 7.1 Examples of different types of skill

Type of skills	Descriptors/some examples
Bodily and practical skills	Fine and gross motor skills, dexterity, balance and coordination, movement skills, muscle memory, effective tool use in all fields (e.g. needle and thread, carving knife, power drill, laptop, driving a vehicle), practical skills in various fields (e.g. cooking, gardening, household repairs), and craftspersonship
Social and personal skills	Communicative skills, proficiency in other languages, relationship skills, team skills, expressive skills, intercultural skills, sense of fairness and social justice, self-managing and personal organization skills, empathy, ability to construct and maintain stable identities, acting autonomously, planning for the future, democratic skills
Procedural skills	Procedural skills, organizational skills, scientific methods, organizing and curating information, research skills, presentational skills, aesthetic skills
Subject-specific skills	Reading, writing, oracy, numeracy skills, scientific, technological and artistic skills, historical awareness, geographical consciousness etc.

Constrained skills are the basic skills in a field of learning that are necessary for the subsequent open-ended development of unconstrained skills. Constrained skills are usually only learned through explicit teaching over relatively short periods of a few years, compared to life-long learning of unconstrained skills. An example is learning to read, which involves a series of specific constrained skills. Once a person has learned to decode text and extract meaning with a degree of competence, the further development of the skill depends on opportunity, motivation, guidance and feedback, which involve less explicit and more indirect teaching skills. There is then no theoretical limit to what a person can read. All fields of school learning involve constrained skills. It is important that teachers identify which constrained skills belong to which field, how they are taught and when this process should be complete; this also involves monitoring of the learning process, where it becomes important to assess how the person uses the skill.

It is helpful to map the notion of constrained/unconstrained skills onto the wider framework of learning stages and preconditions for learning (see Chapter 9). This understanding understands learning as an agentic activity of the learner located in a learning community.[7] This sociocultural account of learning incorporates the conditions for learning through observation and joining in.[8] Drawing on and modifying Rogoff's three planes of sociocultural activity in learning (apprenticeship, guided participation and participatory appropriation),[9] it is possible to describe four basic modes of learning and relate the learning of constrained and unconstrained skills to this. The important aspect of this approach is that it combines the qualities of traditional, informal participatory aspects, akin to indigenous modes of learning[10] with formal classroom teaching that engages the whole person. This can be described as an ecological, relational and practice-based approach, as opposed to the instructional and instrumental approach, or what Rogoff[11] calls the assembly-line instruction model.

The following iteration of learning (see Table 7.2 below) offers teachers a differentiated basis for planning and assessing teaching and learning of practical, social, personal and subject-related skills, and offers a terminology and framework for observing and talking about a wide range of manifestations of development.

Table 7.2 This shows the correlations between the modes and types of learning

Mode of learning	Brief description	Constrained/unconstrained
Participation as novice	Peripheral, intended and welcomed participation in a learning community (the Waldorf class). Taking part in classroom practices and routines. Observing, listening, being shown something in context (mimetic learning), being told something using narrative.	Unconstrained skills - 'caught'
Guided discovery	Teachers create learning situations in which students are guided in a friendly way through specific learning steps including rich experiencing, recalling (retrieving), sharing, naming and characterizing. This differs from typical instruction in that the teacher does not start with the intended outcome but affords the children's discovery of it. The teacher's choice of material, its preparation, her inner commitment to this process and artistic structuring of the lessons all contribute to creating an 'inviting' rather than directing atmosphere.	Constrained skills – taught
Guided application of what has been learned	This follows closely on from the previous mode through applying what has been learned in varying situations to consolidate the skill. Initial stages of applying/practicing are closely teacher-led, later more variation is included and finally students can create their own tasks.	Transition from constrained to unconstrained - taught/caught
Self-directed learning with expertise	Full participation in practices. Learners transform their understandings and expand their skills by applying them in authentic and self-directed tasks. In doing so, they appropriate the values that belong to the practice (e.g. weaving, speaking French, doing chemistry). The role of the teacher is to support and give, useful and constructive feedback.	Unconstrained skills caught

These modes of learning can span longer periods of time and characterize a predominant approach. In Waldorf kindergarten, for example, learning primarily involves participation in an ongoing structure of regular social practices. The participation is free in the sense that the activities occur, and the children are invited to join in as and when they feel able and willing to (like Rogoff's LOPI). The transition to Class 1 involves moving to the next phase, that of guided discovery, for example, in learning the letters and numbers. Here the children are required to take part in the learning activities, though parts of the lessons remain in participatory mode. Though a basic mode of participation in the classroom activities remains, the lessons during the class teacher period involve movement through guided participation to self-activity.

Guided discovery is not necessarily the same as instruction. The Waldorf approach often involves experiencing the phenomenon before analysing it and the guidance is often implicit rather than explicit, in that the teacher's choice and preparation of the material and the way in which it is presented direct the learners' attention to the salient aspects of the experience without explicitly pointing out what they should learn. This strengthens the child's self-activity and identification with the experience. In the subsequent process of recalling, sharing, discussing and characterizing, and then applying what has been learned in exercises, the learners acquire constrained skills and later develop these further as unconstrained skills. Each new aspect in a field that is introduced, recapitulates the phase of constrained skills at a higher level with a transition to autonomous use of the skill. This iterative sequence depends on the subject.

In science subjects, which are taught phenomenologically in the middle school, the constrained skills usually involve observing and describing the phenomena along with some practical laboratory or field work skills and safety awareness. Since we are aiming for knowledgeable action with purpose, the knowledge acquired in middle school science is contextual, including practical usage of the knowledge (e.g. in hygiene, body care, nutrition, the uses of plants and plant material, electricity, chemistry in daily life, map reading, weather observations etc.). In the upper school, this practical knowledge is supplemented by theoretical knowledge, complex techniques and terminology (including the use of formulae and maths in statistics, graphs, use of data etc.), as well as an understanding of the social, economic, ecological and ethical aspects of the field.

In the appropriation mode of learning students should have a sense for the professional values and culture relating to the field – for example, what geologists or chemists or writers do. Full expertise is unlikely within school learning but the students should be able to develop a feeling for what professional expertise involves among artists, craftspeople, scientists, writers and journalists, doctors, architects and teachers etc.

It is important within each subject to establish what constrained skills need to be learned and by when. Secondly, adequate opportunities need to be provided so that unconstrained skills can be encouraged to develop further and be monitored. Not least because enhanced skills, potentialities and capacities are the basis for more advanced forms of learning in the high school and beyond. In lesson planning, teachers identify when constrained skills need to be taught and when to allow students to apply them. This is part of the rhythmical balance in the learning process. In terms of assessment, constrained skills need to be more exactly monitored in the early stages of learning, along the lines of *can't yet*, *can with support*, and *can without support*. With unconstrained skills, assessment modes can vary and include a wider range of criteria and can take a more appreciative and relational form, including self-assessment, because the outcomes are less standardized and more open.

Knowledge and knowing – the roles of subjects in learning

Doing and knowing are different activities yet belong together. In Steiner's pedagogical anthropology, thinking and knowing belong to the cognitive processes connected with the nerve-sense system, centred in the brain, whilst acting and doing belong to the will and the forces of volition and are related to the limbs and metabolic processes of the body. Mediating between these systems is feeling, which is less conscious than thinking but more conscious than willing. In pedagogy, knowing is obviously a particularly important part of learning. Knowing is the ability to apply understanding in meaningful situations, whereas knowledge, as such, is a representation of what is known. Knowledge is reified so we can reflect and communicate about it, whereas knowing is more immediate and intuitive (knowing-in-action, knowledgeable action, artistic activity, skilled artistry). Understanding can be communicated and related to other knowledge using reified knowledge, usually expressed through language and mathematical symbols.

We distinguish between surface knowledge (e.g. terminology, simple disconnected facts, number bonds, vocabulary, simple procedures) and deeper knowing, which is contextual, has its own particular methodology and can be linked with other knowledge. Deep knowing influences ways of seeing and thinking and is thus linked to our dispositions and abilities (e.g. geographical knowledge enables us to access unfamiliar geographical phenomena; knowledge of methods of interpreting literature can be applied to novels we haven't previously read). The function of block teaching in Waldorf education is to dispose the learner to specific ways of seeing and understanding the world and this is linked to practice and skills in this field. The transfer of knowledge, or rather the ability and capacity to understand different but related situations, comes from these ways of seeing linked to subject specific skills and knowledge and the ability to apply this. Generic abilities enable us to generate and use knowledge effectively. Thus, specific knowledge about aspects of the world can be applied through knowing-in-practice in life situations.

Abilities, capabilities and capacities

Abilities (also called capabilities and capacities) are often understood as synonymous with skills, except for the sense that a skill is more technical and specific and an ability or capability is more comprehensive and broader – for example, being a skilful violinist and having considerable musical ability.

A capability is a combination of personal characteristics, technical skills, knowledge and behaviours that are deemed necessary for success in particular work settings. The philosopher Martha Nussbaum uses the term in her capabilities approach,[12] which are understood as the preconditions of wellbeing and involve what people can do and be, within what the socio-cultural-economic-political context affords, and which are the basis for their freedom. Though the global influence of Nussbaum's capabilities approach is massive, it has had relatively little impact on education, not least because access to education is an important freedom that enables wellbeing, and is therefore considered to be more fundamental. Actually, an educational version of this approach would be similar to the approach in this book, which starts from the nature of the human being, makes assumptions about human flourishing and demands an educational provision that affords flourishing.

Skills that are honed through practice become abilities, which are more generalized capacities. Abilities often blend a range of specific skills into a more comprehensive aspect of personality. Someone who has a learned ability is often in a position to teach others because they understand the detailed steps of skill that belong to an overall ability. An example of an ability is being able to play a musical instrument well. This is based on a number of specific constrained and unconstrained skills, from manual coordination and movement, breath control, hearing melodies and being able to pick them up, keeping time, recognising if an instrument is in tune, reading music notation, playing with other musicians, recognising different musical styles. Musical ability then becomes a capacity and changes the person and her relation to self and the world, when a person can describe herself as, "I am a musician". Something similar can be described for ability in a particular sport, or for the literacy skills that enable a person to become a writer, or science and empathy skills that enable a person to become a doctor, or the practical and theoretical skills and knowledge to become a designer or architect. Being a teacher requires a wide range of skills, that in themselves do not make a good teacher, though they are preconditions. The transformation required, as in other professions, from being skilled to being expert marks the transition from skills to capacities. Enhanced capacities alter a person's dispositions and thus the nature of what they can subsequently learn life-long.

Competence

A competency is usually defined as a particular combination of knowledge, skills, attitudes and personal attributes that are deemed essential for the economy or a particular profession. It is often used to measure performance and is favoured by education systems that orientate themselves to the world of work.

Ways of seeing require a more conscious, probably scaffolded, approach, in which the learner is given regular tasks involving certain procedures to be carried out in a certain way, such as accurate observation, careful listening or by regular contemplation on certain ideas. Motivation is certainly a factor in developing habits of mind, and one could say that self-motivation is a habit of mind in itself. Therefore, a learning climate in which doing one's best, craftspersonship – that is the belief that if something is worth doing it is worth doing well.

Skills, like other habits, can also be learned through deliberate repetition of applied certain procedures, such as using a tool such as a paint brush, pencil or plane, or certain ideas by internalizing them consciously.

Dispositions

Dispositions are embodied habits of mind, ways of seeing and attitudes that are embodied through participation in a community of practice in which certain values, attitudes or behaviours are embedded. They may or may not be prompted by biographical intentions that direct us towards one field of activity or another. Like Guy Claxton and his colleagues, we believe that the basis of powerful learning is the growth and development of dispositions, and we agree with most of what they have to say on the matter.[13] Even if the terminology varies somewhat, the intention and general understanding are very similar. They write that the challenge is to turn skills into dispositions, into what they call 'learning muscles', which in an analogy to physical fitness training, need regular stretching, exercise, and training schedules, focusing on the various elements of fitness, such as nutrition, condition, stamina, strength, focus, ability to withstand resistance and so on. They emphasize the need to move on from a thinking that sees learning as a set of techniques and skills that can be trained, to a set of dispositions, interests, and values that need to be cultivated.[14] In an earlier publication, Claxton suggests that terms such as skills and training suggest a process of industrial apprenticeship that can be practically implemented in a relatively short period of time. He makes the very important point that the kind of learning that matters, that is relevant for life-long learning, that enables flexibility and adaptability across changing situations, is dispositional. Attitudes, values and motivation are far more important that the mere acquisition of skills. As Claxton sums it up, "there are ways of going about raising standards that undermine the development of children's 'learning power'. They become more 'able' but less 'ready' and 'willing'."[15]

Claxton, along with Arthur Costa and Bena Kallick, was one of the first to coin the phrase 'habits of mind'. His approach to dispositions has been instrumental in shifting the paradigm in education (though not yet fully acknowledged by education policy makers). Faced with sceptics who consider dispositions not tangible enough, he makes the important point that disposition is best used as an 'adverb of mind', rather than as a noun, which suggests that learners have *something* which others perhaps do not possess. Dispositions, he explains, are not separate from skills and knowledge; rather, they are "indicators of the degree to which one is disposed to make full use of that skill or knowledge". They are adverbs that qualify how, when and where we do something using knowledge. To be disposed to persist means showing persistence across a broad range of situations, to tend to persist in the face of obstacles and "to have a rich repertoire of ways of supporting and encouraging one's own persistence".[16]

Claxton's well-known graphic showing the river of dispositions, with small containers of subject knowledge floating on the surface, with a middle layer in the river of skills and literacies, with dispositions and attitudes at the bottom offers an important perspective. The interesting thing would be to show how the currents in the river's flow interact vertically, from the depths to the surface and back down to the depths. Is this movement accompanied by a corresponding level of consciousness? And how does this consciousness manifest in thinking, feeling and willing? Furthermore, if we stay in the metaphor of a river, a developmental approach suggests that there is a different dynamic from the source as a stream in mountains to the estuary and the sea or when the river as a tributary flows into a bigger river. Metaphors have their limits, but there is much to be gained in terms of pointers to more profound knowledge before the limits are reached. Let us briefly expand this metaphor.

When the child is young, the learning is rapid, powerful and high-energy but barely reflected upon. The three layers would probably not yet be distinguishable. When it is young and in spate in spring after the snows melt, the mountain stream transports large quantities of silt and pebbles. In its middle course, the river starts to meander and the material it is transporting begins to be sorted, graded and deposited according to size, wherever the energy of flow reduces. The action shapes the stones and carves out a river valley or gorge. As the volume of water increases in width and depth, we find the layered structure in Claxton's graphic, with different depths of consciousness, and ultimately the river flows back into the sea of collective unconsciousness. That means that in early years, learning is global and undifferentiated; in primary school education the main focus is on learning basic constrained skills and learning to participate in the learning community; and after puberty, the learning becomes much more differentiated, with many more specialist subjects building on the unconstrained skills.

But to return to the original image: is the movement and relationship between the layers one in which the dispositions carry the literacies and skills and these carry the knowledge or is the movement from the knowledge down to the dispositions, falling as sediment, as it were?

In Steiner's layered model of transformative learning outlined above, we have a layer of memories, with long-term memories in the form of habits (within the body of formative life processes), then the Self selects those experiences that can serve the longer-term development of the person, and these are transformed into abilities, though the specific experiences and memories themselves are forgotten. In his further development of the nature of the higher faculties of the human being, what Steiner calls abilities undergo a further transformation. In his iteration of the will, in the pedagogical anthropology he developed for the teachers in the first Waldorf School in 1919,[17] Steiner starts with instinct, followed by drive, desire, and then motive, meaning the underlying dispositions and attitudes that guide our behaviour – for example, the sense that we could do something better and develop the intention and resolve to act differently in future.

Particularly after puberty young people begin to develop biographical intentions that, on the one hand, are wishes to realize this or that aim, but are also the inner force of an ideal to become someone. They begin to develop what one might call conscience, in the sense that they can start to take responsibility for their actions and their impact on those around them. As adults, we may, in retrospect, recognize such intentions, perhaps as idealistic and altruistic wishes to change the world, but also egotistic and perhaps unrealistic ideas of who we wanted to become. The underlying emergence of a desire to become someone different, someone who can make a difference, is a signature of the Self active within the structures of the personality. For Steiner, the development of the will was the highest aim because this is the source of both ethics and self-realization. The will, however, cannot be educated or formed from outside, at least not in ways that leave the person free. One can train, condition and manipulate children and young people, but this takes away their possibility of becoming autonomous persons capable of acting ethically out of insight, rather than duty or social conditioning or convention.

In Waldorf education, the will is activated indirectly through the feelings, in that an affective response prompts us to become active in thinking. The feelings and the will can be activated through direct experience through the senses, through narrative, through meaningful movement such as Eurythmy (a special form of dance), arts and artistic activities and practical work such as gardening. Pestalozzi's famous notion of head, heart and hand takes concrete form in Waldorf education, as follows:

- Heart: this refers to experiences that address the feelings, through aisthetic/aesthetic education, narrative, personal relationships and the commitment of the teachers, as well as the rhythmical structuring of lessons, the school day, the week, the month and the school year. Rhythm doesn't only involve music, but involves a balance of attention and relaxation, listening and speaking, group work and solo work, humour and seriousness, through the celebration of festivals connected with the cycle of the seasons, and through rituals (verses and mindfulness exercises). Heart also refers to the development of character.
- Hands: is literally hands-on learning in handwork, crafts, arts, practical work, work experience and field trips. The aim here is the 'aisthetic' schooling of the senses as a basis for knowledge generation, and also for the cultivation of a disposition to craftspersonship. The practical, real-world, manual work in crafting not only gives shape to materials but also shapes the maker, as we have discussed throughout this book.
- Head: the term 'thinking' covers a wide range of cognitive activities from processing sensory data, forming mental images, recalling memories, imaginative thinking, practical thinking, logical thinking, holistic thinking, reflection and so on. Thoughts are almost always accompanied by feelings and always require the application of will and mental work. Reflective thinking is a productive activity that is part of being competent in any field and is therefore – in age-appropriate ways – an element on all subjects and activities.

The Waldorf approach to learning, therefore, requires all three dimensions – heart, hand and head – and does not privilege the head.

Where our approach differs from Claxton's is that we build on the pedagogical anthropology outlined above. We start with the spiritual core of being, the Self, which seeks to bring itself into being by engaging with the world and thereby learning. Through this continuous process of acting, experiencing and communicating, the different potentialities emerge. Dispositions are ways of describing *how* the person acts, learns and communicates; that is, with more or less interest, attention, resilience and persistence, curiosity, creativity, enthusiasm, passion, personal commitment and self-expression. Students are more or less disposed to act responsibly, imaginatively, critically. These adverbs tell how us how learners engage with the world and how they apply the knowledge they have gained skilfully.

Why is this perspective important? Wouldn't it be enough to follow Claxton's good ideas about learning-powered schools? We think the approach we are suggesting here, derived originally from Steiner, complements Claxton's (and others we refer to) by adding the spiritual dimension, not just metaphorically or aspirational, but as a practical fact. As we tried to show in Chapter 4, recognizing the Self (or whatever one chooses to call it) as a spiritual being that is both embodied and distributed in the world has three main implications for curriculum, once we've understood the holistic nature of the human being:

1 The first is epistemological – being a 'citizen' of both worlds, the spiritual and the material, enables people, with practice, to form their own reliable knowledge of both worlds in ecological ways that overcome the separation of human beings and world that came with modernity.
2 The second is biographical – people can give meaning to their lives and ground their personality on an inner certainty that was previously only available through religion and belief. We can base our lives on a secular source of meaning.
3 The third is psychological – if we accept the hypothesis of the Self as the agentic core of the human being, then this has implications for our understanding of learning, whether of dispositions, skills or knowledge.

How do we learn dispositions and habits of mind?

'Cultivating' dispositions, interests and values requires moving from learning a skill – being able to do something that one couldn't do before – to having a disposition or habit of mind which inclines one to use that skill and influences whether one uses the skill reluctantly and only when externally necessary (e.g. learning for a test) or willingly (as in expanded learning based on self-motivation). A resilient learner will persist in the face of setbacks and difficulties and will actively learn from mistakes. A learner disposed to playfulness and creativity will experiment, try out different solutions, be creative. Dispositions also include values and beliefs. If people find skills important and socially and culturally valuable, they are more likely to develop dispositions to using them. Values also influence the way we do something. It makes a difference whether we do something with care and pride in the outcome, with the sense that if it is worth doing, it is worth doing well, or whether it doesn't personally matter to us how we do something and the consequences this has. Someone who takes pride in doing something well may also care for the tools, materials and workspaces, will clear up afterwards, will find pleasure and affirmation in whether others appreciate what we do. Notions such as vocation, service and doing good, as well as awareness for the consequences of our actions, are values that enhance skills.

Learning dispositions are acquired through doing something regularly, like any habit, and this can involve using learning techniques regularly. In Chapter 8 on learning we show how the learning process can be structured into regular activities that can be thought of as techniques, which obviously vary from subject to subject and depend on the age of the students. The assumption is that dispositions and learning techniques support each other iteratively – a regularly practiced technique can lead to the growth of a disposition, and a learning disposition will enhance and develop the technique.

Through application and frequent and varied practice, skills and dispositions become abilities or enhanced capabilities – or what Claxton refers to as "the sum total of one's habits of mind".[18] Having such enhanced abilities means a person is a more capable learner, which drives the learning process onwards towards the development of potential through transformative learning.

The educational approach we are suggesting is designed to afford, encourage and support students to, as Claxton describes, "learn more robustly, more broadly, more skilfully and more flexibly". The pedagogical task is what Claxton refers to as teaching to expand learning capacity by creating epistemic cultures – that is, school cultures that foster powerful learning. Since dispositions and inclinations may be tentative as well as strong, it is important that a school culture encourages and avoids hindering and blocking dispositions that are vital to classroom learning, such as asking questions, questioning assumptions (even those of the teacher or other authorities), imagining how things could be different (or could have been different in the past), the courage to risk a minority view and go against the common discourse, trying other ways of doing things and not being unduly reticent if they don't at first work out or make sense to others. In fact, making the learning process transparent, by for example establishing a clear vocabulary for talk about learning processes, is a precondition for enhancing learning dispositions. Claxton and Carr[19] refer to learning cultures that have a "potentiating milieu" in which "there are plenty of hard, interesting things to do, and it is accepted as normal that everyone regularly gets confused, frustrated and stuck".

Like potentialities, dispositions also grow over time from a basic moral relationship to the world and others that brings to expression the notion that 'the world is good'. This doesn't mean that the world is good, because a lot of it obviously isn't. However, the pedagogical gesture of the teacher is to try to establish that we can make the world good and nourish ourselves on its goodness. Perhaps good here means fruitful, well-balanced, healthy. One could say the primary function of early childhood provision is to establish healthy dispositions. In primary education, these dispositions transform into the sense that the world is interesting, perhaps even aesthetically beautiful, if we learn to approach it in an open-minded way. In adolescent education, the core disposition is the question for truth. Young people should learn to be disposed to seeking the truth by generating knowledge. All these dispositions flow together into the foundational belief in social justice, service and the capacity for conflict resolution, and also into democratic values, holistic thinking, a sensitivity to spirituality, and the ability to make autonomous judgements out of insight (Figure 7.2).

Summary: In crafting curriculum thought needs to be given to balancing the range of dispositions and knowledgeable skills and show how these are cultivated across the curriculum.

Tasks for the reader

- What is your account of skills, abilities, competences and dispositions and how they are learned?
- What is your understanding of knowledge and what role the learning of knowledge should play in curriculum?

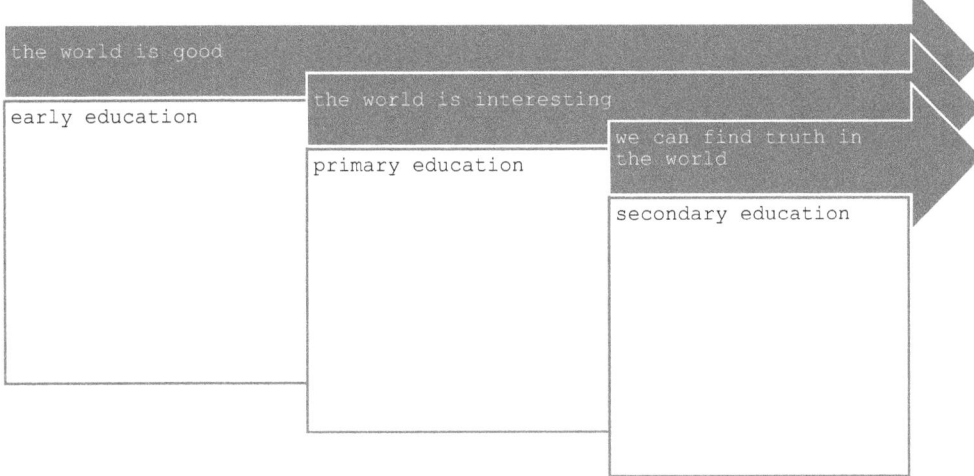

Figure 7.2 The guiding dispositions within education following Rudolf Steiner.

Notes

1 Rawson, M. (2018). Life processes and learning in Waldorf pedagogy. *Research Bulletin for Waldorf Education*, *XV111*(2). Rawson, M. (2019). A complementary theory of learning in Waldorf pedagogical practice. *Research on Steiner Education*, *9*(2), 1–23. Rawson, M. (2021). *Steiner Waldorf Pedagogy in Schools. A Critical Introduction*. Routledge. Rawson, M. (2024). Waldorf Education: New perspectives on a holistic approach. *International Journal of Transpersonal Studies*, *43*(1). Rawson, M. (2025). Embodied Learning. Transforming potentialities into holistic skills through different modes of experience. In K. Nigh (Ed.), *Holistic Education. Enduring Principles and Practice* (Vol. 2). Information Age Publishing.
2 Hoffmann, A.-K., & Buck, M. F. (Eds.). (2024). *Critically Assessing the Reputation of Waldorf Education in Academia and the Public: Recent Developments the World Over, 1987–2004*. (Vol. 2). Routledge.
3 The latest edition in English is Steiner, R. (2011). *Theosophy: An Introduction to the Supersensible Knowledge of the World and the Destination of Man* (M. Cotterell & A. P. Shepherd Trans.; revised 150th anniversary edition ed.). Rudolf Steiner Press.
4 This quote is taken from the online version of Theosophy, Chapter 2 (https://rsarchive.org/Books/GA009/English/AP1971/GA009_c02.html).
5 An example of this is the Australian Curriculum, Assessment and Reporting Authority booklet General Capabilities in the Australian Curriculum https://k10outline.scsa.wa.edu.au/__data/assets/pdf_file/0015/5217/Personal-and-social-capability.pdf, which draws particularly on Gardiner's theory of multiple intelligence and Goleman's work on emotional intelligence.
6 This idea was introduced by Paris in the context of reading skills. We have extended its meanings. Paris, S. G. (2005). Reinterpreting the development of reading skills. *Reading Research Quarterly*, *40*(2), 184–202. https://www.jstor.org/stable/4151679.
7 Rawson, M. (2018). Life processes and learning in Waldorf pedagogy. *Research Bulletin for Waldorf Education*, *XV111*(2).
8 Rogoff, B. (2014). Learning by observing and pitching in to family and community endeavours: an orientation. *Human Development*, *57*, 69–81.
9 Rogoff, B. (1995). Observing sociocultural activity in three planes: participatory appropriation, guided participation and apprenticeship. In J. V. Wertsch, P. del Rio, & A. Alvarez (Eds.), *Sociocultural Studies of Mind* (pp. 139–163). Cambridge University Press.
10 Rosado-May, F. J., Urrieta, Jr, L., Dayton, A., & Rogoff, B. (2020). Innovation as a key feature of Indigenous ways of learning. In N. S. Nasir, C. D. Lee, R. Pea, & M. McKinney de Royston (Eds.), *Handbook of the Cultural Foundations of Learning* (pp. 155–180). Routledge.

11 Rogoff, B. (2014). Learning by observing and pitching in to family and community endeavours: an orientation. *Human Development, 57*, 69–81.
12 Nussbaum, M. (2011). *Creating Capabilities: The Human Development Approach*. The Belknap Press of Harvard University Press.
13 Claxton, G. (2009). Cultivating positive learning dispositions In H. Daniels, H. Lauder, & J. Porter (Eds.), *Educational Theories, Cultures and Learning* (pp. 177–187). Routledge. Claxton, G., & Carr, D. (2004). A framework for teaching learning: the dynamics of disposition. *Early Years, 24*, 87–97. Claxton, G., Chambers, M., Powell, G., & Lucas, B. (2013). *The Learning Powered School*. TLO Limited.
14 Claxton et al (2013), p.37.
15 Claxton, G. (2006) *Learning to Learn – The Fourth Generation. Making Sense of Personalized Learning*. Bristol, TLO Ltd., p17.
16 Claxton,G. (2006), p 17.
17 Steiner, R. (2020). *The First Teachers Course. Anthropological Foundations. Methods of Teaching. Practical Discussions* (M. M. Saar, Trans.). Ratayakom. Thailand. A project of the Education Research Group of Bund der Freien Waldorfschulen, Germany and the Pedagogical Section at the Goetheanum, lecture 4.
18 Claxton, G. (2007). Expanding young people's capacity to learn. *British Journal of Educational Studies, 55*(2), 115–143, p.124.
19 Claxton, G., & Carr, D. (2004). A framework for teaching learning: the dynamics of disposition. *Early Years, 24*, 87–97.

8 Teaching and learning
Some generative principles

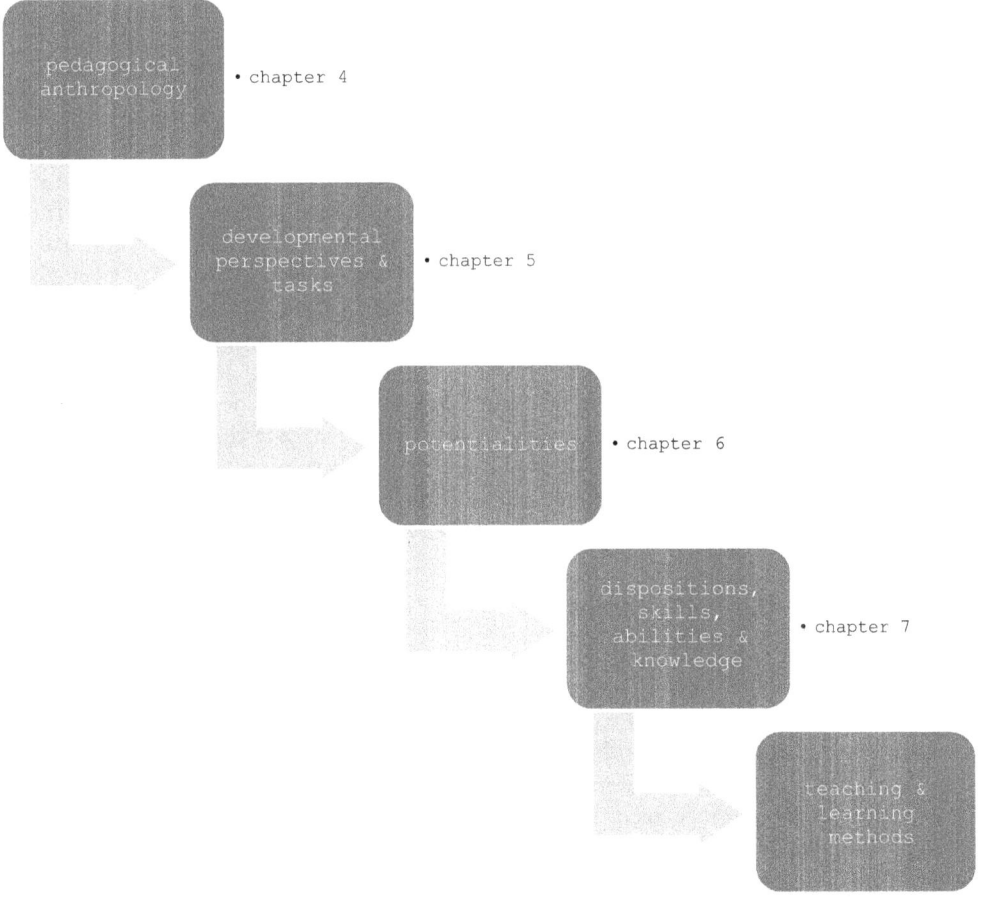

Figure 8.1 The iteration from pedagogical anthropology to teaching and learning methods described in this chapter.

Overview

In this chapter we show how a pedagogical anthropology has implications for the teaching and learning process. By way of example we outline a Waldorf understanding of transformative learning and the generative principles derived from this. We break down the learning process into a series of interlocking steps and explore the implications of doing so. We see that the core aim of curriculum is to provide a sequence of learning opportunities in which the students can develop their potential, and learn the important dispositions and essential knowledgeable skills. As we have stated in our definition of curriculum, this includes not only what is taught but *how*, *where* and *when* it is taught, and by *whom* it is taught. Therefore, we suggest a model in which it is possible to balance these aspects when planning curriculum-as-implemented. This has implications for how curriculum is presented, and we suggest some possible solutions.

Key aspects of the ideal-typical learning processes for crafting curriculum

In order that learning is effective there are basic psycho-somatic preconditions that need to be fulfilled for learning anything at any age. The teaching needs to first ensure that these conditions can be achieved as much as possible under the given constraints of time and space, then it is necessary to make the learning as easy as possible, given that transformational and therefore sustainable learning always requires self-activity and usually effort. The conditions conducive to learning vary, of course, according to age, life experience and the subject or set of skills being learned and this would require a whole book to do justice to it. All we can do here is outline a set of generic conditions, more in terms of a question, as to how these can best be attained in any given situation. The conditions for healthy learning are a special case of healthy living and follow the principles of self-efficacy. We also draw on the preconditions for immersive learning through participation, which, as we have already suggested, applies at the entry stage of most learning situations. In particular, we draw on the principles governing language acquisition, which offers a prototype for much learning.

Relaxed alertness to start (and end) with

The basic preconditions for healthy learning can be summarized as a state of *relaxed alertness*. In Buddhist terms, this is known as a state of mindfulness, and in medicine this is called a calm-alert state (described as the window of optimal arousal and sensory processing). This, of course, is a kind of paradox, which implies that it is a dynamic rather than a static state. We need to be relaxed in body and mind so that we are unpreoccupied by bodily or psychological needs and are therefore open to what comes, but not too relaxed! We also need to be alert to what is going on, focused on what is salient and essential and attentive to the complexities.

In terms of situational awareness, learners can move along a spectrum from 'under arousal' either through being sluggish and unfocused to being over-aroused or overactive, which shows as anxious or disorganized behaviour, leading to meltdown or avoidance behaviour. At one end of the spectrum, the student can experience the social or physical environment as too demanding, with an overload of sensory impressions. The child may respond with hyperactivity or being distracted, by becoming withdrawn or overly emotional. Since the ability of self-regulation develops only towards the end of young people's time at school, children need a supportive environment, which provides conditions for calm-alertness. Interestingly, when children are motivated and when their interest is self-directed, they can concentrate in noisy environments on activities that engage them.

Regularity and familiarity with routines and sequences of activities that students have experienced as conducive to their positive participation help them to adjust to the situation faster. In Waldorf schools every school day starts with a period of attuning to the social group, of warming up and waking up, of inner anticipation of the day ahead, getting into the mood for constructive participation and anticipation of interesting experiences. Depending on the age of the students, this can involve speaking verses, making nature observations and reflections through the year, singing together, doing rhythmical exercises and other forms of movement, balancing, speech exercises, coordination and listening exercises, and retrieval and recall of new input in previous lessons. This is done for as long as it takes for the group to approach an optimal state of relaxed alertness, whilst also leaving enough time for the rest of the learning process. This combination of routine, ritual, warm-up exercises and emotional attunement makes a significant difference to the quality of learning. Furthermore, by balancing the activities throughout the school day, with phases of focused head work and activities in which the emotions and feelings are activated (e.g. through storytelling, artistic work, practical work, group work and solo working, listening and attending and speaking and presenting) the school has a rhythmical structure, which chronobiology shows has salutary effects.

The mindfulness classes that are offered in some schools may be useful, but we believe that an integrated approach would be more effective. Mindfulness classes as a 'bolt on' implies that we have to accept that school, like life, is of necessity stressful, and that we need to create small retreats like islands of calm in a troubled sea. Wouldn't it be more effective (not just nicer or utopian) to do school in a way that actually minimized the stress in the first place? Some curriculum approaches 'teach' wellness and resilience primarily as a mechanism to allow children and young people to access the academic curriculum, rather than as an end in their own right. Other national curricula give the impression that children must learn wellness and resilience in order to compensate for the fact that life and the world of work are going to be stressful. This gives the impression that children should be prepared for disappointment, insecurity in the workplace, the fact that most people are not going to be able to fulfil the dreams and expectations promised by consumerism and populist politics, in other words, cruel optimism.[1]

So, how can we attain relaxed alertness as a normal state in teaching and learning? The short answer is to structure school life rhythmically, enabling the students to grow a sense of coherence and enable them to develop their potential.

The preconditions

Each lesson starts with a check-in phase, routine activities that help everyone feel as relaxed and alert as possible (see above). Even before we start teaching anyone anything we have to ensure, under whatever conditions apply externally (this may be having lessons in a subway station during drone attacks, gathering in a tent in an overcrowded refugee camp, or a custom-built, architecturally optimal space with the right kind of light and heat, school furniture, and healthily nourished students and teachers), that basic needs are adequately met.

Each learner needs:

- to feel safe and secure in the social setting or learning group,
- to feel seen, heard, accepted and understood, whatever their gender, ethnic or social background,
- to be as comfortable in their body as possible under the circumstances (whatever they may be),
- to be assured that someone (their teacher, their peers, others in the school community) is happy that they (the child/young person) are there.

These are not absolute conditions but always relative to the content and individual need. One does one's best as a teacher under the circumstances to meet these basic 'Maslowian' needs,[2] starting with physiological, safety and love and belonging needs. These are the basis of self-esteem and self-actualization, which education should also provide. Meeting these needs within the possibilities of schooling is a long-term task requiring institutional structures. This means, for example, starting the school day with social activities, shared tasks and exchange. It means creating a school culture of collaboration, mutual acknowledgement and interest in others, and acceptance of all forms of diversity.

The requirement that children need to be physiologically relaxed and calm-alert can only be established in the medium term by observing what state the students are in, whether they need waking up or calming down, and whether they need to fine-tune their senses of listening, balancing, and coordinating through exercises involving these senses. Movement of all kinds is helpful in this, but particularly rhythmical movements and those involving balance and coordination.

Stages in the learning process

Making a connection

Having enabled the students to approach the state of relaxed alertness as closely as possible, the first step in the learning process is recalling what is already known about the topic in hand. This may be from the previous lesson, from a theme worked on some time ago, but it might also be gathering what the students already know, even half-knowledge, and especially whatever questions they may have about the topic. It is rare that students know absolutely nothing about any given topic and if they get used to the teacher asking them to reconstruct this, they feel more involved, more respected as people with prior knowledge and experience in response to the inclusive question, what do we know about this?

As we have already indicated in the introduction, we take a Bildung position on education as being in essence about relationships, between teachers and students, between the student and the object of inquiry, what Herbart referred to as the 'third thing'. Education usually focuses on the binary relationship between the student and the knowledge content, with the teacher's job being to facilitate this effectively, but even this relationship is often very one-sided, because the student is in effect being 'made' to engage with the topic, to grasp and internalize the object of knowledge, and then be able to repeat it when required. This is not so much a relationship; it's more a colonial act of taking possession of the knowledge and controlling what the learners do with it. The system says it is in the interests of the students, but they might not see it that way, especially if there is a tacit element of coercion (if you don't learn this, you will get bad grades and fail...and you don't want to be a loser, do you?).

The basic gesture of education, as Herbart put it, is that the teacher directs the student's attention to something that the teacher personally considers important (as opposed to simply implementing the curriculum of the 'five thousand things every citizen needs to know'[3]) and invites them to enter into a relationship with it. For this to be truly effective, the teacher themselves has to have an active and tangible relationship to the 'third thing', and, of course, be interested in the student, not just as a problem or challenge to ensure that they get the grades required, but as a person. This idea relationship between teacher, student and 'third thing' is shown in Figure 8.2).

In this triadic relationship, the teacher needs to have an experience of the subject that is tangible to the student. It is not sufficient for teachers to have once studied the topic, perhaps many years ago in their university studies. It is important that teachers maintain an interest in their subject so that, whenever they teach something, they can signal that they have an ongoing inner commitment and interest and that this is not just professional routine but is based on real interest. This can be expressed, together with their interest in the students, in the way they prepare and present the topic, both communicating the value of the subject and showing their respect of individual students' needs by the way they are addressed. Students don't have to be equally interested in everything that happens at school but there have to be significant moments in each day, when they sense that this is relevant and an opportunity to develop. If students are not involved in generating knowledge but are only expected to learn standardized, prescribed knowledge and if they don't have the sense that what they are being asked to do and learn reflects their interests, they will feel alienated from the learning process, with corresponding lack of motivation and little self-directed, expansive learning.

Having said that teacher and students should develop a relationship to the subject matter, we need to ask an epistemological question regarding the kind of knowledge that is sought through the engagement. Following the German educationalist Horst Rumpf[4] who wrote a book with the intriguing title, *How would Einstein have thought if he hadn't played the violin?*, there are basically two approaches to learning. The first involves going out into the world and capturing things, mastering them, taking them out of their context, taking them apart and analysing them and then exploiting and instrumentalizing them for our egotistical purposes, or bringing reports of their capture into the classroom. This attitude treats the world as a resource (and also as a waste disposal system) that we can use however we want if we have the power. This is how the scientific method has approached the world since the Renaissance. The world is seen as a potential resource, we just

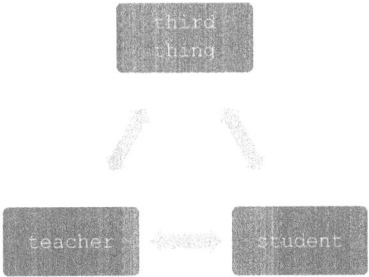

Figure 8.2 The ideal-typical relationship between teacher, student and 'third thing'.

have to learn how best to use it. It is an approach that has been applied to plants, animals and people, especially those other people who are 'not like us' (and scientific ethics is a very recent improvement). The second method of learning about the world is to approach phenomena respectfully, carefully and in context, metaphorically learning 'their language', inviting them to share their ways of being, forming partnerships with them.

Rumpf's purpose in polarizing these two different approaches is twofold. On the one hand, he wishes to recommend a phenomenological and interpretive rather than a reductionist, positivist approach. On the other hand, he wants to show that teaching and learning should not be reduced to the transmission of generalizations, whose authority is based on an assumption that someone did science to arrive at them. Generalizations have their place and use, but in the learning process, rich experience of concrete, real and authentic examples in context on which students can have tangible experiences are more important if we want them to form a respectful relationship, perhaps even based on wonder. The head can sort things into categories, but the heart and hands enter into long-term meaningful relationships. For example, modern societies and the present-day education system have not yet grasped how to educate the young generation to really care for their environment. If they had done so, young people's subsequent behaviour as adult consumers, as farmers, as people in industry, as politicians would not so readily ignore all the warning signs about human-made climate change, the destruction of habitats, pollution of the oceans, and destruction of the forests. We – or enough of us – are still colonizing nature and electing politicians who allow this. Ironically, many of this same generation have now allowed themselves to be persuaded that science is fake and that objective facts that don't fit our interests can be ignored.

At the same time, it doesn't require great scientific knowledge to recognize that there are ways for humanity to live sustainably and that science and technology can make this possible, creating jobs and giving people meaning in their lives. Instead, vast numbers of people have been educated in the so-called free Western world to have no powers of judgement and discernment, no abilities in joined-up, holistic thinking and only short-sighted, short-term, brute self-interest. This may seem harsh on the many dedicated teachers and curriculum makers who are doing their best, but we must be honest and acknowledge that evidently too few people have learned to think holistically or behave like adults, who are presumed to be responsible for their actions.[5] One does not need to take any particular political stance to see that populist governments thrive by appealing to people's *inability* to discern truth from fake news, fairness from self-interest, sustainability from 'gangster capitalism',[6] but easily blame the depersonalized 'others', want to throw them out, put them back in their place, appeal to mean self-interest and ridicule and demonize anyone who objects. That was the message of fascism and it is now the message of populism again today.

This puts a great responsibility on the classroom and how we structure the learning process. If we reduce learning to banking educational capital based on knowledge which can be quantified and transferred into credit points, converted into certificates and awards. If the education system valorizes competition and belittles collaboration, if the message is; without these credit points, grades, exams results, you will be a loser, then we can hardly wonder if so many people come out of the system with competitive personalities, admiring dominant and strong leaders.

Rumpf wants to make the link between the way we teach knowledge and the mindset this cultivates. His point is one of identity: that of the teacher in their relationship to the subject they are teaching and that of the students, for whom the way they are taught either nudges them towards certain neoliberal individualist identities, or who see what (and how) they learn at school as quite separate from their own identity work, which leads to alienation. Rumpf belongs clearly in the Bildung tradition that understands education as self-formation in the (age-appropriate) critical engagement with the world and culture and that includes questions of epistemology and learning dispositions towards how we relate to the world.

The Bildung tradition also emphasizes the importance of relationships between people, and between people and the world. In the Bildung tradition of didactics, that is, the way subjects are taught and the purposes that shape this subject disciplinary approach, teachers choose content that is exemplary, typical, essential or meeting some other criteria, with the expectation that the content provides the students with rich experiences. This has tended to lead to a classical canon of art and literary works, such as 'Bildungsromane' – that is, novels with a Bildung theme in the narrative of the protagonist, often focusing on stories of individuation and emancipation, that also display 'literary value'. More recently, this classical canon has been supplemented by 'modern classics', that is, literature, works of art, or pieces of music that have high artistic merit and addresses themes that enable young readers to address issues relevant to their own development.

The danger in such approaches is that the choice of 'set works on the syllabus' tends to reflect mainstream and establishment works – representing and promoting the cultural capital of the already privileged.[7] The reception of these works also becomes standardized (and the internet is full of study guides to classic works of literature). Critical, disruptive, challenging, minority-orientated material and genres tend to get marginalized or tokenized (i.e. in which the canon includes one example of minority works acceptable to the mainstream, preferably set in a historical period, which is anything older than the current generation). Whether students can have transformative experiences – as literary theory hopes – through this kind of tokenism, depends very much on how such material is worked with in class, and whether the material actually captures the interest and imagination of the students. And is school, with its exams, really the place for transformative learning. Martyn posed this question in the context of marking exam essays (in a school in Hamburg, Germany) on a Black Lives Matter text back in 2021, whilst people were still protesting following the murder of George Floyd.[8] There is a kind of double bind in the idea that students should encounter possibly transformative texts and that they get points for successfully analysing them. Interestingly, some teachers think this is exactly what we should be doing in bringing relevant and up to date topics to students, and there are some like Martyn, who see the exam system itself as a form of estranged labour,[9] basically alienating students from the fruits of their spiritual, i.e. autonomous mental activity. Something similar happened this year, when the English Abitur exam had a heart-rending, almost unbearable text by a Black man who had been in solitary confinement for 12 years. Many of the students were deeply affected and one student broke down in the exam and could barely continue. Martyn's task was to award points for the analysis of stylistic devices used by the author (who had not done a course in creative writing whilst in solitary). As Bob Dylan put it "it is easy to see without looking too far, that not much is really sacred".[10]

Perhaps an even greater danger is that many works of literature are simply deemed too difficult for modern readers used to short episodic narratives, and the tendency is to read commentated extracts or highly abridged versions, or to watch the film of the book. Ease of access may make it easier to teach and assess the accompanying assignments but may limit or even rule out the possibilities of transformative learning with opportunities for affording 'subjectification events', as Biesta[11] calls experiences that interrupt the flow of consciousness and challenge the person to stand up, engage, take a stance and exercise their agency.

Martyn's experience of teaching literature and art is that taking works that do not belong to the classic canon and using hermeneutic approaches that cannot be standardized and require the students to engage personally with the material, are often more likely to be transformative.

What makes a learning process transformative has to do with how the learner encounters the world. If the meeting leads to an interruption of the learner's existing world view or understanding and prompts a realignment of knowledge and relationships, rather than simply an addition to the existing body of knowledge, then it can be considered transformative. This is an idea that exists not only in the European educational theory of Bildung but also in the tradition following John Dewey, who spoke of education having the task to perturb the learner. We remind the reader of our discussion of aesthesis in Chapter 1, in which we spoke about experiences that affect the whole person.

Avoiding alienation

If we take the theory of alienation seriously and apply it to education,[12] then we have to recognize that alienation occurs when the human being's productivity as a self-forming, agentic being is denied the fruits of its own spiritual activity, and school is every bit as much a place where this occurs as the workplace. Learning is the equivalent to work or labour:

> just as the result of alienated labour is embodied in the things produced, so the object of alienated learning becomes material in the things learned – as lessons with exchange value. Just as a product becomes a market thing, so learning becomes a school thing, and just as labour itself becomes a product, so being a pupil or student is a thing one becomes. Similarly, learning becomes embodied in a credential, and being credentialed is a thing to become…The learners become all the poorer the more they become subject to the whim of the educational system…[13]

An alienating learning process is one in which the learning is externally determined rather than being freely undertaken. The bodily and psychological effort involved does not serve a real need, nor does it arise from the intrinsic biographical interests of the person. Students learn because they have to if they wish to participate fully in society, and not because it is an expression of a real inner need. Students don't write essays about Shakespeare because they really have something to say. It does not come from their Self, nor does it serve that Self in its desire to engage with the world and in so doing brings itself into being. Learning is alienating if it conceals or denies or marginalizes the direct relationship between the Self as learner and the productions that we call learning. At the same time the competitive nature of alienated learning alienates the learner from their peers – they become competitors – and thus lack the basic empathy and solidarity to enable collaboration, teamwork, and shared solution-finding to wicked problems. The distribution of alienated learning through standardization and the testing of fixed stocks of predetermined knowledge reprocess alienation at all institutional levels. In the process of which, this kind of learning – Rumpf's first mode of learning as colonization – also alienates the developing human being from the natural world.

Alienation can also occur where students' existing cultural capital does not align with that of the dominant and/or powerful group. Buras, writing in response to E.D. Hirsch's list of '5000 things that every American citizen needs to know', found that children from marginalized sectors of society have to replace their existing cultural knowledge with knowledge of the privileged culture.[14] Research has shown that where students' cultural capital does not align with the knowledge promoted in schools, they face an academic disadvantage and are at risk of disconnecting from education altogether.

To counter alienation and alienating learning, we need a curriculum that addresses the Self's biographical intentions, which respects existing cultural capital and funds of knowledge, and that enables the Self to be active in the learning process in growing dispositions and knowledgeable skills. This enables the Self to construct robust coherent identities in and through learning, and through growing relationships (growing because they are developmental) to the body, to other people and to the world. The 'beautiful risk' (to borrow Gert Biesta's evocative phrase again) of education is that if we allow a non-alienating education, that is, one that affords opportunities for agency in forming free, as opposed to forced, relationships, society as a whole can only profit from committed, engaged, interested, young people capable of being critical of the existing limiting structures.

Promoting connection

There are several ways that Waldorf education seeks to promote connection which we will outline here as examples or perspectives.

Sense of coherence

As we have seen in the section on the transformation of the life processes into learning processes above, Waldorf education has always sought to strengthen the health-creating forces in the person in a psycho-somatic way – that is, in an embodied way. Steiner gave many lectures about the ways in which education can promote bodily and psychological wellbeing, and also pointed to ways in which certain habits of mind can lead to long-term health problems. As we discussed in Chapter 2, the notion of salutogenesis – a word which means origins of health or wellbeing – that Aaron Antonovsky[15] developed in the context of public health has been widely applied in youth studies, and a number of social and therapeutic fields, is a useful model for assessing the extent to which the teaching is promoting sense of meaning.

Students who generally have the feeling that the tasks they are given are meaningful to them personally, who find them manageable (or they feel they have the resources and support to cope) and who understand what they are being asked to do and why, will have a stronger sense of coherence and may feel less alienated from the learning process – they may even feel fulfilled by it.

The question as to how teachers know that their students feel that the tasks they have are comprehensible, manageable and are meaningful is a question of careful, observant assessment, an aspect of pedagogical connoisseurship, as we discuss in the next chapter.

Teaching economy

One of the generative principles of Waldorf education[16] is teaching economy. This basically says that the teacher can present the maximum amount of new material, in the shortest possible time using the least effort and resources as long as no student loses the overview, which means, in effect, that the teaching does nothing to undermine the students' sense of coherence. In other words, the teaching should not leave students feeling that they don't and can't understand, that they can't cope with the demands, that their learning is disconnected, and that they find no personal meaning in what is being taught. Most teachers would agree that this is a tall order. Nevertheless, as a systemic issue, taking the whole educational situation into account, this highlights several important factors that can be addressed.

Learning culture

This is part of the overall school culture which comprises lived practices, attitudes of teachers towards students, the aims of the school, the quality of a supportive and serving leadership, whether the basic preconditions for healthy learning outlined above are generally fulfilled (students feel seen, heard, recognized, accepted and encouraged to participate, criteria of sense of coherence etc.), a learning culture that is supportive, offers useful and personal feedback, expects mistakes as a normal part of learning and addresses these constructively, and students feel involved in the learning process. If this sounds like a 'to-do' list for several years of professional development, it is. We don't imagine that a school culture can be implemented from the top down quickly, but that it grows with insight and shared values over time. The learning culture in a school is part of the meta level within which curriculum is embedded.

Teacher preparation

The teachers prepare their lessons by forming a strong personal relationship and commitment to the topic in advance. As we have seen in the section on teaching being about relationships, the teacher's connection to the subject matter is important for the students' relationship both to the teacher and to the subject matter. The more the teacher makes a personal connection to what will be taught, the more authentic this interest will be. Furthermore, by thinking through the material in terms of the educational aims, the teacher can choose material they feel is particularly relevant to specific learning groups and then organize this in ways that optimize the learning. That means knowing how this group of students learn, how best to arrange the presentation of the new material for optimum effect (and minimum outlay of effort and resources), and how to signal what is salient and essential *without* necessarily telling the students what they are going to learn, because this would reduce their need to apply their will and self-activity, which would weaken the overall learning effect. The presentation should be so effective that the key message is apparent to all learners by virtue of the way the material is arranged, which is why teaching is an art – the art of directing attention to what is important without doing the work for the students. Art gives expression to meaning without defining what that meaning is. This is one of the reasons that Waldorf education tries to avoid using course books or pre-made lesson plans (except for novices or in special circumstances) because no course book designed by people working for a publisher remote in time and space from the actual situation can know what this particular learning group needs, and we believe that one size does *not* fit all. We know it can be timesaving for busy teachers, but it does not replicate the important function of tailor-made, bespoke lesson planning, not least because of the aspect of relationships described above.

Another aspect that we work with in Waldorf education is the role of unconscious intentionality. Human beings have the capacity to interpret the intentions of other people they are communicating with that precedes linguistic expression. This ability of shared intentionality is the basis for language acquisition but also the use of gesture, signs and symbols.[17] In preparing a lesson, the teacher keeps the actual class in mind and this personalized focus of attention becomes noticeable at an unconscious level by the students, especially when the relationship to the teacher is one that has grown over time and multiple shared experiences. Part of the pedagogical anthropology that we are suggesting here is that the unconscious cognitive processes are a factor to take account of. We will return to this in the question of forgetting and the retrieval of experiences. Experience shows that a conscious evocation of a class or individual students for the purpose to directing attention to the learning process is noticed and has a tangible effect on their learning behaviour.

Rich experience

After making a connection, the next stage in the learning process is that students have rich experiences. New material needs to be introduced in the right proportions at the right time, in a way that makes maximum impact. Simply the fact that we are in school and have to learn does not guarantee that students will be any more than superficially interested in what the teacher wants to draw the students' attention to, though many teachers may assume that they know that they should be interested. Our anthropology tells us that rich, transformative learning works best when it is not directly addressed to the head but appeals first to the feelings and from there to the will and rises into active consciousness. Children are bombarded by impressions seeking to grab their attention and school is just another channel in the continuous programme. It doesn't help if we aim to make an even bigger splash! This only leads to sensory inflation and overload. Rich experiences also means not explaining new content at first, but allowing the experience to sink in then recalling and reconstructing it on the next day.

The aim is to awaken the students' attention, curiosity and interest by creating an affect and activating their will to engage. One way has already been mentioned above – the careful preparation of the material and the teacher's clearly signalled intentions. The presentation needs to activate the students' self-activity, which does not necessary happen by exhortation – "pay attention, this is important" – even among a captive audience like a school class. One can generate expectation, offer teasers, promise rewards, which is how advertising functions, but students are usually so media-savvy that they can ignore such promptings (which would at least be a sign that their self-activity was activated), or, more likely, their attention energy is generally low, so that even if they pay any attention, it will be low-level and passive in nature. The aim is to create opportunities for rich experience that increase the energy levels, in a way similar to those that unexpected occurrences, surprises or shocks achieve.

This can basically be done using one of three primary methods of having experiences: through directly sensory impressions, through narrative and through media such as text or images (Figure 8.3).

Direct experience can make a powerful impact, though there are limited opportunities in a classroom situation. This is more likely through field trips or visiting places, art galleries and so on, in which the real things can be directly experienced. Even in the field children are often so used to sensational things in film (e.g. wildlife documentaries, or

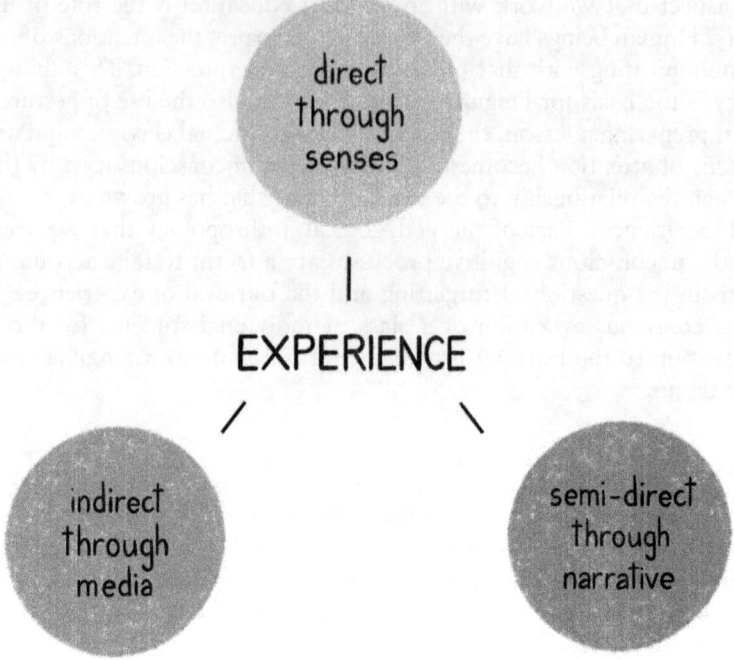

Figure 8.3 The three possible modes of generating experiences. Credit: Aristea Klanac.

simulations) that real life may not immediately have much impact. Therefore, it is often necessary to prime them with narrative to create an atmosphere of attentiveness: "the creatures in the woods are very shy and observant, they see, hear and smell us before we see them and then they hide. They'll only come out if we are very quiet and if they feel that we do not threaten them in anyway" or "if you look very carefully you may find small pieces of amber on the beach" (assuming that is likely). The more students have the sense that they can discover something interesting and relevant, the more likely it is that the experience will be rich and rich experiences leave longer, even lasting impressions. Guided instruction is essential before students are able to design their own exploratory activities and take the initiative.

Narrative is an incredibly effective way of gaining attention, especially if the students are used to being told stories. Even with older students, historical narrative, or accounts of how scientific discoveries were made, are more likely to gain their attention than text or even image (and where direct experience is not possible). Waldorf teachers undergo training in storytelling and historical and scientific narration. Text and images also often require some contextualization to ease access, so a balanced blend of the three modes of experience are almost always necessary if we want the experience to be rich.

Another aspect of gaining rich experience is being immersed in activities and practices in which rich experience is assimilated in context but not yet made fully conscious. A classic example of this is participating in a particular language community and assimilating the language in an unreflected way. In Waldorf schools, second languages are taught by immersing children in a language environment of age-appropriate practices for three years before formal literacy instruction in the language starts.

Retrieving, recalling, reconstructing

We have made the point that rich experiences leave lasting impressions, but whether these are recalled in the stream of life is not guaranteed. In order for learning to become sustainable students need to use their self-activity and apply their will to retrieve, recall and reconstruct things they have intentionally experienced in previous lessons. Therefore, a very important aspect of learning is getting students to make the effort to recall what they have experienced. The mind is not simply a storage bin from which one can retrieve stuff that has been deposited there and forgotten – memory is a far more complex and deliberate process. Steiner offered a remarkable account of this process in his terms and modern neurology has elaborated on it.[18]

Memory is different from a photograph or video because it retains what we pay attention to, how we perceive a situation or object, what we felt when we had the experience, and what meaning our mind – that is, our Self – gave to the perception. Furthermore, memories change both in the unconscious mind because they get linked to existing embodied memories and further modified. When we recall we create a new perception, this then overlays the original which means our memories change over time. This has some negative aspects but, in terms of learning, also positive consequences. If we add more knowledge to each act of recall, the memories grow into concepts that can be generalized. Motor or muscle memories of actions improve the more we practice the activity. Skills become more fluent with practice, which means retrieving the memory of an experience, applying it, acquiring more skill, forgetting and then recalling again.

This is the process referred to as the Self harvesting the fruits of memory and converting them into abilities, in which we then forget the inessential details of the act of practicing and only need to reactivate the skills. Thus, ways of seeing and responding can become habitual and become dispositions. The brain prunes unnecessary neural connections once a higher-order structure – the skill – has been established (not only to save energy but also to increase effectiveness). The vast majority of sense impressions are not reinforced by repetition and therefore not retained – only those that made a subjective impression on us for whatever reason. A subjective impression is one that our Self as subject associates itself with. This is the reason why Waldorf education steers learning by prompting self-activity, rather than just through rote learning and superficial recall of facts that are neither fully understood in their significance nor particularly meaningful to us personally.

Therefore, calling on students to engage their will and recall experiences requires good classroom techniques so that they all do this individually. Students are asked to formulate what they have learned in their own words and pictures or enact what they thought was important. In some cases, non-verbal recall involves the embodied mind more actively than linguistic memory, so re-enacting, finding gestures, making drawings or graphics can go deeper.[19] As one neurological study puts it, "when we form new memories, their mnestic fate largely depends upon the cognitive operations set in train during encoding".[20] Mnestic (from the Greek *mnēstis*) means memory or related to memory. What this means is that items that use semantic operations which emphasize meaning are better remembered than items that are encoded in a shallow way, such as merely retaining a fact. Deep memory conserves meaning; shallow memory retains the appearance of words and how they are spelled. Deeper connections strengthen memory and emotions enhance the mental encoding process. Memory research also tells us that mindfulness enhances personal growth and meaningful learning supports wellbeing.[21] There is a vast amount of research on this, but we think the message here is clear.

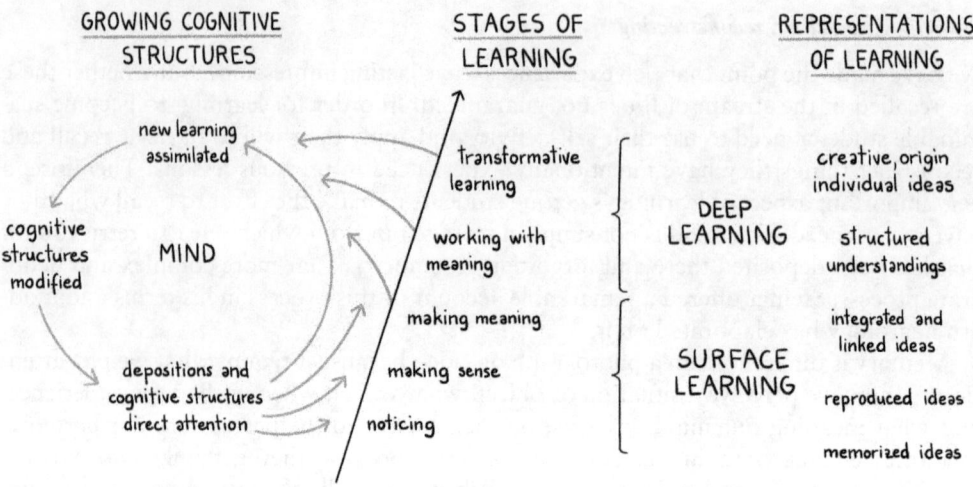

Figure 8.4 The stages in learning and what has been learned. Between noticing and making sense is the process of recall. This graphic draws on work by Jenny Moon and John Hattie.[22] Credit: Aristea Klanac.

Learning techniques, such as non-verbal methods of recall, regular pair work in which students recall to each other and compare their experiences with other pairs, strengthens not only memory but also the subsequent process of meaning-making.

Following on from immersion in rich experiences, recall provides opportunities for emergence, that is, raising what has been unconsciously assimilated to conscious attention, in order that structures and patterns can be made conscious. To follow up the example above, in Waldorf second language learning, after three years of immersion in a second language-rich environment, the children then learn to write and read what they already know by heart, thus becoming conscious of individual words, their sequencing in sentences, how they are spelled, and how verbs are structured. This leads to the next stage: meaning-making.

Shared meaning-making

Once students have recalled their experiences, articulated these in words and shared them with peers, they are in a position to start making meaning. This is an iterative process in which the memory is brought into relation with other knowledge and contextualized, thus enabling students to generate knowledge and concepts and supporting the growth both of dispositions and of living concepts. We can show this graphically as in Figure 8.4.

An important aspect of the cycle of recall and meaning-making is reflection. Here are some examples from Waldorf education:

- At regular intervals (e.g. the end of the lesson, the end of the week, the end of a three- week block, the final weeks of the school year), the students are asked to summarize what they have learned that was new, what built on what they already know, perhaps, how this has changed over time. Age-appropriate forms of reflection are used.

- Students document their learning using self-made books, folders, online platforms, images in age-related ways rather than relying on textbooks or course books.
- Students document their own learning and choose what they think was important, preset it in a portfolio and explain their choice of examples.
- Students share their experiences and learning with peers and not always with the teacher.
- Practical work (arts, crafts, gardening, technology, field trips, work experience practicals) often involve a learning journal (that is not assessed) to document the subject aspects of the experience.

Practicing and applying

Once a constrained skill has been learned, and this always involves relevant knowledge, what has been learned needs to be practiced and applied, ideally in real situations in which the skill is actually required, for example in carrying out projects. The process of practicing, applying and reflecting is an iterative one in which both dispositions as habits of mind and abilities grow, and the concepts that are involved are deepened by being connected to other related concepts. Applying what we are learning leads to our ability to demonstrate the skills we've learned.

To continue our example from Waldorf second language learning, following immersion and re-emersion, skills are acquired and consolidated. The process is continued in that the constrained skills are embedded in real language (both verbal and textual) situations and then subsequently refined and extended into unconstrained skills which can be used creatively and develop in unlimited ways.

Applying knowledge and skills in meaningful contexts, as an expression of expansive learning, provides students with an opportunity to demonstrate what they have achieved, and can be understood as 'performance'. Students' work can be evaluated using appropriate criteria, agreed in advance, and valuable feedback given and received to further develop understanding. Authentic performance, in the form of sharing the results of students' work, is a very important element in making learning personal and embodied, whether that be the presentation of independent projects, a display of artwork, drama productions, musical concerts, dance recitals or the taking home of a beautiful and/or useful crafted artefact. Waldorf students from an early age are experienced performers and this shows in their levels of self-confidence, and probably explains why a disproportional number of alumni work in theatre, film, news media or are working artists. Many Waldorf schools maintain the tradition that every student plays a musical instrument in the school orchestra and/or sings in a choir, and the styles of music played and sung, usually covers the full range. At student social events, there is almost always a dance band, often with rotating performers.

We can show this sequence of learning skills graphically as in Figure 8.5. It can be applied to the growth and development of any skills, as we have seen above in terms of learning dispositions.

Locations of learning

Curriculum design should also consider where the learning occurs, and how the spaces are organized. The location and the setting often contribute implicitly to the learning process. School architecture is rarely something that one is likely to have influence on. If this happens, then the architects will require a brief that, alongside the budget, includes aspects of the school's ethos and intended learning culture. Should it be an open, friendly space with

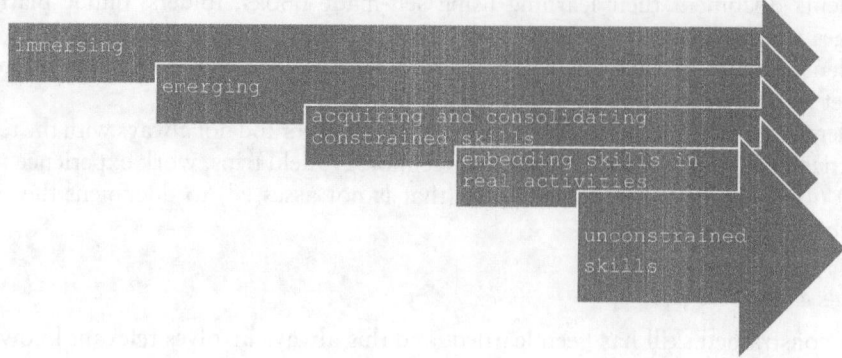

Figure 8.5 The sequence of overlapping learning actions.

plenty of room for circulation, personal encounters, informal meetings, and small- and large-scale presentations and performances? Should the activities in the rooms be visible from outside (not only for reasons of safeguarding and child and teacher protection, but also so that younger students can see the older ones working)? One Waldorf school we know in Sweden has placed all the arts and crafts workshops and studio, including a blacksmithy, in the centre of the school with large glass walls and outdoor workspaces so everyone can see the activities and the extent to which these are valued. That is a statement. Other schools ensure that the parking spaces are at a distance from the school so that everyone has to walk the last kilometre in all weathers (also in Sweden). Another school, in northern Germany, is designed like a village of wooden pavilions around a centre 'marketplace'. Inside many Waldorf schools, the walls are painted in colours that create a desired mood in the room. And instead of having standard rectangular functionalist space, the internal spaces are shaped and clad with wood for both acoustic reasons but also so that the effect of the space is not standardized and feels more intimate.[23]

Special furniture has been designed for the so-called moving classroom, which allows the desks to be quickly converted into balancing equipment (Figure 8.6). The students sit on the floor or on special cushions, which is apparently, according to research done by the medical department of Witten-Herdecke University, much better for their posture.

A further aspect of location is important. In the sense of experiencing authentic learning situations, the practice of having artists and craftspeople have their studios and workshops as teaching spaces has much to recommend it. The ambiance of such spaces, the tools, the materials, the work benches, the artefacts at various stages of the production process visible in the room, the smell of oil, wood-shavings and so on already make an impression on the students. The expertise of the teacher as artist/craftsperson is embodied in their very appearance and manner. The same applies for gardeners in the garden, musicians and drama teachers in their studios and on the stage and even scientists in their labs. In a number of Scandinavian countries, professional artists and craftspeople are also qualified teachers and Waldorf education has followed this tradition.

Structuring and documenting learning

When designing and writing a curriculum, important decisions have to be taken about how to articulate, structure and describe the teaching and learning process over time.

Figure 8.6 Inverted desks can be used for balancing in the 'moving classroom'. Pictures courtesy of Justin Knight.

The choices made will depend on the context for the document. We would like to demonstrate this using two examples from Waldorf education.

Traditionally, in England, a curriculum is elaborated into programmes of study, which are then implemented through a series of learning objectives, which allow teachers to assess whether a lesson or series of lessons have been successful. John Hattie argues that learning objectives make teaching and learning 'visible',[24] but the validity of an 'objectives model' of curriculum design has been contested since it was first described in Bloom's Taxonomy in 1956.[25] There are three key arguments about the limitations of a 'learning objectives' approach:

Setting learning objectives risks disregarding any learning not intended by the teacher

Learning objectives are highly effective in increasing the retention of information about a specified objective. Proponents of the learning objective approach, such as Bob Mager in his influential and best-selling book 'Preparing Instructional Objectives', argue that learning objectives should always be determined by the teacher, and any learning that is not in the desired direction is 'unwanted side effects' or even 'harmful instruction'.[26] Controlling students' learning in this way by the explicit setting of objectives has been criticized as limiting and behaviourist, and certainly does not contribute to the kind of educative self-formation that we advocate for in this book. Learning objectives also decrease the retention of any information not specifically related to the objective,[27] meaning that in many ways they limit learning. Research has shown that where learning objectives are a dominant part of classroom life, the result for children and young people can be increased stress and a decreased desire to participate and learn.[28]

Learning objectives do not suit tasks that involve complex learning where questioning, uncertainty and innovation are necessary

Learning objectives often fail to reflect the complexities of the teaching and learning process: whether it is individual or social, memorization or application, performance or problem-solving, cognitive, haptic or affective, involving values, motivation and/or effort. Learning objectives, although well suited to the teaching and learning of highly constrained skills, cannot be applied to unconstrained skills such as critical thinking.[29]

Learning objectives shape the curriculum, not vice versa

Learning objectives are highly effective for the teaching of specified constrained skills. They create a linear relationship between planned teaching, direct instruction and learning outcome. However, learning objectives, with their consequent emphasis on measurable outcomes, have been shown to exert influence on curriculum, teaching and therefore learning. If, as the research shows, complex learning is difficult to observe and assess,[30] then a curriculum constructed around learning objectives and constrained skills risks distorting curriculum and teaching towards learning that is easily defined and measured. Gert Biesta warns that in defining learning only through objectives, we risk losing sight of desirable educational outcomes that cannot be easily quantified.[31]

In crafting the national UK Waldorf curriculum framework, we wanted to break, or at least loosen, the causal link between teaching and learning outcomes, acknowledging that this is a complex multifaceted process. We therefore created a new approach of 'Learning Journey Descriptors' and 'Age-Related Learning Opportunities'.

For each curriculum subject, a description was created of the typical progression of learning from emergent to growing independence and maturity. The different stages of the 'learning journey' were not linked to students' age, creating the space to acknowledge the natural variation in development and learning. This provides a framework for ipsative (individual) and formative (process-orientated) assessment so that teachers can identify students' progressions. These are not norms that have to be attained.

Whilst recognizing that children and young people's learning journeys might be highly individual, Waldorf education also understands that within the institution of school, healthy learning takes place in a class learning community. Students' developmental journeys are shaped and harmonized by a common curriculum, even if this is accessed at different levels. To support this, running parallel to the Learning Journey Descriptors, a framework of 'Age-Related Learning Opportunities' (ARLOs) was created for each curriculum subject. Very different to learning objectives or outcomes, the 'ARLOs' tend to use active, open-ended verbs such as 'explore', 'encounter' and 'experience'. They relate to the child development perspective and understanding of the learning process that underpins the curriculum, with the aim of providing rich learning experiences that prompt and support development.

Together, the Age-Related Learning Opportunities and Learning Journey Descriptors also take account of the statutory and cultural expectations of a contemporary UK context, forming the meso-layer of the curriculum (see Chapter 3). This structure, however, creates a space for the design and construction of a micro-curriculum by the teacher. Recognised as someone with a deep knowledge and understanding of each child's development and learning, the teacher is provided a degree of autonomy that is rare within schools that follow the English National Curriculum. Rather than being provided with a pre-written scheme of work, a list of content and resources, and a ladder of learning objectives, the teacher's role is to support learning and prompt development through providing the right learning opportunities, at the right time, using content that is relevant to the context and engaging for this particular group of children. Teachers are challenged to use a wide range of teaching and learning strategies to facilitate the development of skills along the whole continuum, from constrained to unconstrained. In Waldorf education this is often referred to as the 'art' of teaching.[32]

Below is an extract from the UK Waldorf Geography curriculum, showing how the Age-Related Learning Opportunities and Learning Journey Descriptors run in parallel.

Geography Age-Related Learning Opportunities	Learning Journey Descriptors
Class 1: Children should have the opportunity:	**Beginning Geography**:
• To have practical, physical experiences of exploring the school grounds and local area on foot • To learn simple geographical terms for local physical and human features • To draw and write about their experiences of the local environment • To have practical experiences of the changing seasons	Children can talk about places that are important to them, e.g. school and home. Children discuss elements of the local environment. They talk about the boundaries of the spaces they live and play in. Children draw pictures and/or write about what they have seen and experienced, using the geographical term for and name of some local features, e.g. local river, town/street name. Children talk about the changing seasons, the weather and the effect on the local environment.
Class 2: Children should have the opportunity:	**Early Geography**:
• To have practical, physical experiences of exploring the wider local area on foot • To learn additional simple geographical terms for and names of local physical and human features • To draw and write about their experiences of the local environment • To have practical experiences of the changing seasons	Children can compare and contrast several places that are important to them, e.g. school and home, holidays, families and visits. Children discuss, compare and contrast elements of the wider local environment. They explain the boundaries of the spaces they live and play in. They can show that they know the difference between, for example, public and private land by talking about where they can and can't go. Children draw pictures and/or write about what they have seen and experienced, using the geographical term for and name of some local features, e.g. local river, town, street name, and talking about comparative sizes (e.g. stream/river, village/town/city). Children talk about the changing seasons, the weather and the effect on the local environment in some detail. They make some connections between sun, warmth, light and dark, day and night, the seasons and months of the year.

(Continued)

Geography Age-Related Learning Opportunities	Learning Journey Descriptors
Class 3: Children should have the opportunity: • To have practical, physical experiences of exploring the wider local area on foot • To explore the possible uses of local raw materials in local archetypal trades, crafts and occupations • To explore ways of meeting basic human needs of shelter, warmth and food in the local natural environment • To explore technical vocabulary around local trades, crafts and occupations, e.g. tools, materials, etc • To draw and write about their experiences of the local environment • To experience and talk about a range of weather conditions	**Developing Geography:** Children can talk about aspects of human interaction with the local environment, including identifying land that has been farmed, materials that have been used for building, the use of different buildings, and trades that are dependent on local resources. Children discuss elements of the wider local environment and places they have visited, e.g. on school trips and visits. Children write about what they have seen and experienced, using the geographical term for landscape features e.g. hill/valley, plains/mountains, village/town/city, port/harbour etc. They talk about how the land is used, e.g. farming, boat building, forestry. Children can describe the seasons, the weather and length of the day in the context of the archetypal farming year, e.g. harvest time. They talk about the impact of weather conditions on land and at sea, making connections to human activity (e.g. high winds, rough seas and fishing)
Class 4: Children should have the opportunity: • To physically explore the local environment, e.g. on foot, by bicycle, from high vantage points (church tower, viewpoint) etc • To explore the origins and connections to the local physical geography of local industries, transport routes (roads, railways, canals, airports, harbours) and settlements • To explore local legend and history • To encounter and use appropriate geographical vocabulary for local features • To explore geographical connections between the local area and other places • To draw and write about their experiences • To explore the construction of maps from simple imaginative portrayals to more accurate scaled representations showing different topographical and human geographical features • To explore cardinal directions and the use of a compass • To experience and record local weather throughout the year and its impact on everyday local life (e.g. clothing, road gritting, vernacular architecture etc)	**Progressing Geography:** Children can talk and write about the origins and character of the place they live in, using appropriate geographical vocabulary. They can describe the origins of local traditional industries and their connection to the availability of natural resources. Children can represent their concrete and experiential geographical understanding of the local environment by making simple maps, using legends and cardinal compass directions.

Teaching and learning 175

In the graphic below, the highlighted text shows how the children in Class 2 share similar learning opportunities, but their learning outcomes differ: the majority of children are working within the 'Early Geography' stage, but some are still at a 'Beginning' level, and some 'Developing':

Age-Related Learning Opportunity	Learning Journey Descriptor
	Beginning Geography:
	Children talk about the changing seasons, the weather and the effect on the local environment.
Class 2: Children should have the opportunity: • To have practical experiences of the changing seasons	**Early Geography:** Children talk about the changing seasons, the weather and the effect on the local environment in some detail. They make some connections between sun, warmth, light and dark, day and night, the seasons and months of the year.
	Developing Geography:
	Children can describe the seasons, the weather and length of the day in the context of the archetypal farming year, e.g. harvest time. They talk about the impact of weather conditions on land and at sea, making connections to human activity (e.g.) high winds, rough seas and fishing)

As part of the Curriculum Working Group for the European Council for Steiner Waldorf Education (ECSWE), we were involved in producing a Common Core Curriculum Framework for a very different context. This time, rather than teachers, the audience was politicians and policy makers. The project had two aims:

- creating an 'established' Waldorf curriculum that schools could use to advocate exemptions from and modifications to national curriculum requirements; and
- demonstrating how Waldorf education delivers cross-curricular competences in line with European frameworks and priorities (e.g. digital competences, entrepreneurship and GreenComp – the sustainability competence framework).

For this project we chose to use the language of 'Learning Aims' and 'Teaching Strategies', giving more familiar and practical exemplification that would be comprehensible and accessible to an audience outside of Waldorf and teaching.

For example, in the history and social science curriculum, students at the age of 9 (in Waldorf grade 3) are given opportunities to be able to learn various knowledgeable skills related to the overall aim of developing a consciousness for historical processes. The Common Curriculum Framework from the European Council of Steiner Waldorf Education (reproduced here with permission of ECSWE) states:[33]

Learning aims

The pupils are able to:

- Understand the concept of origins and beginnings in history and culture, recognizing that previous periods had different conditions, such as technology, tools, and lifestyles.
- Appreciate traditional ways of procuring food, building houses, and using tools.
- Understand the cyclical nature of time and the connection to traditional farming calendars.
- Recognize and name units of time (days, weeks, months) and relate them to traditional activities.
- Develop an awareness of how human life has evolved over time and the relationship between past and present.

Teaching strategies

The teachers:

- Use stories, legends, and creation myths from various cultures to illustrate the notion of origins and different ways of living.
- Organize practical activities such as model-building, gardening, or food preparation that reflect traditional methods of living (e.g., planting, harvesting, or simple construction techniques).
- Introduce the farming year through stories and practical demonstrations, focusing on seasonal activities and the rhythm of nature.
- Create activities that link units of time to specific farming or community activities (e.g., "In spring, we plant seeds; in autumn, we harvest crops"), reinforcing the connection to real-life rhythms and practices.
- Facilitate discussions and storytelling that encourage students to compare and contrast life in the past with their current experiences (e.g., "What did people use before telephones? How were homes built differently?").

For comparison with what this looks like with older students, we include here the text from grade 7 (age 13).

Learning aims

The pupils are able to:

- Understand the European conquest of the Americas and its effects on indigenous peoples.
- Explore the consequences of slavery and the European trading empires in Africa, Asia, and the Americas.
- Examine the European Renaissance, its cultural, artistic, and scientific achievements.
- Study the Reformation and its political consequences in Europe.
- Investigate the emergence of modern states in Europe and the global connections of this period.

- Appreciate advanced cultures in non-European regions, such as the Inka, Maya, Aztec, and Angkor civilizations.
- Develop empathy and understanding through accounts of persecution, slavery, and cultural injustice.

Teaching strategies

The teachers:

- Use texts, including historical sources and indigenous accounts, to provide vivid and realistic accounts.
- Highlight the relationship between colonization, slavery, and the growth of trading empires.
- Use images, maps, and narrations to explain key Renaissance developments.
- Guide students through historical events, emphasizing the Reformation's role in shaping modern states.
- Encourage research and presentations on specific themes using teacher-recommended materials.
- Highlight cultural and artistic achievements from all regions (e.g., Buddhist art, Islamic architecture, Indian mathematics).
- Focus on individual experiences to awaken a sense of empathy and justice while maintaining a balanced historical perspective.

An example of learning aims for cross-curricular competences is shown here text from the Waldorf grade 5 (age 11) curriculum.

Learning aims

The pupils are able to:

- Understand the concepts of migration and trade through local and global examples.
- Recognise the importance of creation and hero myths in different cultural traditions.
- Learn about the history of their local region, including the presence of indigenous people.

For comparison we show the learning aims for Waldorf grade 10 (16 years old).

Learning strategies

The pupils are able to:

- Explore world religions, philosophies, and their cultural-historical contexts to understand their influence on societal values and beliefs.
- Analyse themes of transformation in identity, culture, and society through literature, biographies, and historical narratives.
- Reflect on historical and contemporary challenges such as inequality, social justice, migration, and diversity.

- Develop critical thinking skills by examining global issues and ethical dilemmas from multiple cultural perspectives.
- Create individual or group projects that synthesize intercultural understanding and address ethical, cultural, or societal challenges.
- Reflect on personal beliefs and values in relation to intercultural understanding and global citizenship.

Task for the reader

- How does the framing of the curriculum you work with compare with what we are suggesting?
- What are the similarities and differences?
- What criticism do you have of the way we break down learning opportunities and learning journeys, learning aims and teaching strategies?
- If you had a free hand to craft curriculum, how would you articulate the progression of dispositions, knowledge and skills?

Notes

1 See Berlant, L. (2011). *Cruel Optimism*. Duke University Press.
2 See Maslow's famous hierarchical pyramid of needs Maslow, A. H. (1998). *Towards a Psychology of Being*. Wiley.
3 To paraphrase the core idea expressed by Hirsch, E. D. (1988). *Cultural Literacy. What Every American Needs to Know. Includes 5,000 Essential Names, Phrases, Dates and Concepts*. Vintage.
4 Rumpf, H. (2010). *Was hätte Einstein gedacht, wenn er nicht Geige gespielt hätte? Gegen die Verkürzung des etablierten Lernbegriffs*. Juventa Verlag. Rumpf's argument in this book is also that cultivating artistic/musical capabilities enhances creative thinking, which is what Einstein himself asserted.
5 This is a point Gert Biesta has frequently made, but particularly in his book, Biesta, G. J. J. (2022). *World-Centred Education. A View for the Present*. Routledge.
6 Henry Giroux uses this phrase, and its related 'cannibal capitalism', to refer to the virulent version of Neoliberalism whose obsession with privatization, deregulation, asset stripping, marketing of unsound financial products increasingly goes beyond the law and social consensus in the quest of profit at any cost in human suffering or environmental destruction, feeds on corruption and is often aligned with authoritarian anti-democratic forces- much as the Mafia traditionally does. See Giroux, H. (2025). *The Burden of Conscience. Educating Beyond the Veil of Silence*. Bloomsbury Academic. pp 2–3, 11.
7 Bourdieu, P. (1986). The forms of capital (R. Nice, Trans.). In J. C. Richardson (Ed.), *Handbook of Theory and Research for the Sociology of Education* (pp. 241–258). New York: Greenwood Press. (Original work published 1973).
8 Rawson, M. (2021). A forgotten German philosopher: a self-critical reflection by a high school teacher on Black Lives Matter. *Waldorf Research Bulletin* 26(1).
9 See Lave, J., & McDermott, R. (2002). Estranged Labor Learning. *Outlines*, 1, 19–48.
10 Bob Dylan "It's Alright, Ma (I'm only bleeding)" (1965) on the album *Bring It All Back Home*.
11 Biesta, G. J. J. (2022). *World-Centred Education. A View for the Present*. Routledge.
12 As Jean Lave and Ray McDermott have done in this article: Lave, J., & McDermott, R. (2002). Estranged Labor Learning. *Outlines*, 1, 19–48.
13 Lave, J., & McDermott, R., *Outlines*, p. 34.
14 Buras, K. (1999). Questioning core assumptions: A critical reading of and response to E D Hirsch's 'The Schools We Need and Why We Don't Have Them'. *Harvard Educational Review*, 69(1), 67–93.

15 Antonovsky, A. (1996). The salutogenic model as a theory to guide health promotion. *Health Promotion International*, 11(1), 11–18.
16 These generative principles are outlined and explained in Rawson, M. (2021). *Steiner Waldorf Pedagogy in Schools. A critical introduction*. Routledge; and in Bransby & Rawson (2025) *Waldorf Education for the 21st Century*. Floris Books.
17 Tomasello, M., & Carpenter, M. (2007). Shared intentionality. *Developmental Science*, 10(1), 121–125; Tomasello, M. (2019). *Becoming Human. A Theory of Ontogeny*. The Belknap Press of Harvard University Press.
18 Schachter, D. (1996). *Searching for Memory: The Brain, the Mind and the Past*. Basic Books; Kandel, E. R. (2007). *In Search of Memory. The Emergence of a New Science of Mind*. W.W. Norton & Company.
19 There are several types of memory that we need in educational settings, which we can't go into here. The readers are advised to read Hattie, J. A. C., & Donoghue, G. M. (2018). A model of learning: optimizing the effectiveness of learning. In K. Illeris (Ed.), *Contemporary Theories of Learning. Learning theorists ... in their own words* (2nd edition, pp. 97–113). Routledge.
20 Galli, G. (2014) What makes deeply encoded items memorable? Insights into the levels of processing framework from neuroimaging and neuromodulation. *Frontiers in Psychiatry*. Online https://doi.org/10.3389/fpsyt.2014.00061.
21 See the website: https://www.enotalone.com/article/mental-health/shallow-vs-deep-processing-insights-from-memory-research-r21930/.
22 Moon, J. (2004) *A Handbook of Reflective and Experiential Learning: Theory and Practice*. Routledge Falmer. Hattie, J.A.C. (2003) *Visible Learning: The Sequel. A Synthesis of Over 2,100 Meta-Analyses Relating to Achievement*. Routledge.
23 See https://www.waldorftoday.com/2018/06/world-of-waldorf-school-architecture/.
24 Hattie, J. (2009) *Visible Learning: A Synthesis of Over 800 Meta-analyses Relating to Achievement*. Routledge.
25 Bloom, B.S., Engelhart, M.D., Furst, E.J., Hill, W.H. & Krathwohl, D. R. (1956) *Taxonomy of Educational Objectives: The Classification of Educational Goals. Vol. Handbook I: Cognitive domain*. David MacKay Company.
26 Mager, R. (1969) *Preparing Instructional Objectives: A Critical Tool in the Development of Effective Instruction*. CEP Press.
27 Rothkopf, E. Z. & Billington, M. J. (1979) 'Goal-guided learning from text: inferring a descriptive processing model from inspection times and eye movements'. *Journal of Educational Psychology*, 71, 310–327.
28 Hirsh, Å., (2020). 'When assessment is a constant companion: students' experiences of instruction in an era of intensified assessment focus'. *Nordic Journal of Studies in Educational Policy*, 2(6).
29 Erikson, M. & Erikson, M (2019) 'Learning outcomes and critical thinking – good intentions in conflict' *Studies in Higher Education*, 12(44).
30 Brockway, D. (2016) 'When Lesson Objectives Limit Learning' *School Leadership Today*, 7(4).
31 Biesta, G. (2009) 'Good Education in an Age of Measurement: on the Need to Reconnect with the Question of Purpose in Education', *Educational Assessment, Evaluation and Accountability*, 1(21).
32 European Council for Steiner Waldorf Education (2023) *Generative Principles of Waldorf Education*. Available at: https://documents.ecswe.eu/ecswe-principles. (Accessed 5 November 2023).
33 From European Council Steiner Waldorf Education, Common Core Curriculum Framework internal website. Content written by Martyn Rawson, Kath Bransby, Trevor Mepham and Margareta van Raemdonck.

9 Teacher Connoisseurship and pedagogical tact

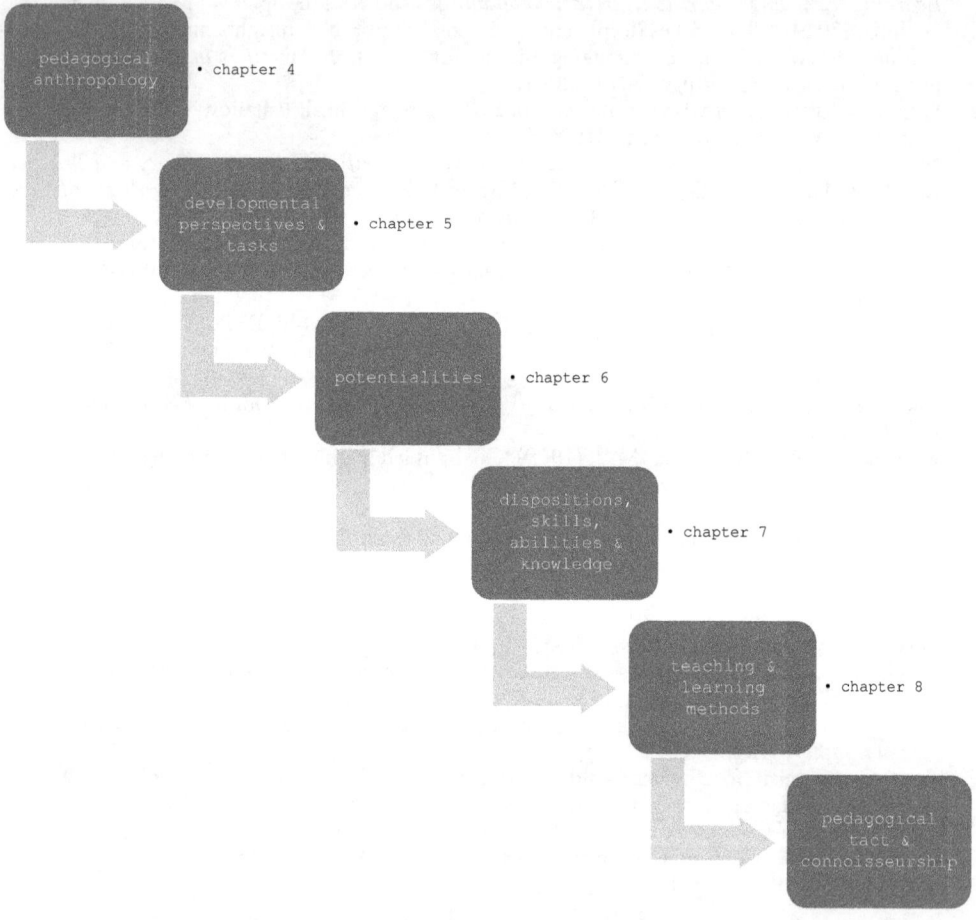

Figure 9.1 The iteration of crafting curriculum from pedagogical anthropology to teacher skills as described in this chapter.

DOI: 10.4324/9781003518471-10

Overview

In order to craft curriculum and teach it, we suggest teachers and school leaders, who we hope also continue to do some teaching, have the skills to read the developmental processes in the actual students and the factors that shape these. The ability to 'read' and respond to the full spectrum of developmental processes and understand the pedagogical anthropology undergirding the curriculum requires connoisseurship. The ability, at the micro level of curriculum, to plan and evaluate lessons and of course to teach, is what is called pedagogical tact. We describe these two abilities and suggest a few ways in which they can be developed.

Connoisseurship

As we outlined in the Introduction, connoisseurship is a particular form of expertise that involves knowledge and appreciation. The American educationalist Elliot Eisner[1] coined this phrase in connection with teacher research in his wonderful book *The Enlightened Eye*. What is important in the term connoisseurship is the aspect of appreciation. Crafting curriculum requires more than just technical knowledge; it also requires holistic thinking. In the German-speaking world in the early 20th century, in which Bildung was the guiding educational philosophy, the equivalent for curriculum was *Lehrplan*, which literally means 'the plan of what is to be taught'. However, *Lehrplan* was very much understood as a whole educational concept, much as we have defined curriculum in this book. At that time – and this is an element we have not adopted – *Lehrplan* was thought of almost as a work of art, a grand total concept by a great educational artist, in which if one was to modify one part, this might risk the integrity of the whole.[2] Nevertheless something of this quality of appreciation is important.

Appreciation is more than just knowledge about something – instrumental knowledge that asks, what can we do with this? or propositional or theoretical knowledge – it is knowledge that matters to the person. It is both subjective and objective and it is situational because it focuses on what is important here and now, it recognizes what is relevant and important in the situation. Like appreciative inquiry,[3] it takes the stance that the stakeholders in an organization, such as a school, can determine the culture and practices through their actions and the relationships these express, and acknowledges that human systems can be changed through the process of thinking about them and through inquiry, they respond to the questions we ask of them. In particular, appreciative inquiry is interested in the stories people tell about the organization, and also about the stories that anticipate the future development of the organization. It is generally a positive force in the development of the organization.

Elliot Eisner's view of connoisseurship in education is similar, in that it seeks to articulate a positive appreciation of the situation, which certainly does not preclude critical thinking. Only through appreciation can a critical way of looking identify what needs to be done to enhance the situation. This approach enables us to see more by drawing our attention to what is salient.

One of Eisner's enduring interests was artistic ways of thinking and thus education as an art and, in particular, the notion of artistry as a skill that teachers need. He wanted to move beyond emotional aspects of art and develop the cognitive aspects, though not to stop at the technical aspects of artistry – what one could call techniques. The word connoisseur comes from the Latin *cognoscere*, to know, and implies not only seeing qualities in a phenomenon but also knowing how to value them, understanding what they mean in context. Artistry, in the teaching profession, is a form of thinking-in-action or knowing-in-context,[4] also known as pedagogical tact,[5] which is the ability to know what can be meaningfully done in a pedagogical situation.

The question is: how can discernment, appreciation and connoisseurship be learned? It clearly can be learned, and it improves through use. Indeed, it can improve with experience and maturity. In Bildung terms – and this was a key contribution of the philosophy of Hans-Georg Gadamer[6] – tact grows through self-formation in the hermeneutic process of arriving at understanding through interpretation, which is always a mode of translation. For Gadamer, all understanding is a form of translation, and all translations are interpretations. Eisner, following John Dewey,[7] argued that connoisseurship involves an expansive, holistic form of knowledge that includes affect and the full range of sensory experience, and not just the visual. In Dewey's view, art is related to a fuller, more comprehensive form of knowledge than mere thinking cognition. The artistic way of knowing is not only relevant to art but is a way of experiencing the world and can be applied in any field, including science and practical activities. This requires an immersion in the phenomenon and the object of our interest and inquiry is best understood in context and by the activity of making meaning of our experiences.

The reader will have noticed that our account of learning also starts from immersion, followed by emersion, leading to meaning-making. This relates to Steiner's theory of knowledge, which we already referred to in Chapter 4. In simplified form, Steiner's theory of knowledge says that we experience the world through our senses and construct mental images to represent what we experience. But this percept (the term used to translate Steiner's specific use of the German term *Wahrnehmung*), initially based on observation, has no meaning. The meaning of the phenomenon is not revealed merely by empirical observation. Our thinking cognition – our thinking *in* cognition – observes the effects of our experiences on the mind and interprets this intuitively by finding a concept that makes sense of the percept and thereby creates our reality – not an *ultimate* reality, but a situated reality that is both subjective, because we as subjects perform the cognitive activity of producing the concept, but also objective because the concepts we produce can be thought and verified as valid by anybody having the same experience (which is why dialogic inquiry is so important).

Bo Dahlin[8] expresses this knowledge process in the simple formula *experience + concept = reality*. Steiner's idealistic take on this was that the Self, being partly in the spiritual world, which contains the sum of everything and all relationships, has access to this knowledge, though the development of thinking is required to be able to do this effectively. Steiner insisted that there are no limits to our knowledge of the world through the development of spiritual thinking, but there is no doubt that this requires a specialized schooling of active mindfulness, which is what the various paths of meditation and contemplation that Steiner offered are aimed at achieving.[9] Our interpretation of this process is a more modest version aimed at daily use for teachers, as it were, which does not assume that the person is advanced in their capacity for spiritual thinking. The Self is firstly embedded in a cultural and linguistic space, a discourse within the lifeworld, which is equally nonmaterial and therefore spiritual, and thus draws on cultural concepts to make sense of experiences. The ideas in circulation and the language they are clothed in within a particular community of inquiry constitutes a particular lifeworld which participants embody by participating in the practices that are informed by these ideas, often as taken-for-granted understandings. These tacit assumptions have to be made conscious and critically reflected, which is why a hermeneutic process is necessary[10] (see below).

By consciously assimilating ideas of pedagogical anthropology these can direct our attention to certain pedagogical phenomena. Each time we do this and critically reflect on the outcomes of our deliberations, we are able to extend our understanding, whilst at the same time contributing to the discourse/lifeworld of our professional community of inquiry. This is the main argument for collegial processes of case study and practitioner research within a school.

We form our knowledge by combining sensory experience with concepts that make sense of those experiences and give them meaning. During the learning process through childhood and adulthood, we assimilated a whole lexicon of concepts, some naturally acquired through experience, others learned through education and self-education (including reading). These concepts dispose us to position ourselves in certain ways, to relate to the world through certain habits of mind, and these dispositions influence what we notice and look for. Not all of these embodied concepts are useful or pedagogically conducive, in fact, some fall into the category of prejudices or stereotypical categories, which is why it is vital in the teaching profession to address unconsidered and tacit assumptions. Peter Kelly[11] recommends, for example, narrative and artistic methods to help make unconscious assumptions visible and thus easier to overcome. Steiner's advice was that teachers should practice various exercises to control their own thoughts, feelings and volition, cultivate openness and positivity, and work with the assumption that the thoughts and feelings we have about other people have as much impact on them as actions.[12]

If appreciation is a form of aesthetic judgement in the sense of *aisthesis*, in the way we have spoken of it in Chapter 1, that is, as rich experience, then the way we make sense of these experiences, in fact the way we actively engage with the world, and the way we respond to it, will be influenced by the quality of our perceptions and the habits of mind we apply to interpreting them. Therefore, if our job is observing and 'reading' complex, multifactor educational situations, it makes sense that we train our powers of observation and assimilate appropriate ideas that become dispositions. How else would pedagogical tact, thinking-in-action, thinking-in-practice work? We don't have time to reflect on propositional knowledge in the moment, or take in multiple factors and analyse them, we have to intuit what is right for the moment, and then evaluate retrospectively whether we were right or not, whether the way we acted was fruitful in the situation. If we are disposed to observing children and young people and classroom situations through the lens of certain embodied dispositions that we have carefully and consciously learned, then we are more likely to make sense of the situation. Using embodied ideas can make us more disposed to applying our imagination effectively to anticipate outcomes and the possible effects of our actions. Using fast thinking we can estimate with increasing degrees of accuracy what meaningful actions to take. Therefore, the preparation for pedagogical tact is embodying the appropriate ideas about child and youth development and the generative principles.

Connoisseurship is, however, not the same as pedagogical tact, if only because it is not required to be done with a high level of spontaneity in the moment. Connoisseurship means taking time, weighing things up, taking a closer look (another sip of the wine in question). Connoisseurship slows down fast, intuitive thinking and becomes considered, deliberated judgement-making. It still requires imagination to anticipate the possible and likely outcomes, but it takes time doing so. And because it is basically a form of theory building, it can be tested in practice using suitable methods of educational research. But it still requires the acquisition of dispositions to noticing and judging qualities. So how can these be rehearsed and learned?

Hermeneutic study

In order that new ideas can be assimilated to the point that they become dispositions we have had positive experiences using the following steps. This can be done with texts or through verbal presentations. When we say student here, we are referring to adults in teacher education- student teachers, but this applies to any one studying a text.

1. Downloading. The teacher student 'downloads', that is reflects and brings to mind and then formulates in words, everything they already know about the topics being studied, all pre-knowledge and as much as possible all prejudices and taken-for granted ideas. This is not done to 'bracket it out' – we don't believe this is possible. It is done because this is our starting horizon. We never start any process from a neutral or fully open position. In matters of education, in particular, we are predisposed by our own embodied experiences, not least through years of schooling and institutional learning, to say nothing of our socialization and enculturation.
2. Empathic understanding. After taking in a text, lecture, presentation etc, the student then attempts to retell the main ideas in their own words, being as fair as possible to the intentions of the writer/speaker. We try to put ourselves in their position and give them the benefit of the doubt. This is a benign interpretation.
3. Dialogic understanding. The student enters into dialogue with the ideas in the text, first by contextualizing them, relating them to other ideas that seem relevant, then by discussing these with other participants, taking account of the relevant literature, looking for possible theoretical explanations that might shed light on the text.
4. Transactional understanding. Using critical reflection, the student tries to articulate what has become of their starting horizon, whether it has changed or moved and, if so, in which direction. The student observes and tries to articulate their own emotional and intentional response to the experience, addressing questions such as: Has my understanding of the situation changed? Has my position changed? What do I now want to do with this experience?

Contemplative meditation

Contemplative meditation[13] involves studying something and then condensing the experience into a question or an image and using this as an object of meditation (this involves holding the thought in mind then dissolving this mental image and keeping an open mind for a certain period of time). This allows the question/image to sink down into the unconscious so that it may 're-emerge' in life in an appropriate situation, in effect disposing the person to notice something relevant to their question. In this way, we can imagine that the assimilation of important ideas in this way can lead to new ways of seeing and new habits of mind. It certainly doesn't happen quickly and requires time to incubate, mature or become enriched through linking up with other inner experiences.

Self-development through artistic activity

Over many years, Martyn has worked in partnership with improvisation and clowning trainer Catherine Bryden, in workshops with trainee teachers in many countries. This method was originally the focus of Professor Peter Lutzker's[14] PhD study, which established the important link between improvisation and clowning and teacher artistry (in Elliott Eisner's sense). Catherine and Martyn collected data over six years from hundreds of participants who also used scaffolded reflection in this process to bring about an emergence of awareness of process from the immersion in the activity. This showed not only heightened sense of self-efficacy, confidence and artistry, but also that the participants noticed more in the classroom processes and thus increased their ability to observe the effects of their teaching on the learning behaviour of the students, which, as John Hattie's famous meta-study[15] indicates, is a powerful factor in student and teacher learning. We have had had similar experiences using other artistic activities, such as land art, though without the formal empirical research as yet to back this up.

Waldorf teacher education has long used methods of observation suggested by Steiner, which to date have not been the subject of empirical research (due to lack of funding). These exercises include modelling abstract forms in clay and describing the processes involved, observing natural phenomena, such as plants or weather, using so-called Goethean observation techniques,[16] which involve patient and exact observation and inner reconstruction of, for example, the processes involved in plant growth across changing weather patterns over time. The basic idea of metamorphosis – or the emergence and change of form – is that something happens for which visible causes are not apparent that leads to qualitative and not quantitative change in the organism or phenomenon. Such exercises can lead to the subtle sensing of autopoietic processes, such as those that occur in the development of children and young people and also in the dynamic of social processes. We would argue that such exercises can attune the mind to new ways of seeing that can be described as connoisseurship. This is a field that would require considerably more research, which might yield important insights into this important aspect of teacher abilities.

Practitioner research

Action research[17] or illuminative practitioner research[18] have been well documented as methods of teacher capacity building as well as pedagogical problem solving, though since we are talking about the growth of dispositions, the effects here are much less known. For dispositions to grow there needs to be a fundamental shift in the way a person sees the world, and this requires significant and long-term practice. Illuminative practitioner research, which aims more at gaining insight and developing capacities, is probably a more likely route to new dispositions than action research, but we admit this is pure speculation.

Exercises in the observation of processes

Our experience in Waldorf teacher education suggests that several methods can be effective.[19] These involve exercises in attention and mindfulness and in the observation of natural phenomena, of artistic processes and of pedagogical situations, all of which are supported by scaffolded reflection. Lesson observation is a particularly challenging but rewarding field of observation. The aim is not to make judgements about what is seen but simply to observe the multiple layers of processes involving students and teachers, as well appreciation of the situation based on background information about the history and context of the class. In such observations, one can focus, for example, on transitions within the lesson, on unexpected and unusual occurrences and how everyone responds to these.

The important aspect of all these exercises is that by observing processes over time, the mind is schooled to notices what happens in transitions from one state to another, the rhythms of change and the new forms that can unexpectedly emerge, since many living or natural processes are basically unpredictable because so many factors are involved. One can improve the ability to be aware of what is emerging as it emerges. Otto Scharmer has developed many exercises for observing social processes using his Theory U approach.[20]

Case studies

As mentioned above, connoisseurship can include case studies of individual students or groups of learners. This has three primary functions.

- To gain a deeper understanding of individual students in their development so that the teachers can offer support and guidance.
- To deepen the pedagogical understanding of those who participate and to develop capacities in the observation of students and pedagogical situations.
- To develop shared understandings within the collegial body, both for coherence of action and for cultivating a sense of shared identity and purpose and, in particular, to be sensitive to what is emergent.

A case study, sometimes called a child study, involves a group of educators who know the student meeting to form a picture of the child or young person[21]. The great Russian psychologist Lev Vygotsky kept detailed notebooks on his conversations with individual students in which he sat down with them at eye-level, as it were, and asked them to talk about themselves and their experiences. One of his students, Lev Zankov, recorded aspects of his method of conducting clinical interviews,

> many observers were amazed how Vygotsky conversed with the child while examining him. These conversations were unique in comparison with the way the child was asked and answered questions…this was an involving, very personal conversation with the little one…Vygotsky was always able to establish an atmosphere of trust in his rapport with the children, he talked with them as though they were equals, always paid attention to their answers. In turn, the children opened up to him in a way they never did with other examiners.[22]

Generally, teachers do not conduct clinical interviews, but the point about taking the child or young person seriously and hearing what they have to say is very important. Likewise involving parents in case studies is also important and appropriate forms have to be found to include them.

In a case study, the task is not simply to diagnose a problem and prescribe a set of measures designed to solve or ameliorate the problem, but to listen to the what the situation is 'trying to tell us', to sense what is coming to expression in terms of underlying processes and what is emerging out of this. This is why the activity does more than tackle specific problems; it builds capacity in those working with the issues. They become, more experienced and this new knowledge guides their attention to what is salient and important. A case study in this sense becomes a form of illuminative practitioner research,[23] which is a way of cultivating connoisseurship.

The point here is that the connoisseurship required for crafting curriculum is best cultivated in the activity of studying students and pedagogical situations, because this enables teachers to assimilate the required pedagogical anthropology and developmental approach as practice, rather than as abstract theory. This shows, if the reader has not already noticed, that the approach we are suggesting really does assume a close pedagogical involvement, in whatever form is possible, if we want to craft curriculum that isn't top-down or abstract but is founded on an understanding of the needs of the students.

Student voice is important too in crafting curriculum at all stages in the process. Students may not know enough about the world to predict what they need to know, though they may know as much as teachers and academics in a more immediate way, but they can certainly offer insight into the curriculum they know (especially in the wider sense we are using here). Though students are busy passing through school, while teachers are generally there for the long haul, they are often capable in short bursts of creative participation that may have the effect of opening our eyes. For them it's often here and now but no less important for that. We need to adapt to their ways of working and be quick to catch them – it is usually worth the effort.

One of the roles of educational leadership is to facilitate case studies. Crafting curriculum does not just happen alongside everything else in the busy life of teachers and school leadership is required to create conditions with which concerted work can occur, that key people have time and resources, back-up, space and time. Multi-stranded curriculum work needs to be coordinated and facilitated.

Cultivating a sense for a possible future

Although Rudolf Steiner could be accused of offering a 'one-man' spiritual science,[24] since the methods of taking a systematic scientific approach to the spiritual dimension of life that he put forward initially appear to only have been accessible to him, we'd like to recommend some aspects of his approach. In his early philosophical work, in 1892 Steiner made a remarkable assertion about human knowledge. He starts from the position that human creative activity,

> is an organic part of the universal world process. The world process should not be considered a complete, enclosed totality without this activity. The human being is not a passive onlooker in relation to evolution, merely reproducing in mental images cosmic events taking place without their participation; they are the active co-creator of the world process, and cognition is the most perfect link in the organism of the universe.[25]

Nearly 30 years later in the First Teachers' Course, Steiner took up this theme again, insisting that human beings are not merely spectators of world events that happen 'out there' and are merely reproduced 'in here', but rather that the human mind is the stage upon which world events take place, an actor in the drama of life, not the audience.[26] This is, in effect, a participatory form of knowledge creation.

Theoretically, the individual human mind can experience and intervene in world events, but until individuals have acquired that ability, the next best thing is a group of human minds working together, intuiting the immediate world events at hand, in the process of their emergence, the aim being to have some degree of agency, be subjects rather than simply being objects of the forces at work.

Steiner seems to have come to the recognition that once the situation arose in which he was being asked to apply his anthroposophical insights in the public sphere, beyond the confines of the Anthroposophical Society that he had founded for his followers to cultivate and practice anthroposophy, he needed to modify the process. Since the Waldorf School was not intended to be a school for the children of anthroposophists but the children of the workers of the Waldorf Cigarette Factory, it was no longer possible to sustain the activity on his insights alone. It was necessary to streamline the process. So, the first thing he did in founding the Waldorf School was to create a college of teachers, whose task it was to work together on the pedagogical anthropology Steiner was about to develop, with the three aims we just outlined above: capacity building, gaining shared insights and creating a culture of awareness of what is emerging.[27] This structure was based on the self-development of the individual but built on this by creating three levels of activity:

- The activity of the individual having the inner strength and capacity to overcome subjective positions.
- The activity of the individuals in the circle being open to allow discourse to flow, in which each takes up the thoughts of the others and weave this into a shared consciousness that then becomes receptive to the emergent future.
- The activity of the circle in being receptive to what is emergent and capable of articulating this as insight.

Though this approach was cultivated within the Waldorf movement for many years as an esoteric practice, and indeed Steiner gave it as an esoteric practice, over the past 20 to 30 years this has been made more explicit. At the same time, however, there has long been a conflation of this presencing function with daily management of schools. What, in our view, was intended as a technique for generating insight and knowledge was frequently interpreted as an insider collective that based every decision on consensus, which may be well-intentioned but is highly time-consuming, often susceptible to hidden power structures and also frankly inefficient. This is far less apparent in pioneer situations, in which the dynamic of the start-up provides momentum, but as the need to consolidate and develop consistency arises, so do myths about collective leadership. As a reaction to this, the pendulum has often swung entirely to the other extreme, with the installation of authoritarian leadership via headteachers or school principals, sometimes with no knowledge of Waldorf practice. Probably nothing has held the Waldorf movement back more than inadequate leadership – of both kinds. Those schools that avoid these twin traps – everyone must decide everything or total delegation to a single manager - develop various forms of distributed leadership with clear roles and responsibilities, and transparent hierarchies of decision making and accountability.

Steiner's insights into working with the dimension of reality that is not yet visible – "a felt sense of a possible future" – has been taken up in a particularly fruitful way by Otto Scharmer of MIT in his Theory U work, which also draws on other insights. The Presencing Institute he co-founded and also the *Journal of Awareness-Based Systems Change*[28] has found resonance in all kinds of institutions around the world. In his most recent publication,[29] he, along with his co-author Katrin Kaufer, outline four modes of knowing, the first three are acknowledged by current scientific thinking:

1 first-person knowledge, which is subjective,
2 second-person knowledge, which is intersubjective,
3 third-person knowledge, which is objective because it can be measured,
4 fourth-person knowledge, which "emerges around the edges of the first three forms of knowledge, blending with but also transcending them. It is trans-subjective in that it is very personal but emerges through you rather than being of you and it gives us access to a deeper form of self-knowledge, of who we really are, and what it is we are here for."[30]

Generating fourth-person knowledge and the processes of working with it, which Scharmer and Kaufer elaborate, are important new tools in bringing about change in systems such as education. Our point is that conventional forms of knowledge are adequate for crafting curriculum in predictable situations, in which most of the factors are known and can be anticipated with a high degree of certainty. Today, however, the world situation is such that we can't know what dispositions, skills and knowledge will be needed by the current generation of school-aged students by the time they enter the world of work and take responsibility for a family.

Conditions of practice

No amount of connoisseurship or pedagogical tact will help teachers master difficult situations if the school environment and culture does not support this. It can make teaching unnecessarily difficult if teachers are not trusted to be responsible professionals and allowed space and time to try new things out, explore alternatives, innovate, and to take a somewhat longer view. If everything has to be reduced to measurable outcomes now or in the very short term, then teachers will inevitably cut corners, and opt for superficial outcomes that may meet targets but miss the whole point of education. We admit this is a difficult idea for politicians and ministry officials, who want metrics to grasp, but the teaching profession must learn to make the case that we all want quality, but like making grass grow faster, this only works using medium and long term sustainable methods, that enable healthy structures to become established, rather than by applying quick fixes that ruin the 'soil' in the long run. Our focus here has been on curriculum, but it would require another book to explore the organizational and leadership conditions necessary to establish, what we are calling here in shorthand, *healthy school cultures* which enable human flourishing for students, teachers and other staff. There are generative principles for good school leadership[31] that we have applied within the Waldorf movement.

Tasks for the reader

- In what ways do you practice connoisseurship in your educational practice?
- How did you learn this?
- What methods of developing capacities do you use in your practice?

Notes

1 Eisner, E. W. (1976). Educational connoisseurship and criticism: Their form and functions in educational evaluation. *The Journal of Aesthetic Education*, 10(3/4), 135–150. https://doi.org/10.2307/3332067; Eisner, E. W. (2017). *The Enlightened Eye. Qualitative Inquiry and the Enhancement of Educational Practice*. Teachers College Press.
2 See Horlacher, R. (2018). The same but different: the German Lehrplan and curriculum. *Journal of Curriculum Studies*, 50(1), 1–16. https://doi.org/10.1080/00220272.2017.1307458.
3 Cooperrider, D. L., Whitney, D., & Stavros, J. M. (2008). *Appreciative Inquiry Handbook*. Crown Custom Publishing.
4 See Kelly, P. (2006). What is teacher learning? A socio-cultural perspective. *Oxford Review of Education*, 32(4), 505–519.
5 van Manen, M. (1991). *The Tact of Teaching*. The Althouse Press; van Manen, M. (2015). *Pedagogical Tact*. Left Coast Press.
6 Gadamer, H.-G. (2013). *Truth and Method* (J. W. and D. G. Marshall, Trans.; revised second edition ed.). Bloomsbury. (2004 (first published 1975)).
7 Dewey, J. (1934). *Art as Experience*. Putnam.

8 Dahlin, B. (2013). Gloves of Ice or Free Hands? A nomadic reading of Rudolf Steiner and Bergson and Deleuze and others on knowledge as nonrepresentational and the importance of Aesthesis. *Other Education: The Journal of Educational Alternatives*, 2(2), 67–89.
9 See for example Steiner, R. (2011). *Knowledge of the Higher Worlds. How is it Achieved?* (D. S. Osmond & C. Davy, Trans.). Rudolf Steiner Press, and.

    Steiner, R. (2014). *Soul Exercises: Word and Symbol Meditations 1904–1924* (M. Barton, Trans.; Vol. Collected Works of Rudolf Steiner 267). SteinerBooks Inc.
10 Space does not permit a fuller discussion of this, but it is essentially a phenomenological process, as described by Maurice Merleau-Ponty (Merleau-Ponty, M. (2005). *The Phenomenology of Perception* (C. Smith, Trans.). Taylor and Francis e-Library, Routledge and Kegan Paul). See also Smith, J. A., Flowers, P., & Larkin, M. (2009). *Interpretative Phenomenological Analysis*. SAGE.
11 Kelly, P. (2011). Unconsidered activity, craft expertise and reflective practice in teaching. *Reflexive Practice: International and Multidisciplinary Perspectives*, 12(4), 557–568.
12 There are many books, particularly in the US about the spiritual path of the teacher. Everyone has to find their own favourites. Our recommendation is Wiechert, C. (2012). *Teaching. The Joy of Profession. An invitation to Enhance Your (Waldorf) Interest*. Verlag am Goetheanum.
13 Zajonc, A. (2009). *Meditation as Contemplative Inquiry: When Knowing Becomes Love*. Lindisfarne.
14 Lutzker, P. (2021). *The Art of Foreign Language Teaching: Improvisation and Drama in Teacher Development and Language Learning* (2nd fully revised edition ed.). Franke Verlag.
15 Hattie, J. A. C. (2023). *Visible Learning: The Sequel. A Synthesis of Over 2,100 Meta-analyses Relating to Achievement*. Routledge.
16 Holdrege, C. (2013). *Thinking Like a Plant: A Living Science for Life*. Lindisfarne Books; Holdrege, C. (2018). A fresh take on the Goethean approach. *In Context*, 40(Fall 2018).
17 Noffke, S., & Somekh, B. (2013). Action Research. In B. Somekh & C. Lewin (Eds.), *Theory and Methods in Social Research* (second edition ed., pp. 94–101). Sage. McNiff, J. (2013). *Action Research: Principles and Practice* (third edition ed.). Routledge.
18 Elliott, J., & Lukeš, D. (2008). Epistemology as ethics in research and policy: the use of case studies. *Journal of Philosophy of Education*, 42(1), 87–119.
19 Martyn has published several articles on this: Rawson, M. (2020). A theory of Waldorf teacher education. Part 1. Learning dispositions. *Research on Steiner Education*, 11(1), 1–22; Rawson, M. (2020). A Theory of Waldorf Education: Part 2. The role of study and artistic exercises. *Research on Steiner Education*, 11(2), 23–36; Rawson, M. (2021). Using artistic, phenomenological and hermeneutic reflective practices in Waldorf (Steiner) teacher education. *Tsing Hua Journal of Educational Research*, 37(1), 125–162. http://edujou.site.nthu.edu.tw/var/file/128/1128/img/1172/37-1-4.pdf; Rawson, M. (2021). A Theory of Waldorf Teacher Education. Part 3. Learning knowledgeable action with purpose through learning-in-practice. *Research on Steiner Education*, 12(2), 1–12.

    Bryden, C., & Rawson, M. (2022). Theatre clowning in L2 teacher learning: An example from Waldorf/Steiner education. *L2 Journal*, 14(3).
20 Scharmer, C. O., & Kaufer, K. (2013). *Leading from the Emerging Future: From Ego-system to Eco-system Economies*. Berrett-Koehler Publishers. See also https://www.presencing.org/.
21 An excellent guide to this process can be found in Wiechert, C. (2012). *Solving the Riddle of the Child*. Verlag am Goetheanum.
22 Quoted in Barrs, M. (2022). *Vygotsky the Teacher. A Companion to His Psychology for Teachers*. Routledge, p. 47.
23 See Rawson, M. (2018). The case for illuminative practitioner research in Steiner Education. *Research on Steiner Education*, 8(2), 15–32, and Elliott, J., & Lukes, D. (2008). Epistemology as ethics in research and policy: the use of case studies. *Journal of Philosophy and Education* 42(1), 87–119.
24 This argument has been put forward by Christian Rittelmeyer, he himself offers ways of making Steiner's approach fruitful, see Rittelmeyer, C. (2023). *Rudolf Steiners Mission und Wirkung*. Info3.
25 Steiner, R. (1963). *The Philosophy of Spiritual Activity and Truth and Knowledge* (R. Stebbing, Trans.; H. S. Bergman, Ed.). Rudolf Steiner Publications, pp. 297–298 (gendered pronouns changed from the original translation, which speaks of man).

26 Steiner, R. (2020). *The First Teachers Course. Anthropological Foundations. Methods of Teaching. Practical Discussions* (M. M. Saar, Trans.). Ratayakom. Thailand. A project of the Education Research Group of Bund der Freien Waldorfschulen, Germany and the Pedagogical Section at the Goetheanum, p. 74. The German original says the human mind/psyche is the 'Schauplatz', which is usually translated as venue, which seems a little neutral. In the spirit of Shakespeare's, we prefer the translation of Schauplatz as stage and imagine the Globe Theatre above which flew the flag with the motto *totus mundus agit histrionem* (all the world's a stage/playhouse).
27 For those interested in the background of this Martyn has provided an analysis of the original context of Steiner's model for collegial school governance, see Rawson, M. (2023). School leadership and governance in Waldorf/Steiner schools. A commentary on Steiner's original ideas and practice. The long read. *Waldorf Working Papers.* https://e-learningwaldorf.de/wp-content/uploads/2023/08/No.4-School-leadership-and-governance-in-WS.pdf.
28 See https://www.presencing.org/uresearch.
29 Scharmer, C-O. & Kaufer, K. (2025) *Presencing: 7 Practices for Transforming Self, Society and Business.* Berrett-Koehler Publishers.
30 Scharmer, C-O. & Kaufer, K. (2025) *Presencing: 7 Practices for Transforming Self, Society and Business.* Berrett-Koehler Publishers. This quote and the one above come from the introduction in the Kindle edition.
31 Martyn outlined these within Waldorf schools in his book Rawson, M. (2021). *Steiner Waldorf Pedagogy in Schools. A Critical Introduction.* Routledge, pp. 138–142.

Conclusions

Reading sparks one's thinking and continuously offers corrections, prompts and nudges. We are continuously knocked off course and pointed in new directions by books we pick up and read (or even sometimes merely browse), and this cannot always be done justice to by a mere reference to some literature. At the end of this book, we have the feeling that we have opened a number of fields of research and inquiry, that we were less aware of than when we started. Writing a book out of the flow of practice brings all kinds of latent thoughts and experiences to the surface that can't always be taken up, without doubling the size of the book and the length of time required to write it. As busy practitioners, never far from the chalk face for long, which brings a certain pragmatic energy, we realize that this would actually be a much bigger project. Publishing this book is like exposing one's consolidated thoughts – though still work in progress.

Our hope is that you, the readers, will likewise feel prompted to different thoughts, even critical ones, about the ideas we have opened up here. We feel passionately about the need to keep education moving, not allowing it to fall fully into the hands of bureaucrats (who have their important tasks to fulfil – and yes, who we do also need) who don't always get what education is really about – not to mention the politicians driving policy (or being seduced down dark policy alleys by forces intent on marketization). If only education could be free of the often wholly inappropriate perspectives and purposes of business and certain branches of the economy. Even if the economy was driven by the idea of human and ecological flourishing, which it manifestly mainly isn't, it would still need to keep a respectful distance from the activity of education. Education is about supporting the process of children and young people becoming autonomous yet ethical individuals by developing their potentialities to their full extent. Only then will they be in a position to bring new energy and capacities to a world that we the older generations have not handled as well as we could have done. If we are honest, we would have to admit that we, both collectively and individually, could have done better. Given the opportunities to realize their potentialities they couldn't do worse than we have, and probably a lot better. That is the beautiful risk of education, that Gert Biesta so eloquently calls for.

Our purpose was to map out some ways in which curriculum can be crafted that might give not only give peace a chance, but also human flourishing appropriate space and time to unfold. We came to this task from our field of experience in Waldorf education, which, as we well know better than most, is far from perfect and is itself in need of revision and renewal. It certainly has no monopoly on high-quality education. Given adequate recognition and funding it could make a much more significant contribution (which some countries happily recognize, but which others persistently refuse to take seriously). However, even in its current state of development, it does offer options which we think are worth exploring. We have tried to make some of these accessible in the book.

We will be following up many of the topics addressed in this book and developing these into online and where possible, in live courses hosted by the non-profit Elewa organization (www.elearningwaldorf.de). The name Elewa, which was originally conceived of as an abbreviation for e-learning-waldorf, turned out to be Kiswahili for understanding and knowing (pronounced ele-wa), which seemed serendipitous. Elewa is a platform for Waldorf educators and teacher students, which offers courses, the Waldorf Working Papers collection of ideas in development, pre-published draft papers put out there for feedback and opportunities to engage in dialogue and exchange, which is open to partner organizations (such as the Alanus University where Martyn works or the European Council of Steiner Waldorf Education, of which Kath is a board member). Elewa is supported by the Association of Waldorf Schools in Germany and via the Erasmus projects it participates in and is open source. A book is a useful resource for reference but interactive courses, are, well interactive!

Index

Pages in *italics* refer to figures.

aesthetics 128; aesthetic education 25–31; aesthetic experience 26, 28–29; aesthetic judgement 29–30, 183; aesthetic perception 2, 30, 37
aisthesis 11, 26–27, 30, 37
alienation 26–27, 32, 46, 69, 84, 161–163; as estranged labour 95, 161–162
anthroposophy 7–8, 14, 71–72, 136
Antonovsky, A. 45, 53, 137, 179

Benner, D. 14, 34, 37–38, 52
Biesta, G.J.J. 14–15, 42, 52–54, 63, 112, 172, 178–179; *Beautiful Risk of Education* 50, 163, 192; Biesta and *Erziehung* 12, 20; Biesta and infantilization 102; Biesta on subjectification 39–40, 43–46, 76, 162; Bildung 4–5, 11–12, 14, 17, 23–26, 29–30, 33–35, 37–38, 40, 51–52, 55, 64–65, 68, 70, 84–85, 93, 95; Bildung and Dewey 162; Bildung and *Erziehung* 11–14, 25, 37; Bildung and macro-level curriculum 106; Bildung and relationships 161; *gebildet* or experienced 140; postmodern Bildung 32; self-Bildung, Bildung as self-formation 67–68, 94–95, 106, 123, 161
biographical intentions 5, 6, 99–100, 141, 148, 150, 163
Bransby 64, 113, 179

competence 8, 11, 21–22, 54, 64, 73; competence-based curricula 51; definition of 148; intercultural competence 61; language competence 121; social and emotional competence 129
connoisseurship 10–12, 31, 36, 41, 50, 180–189
constrained/unconstrained skills 91, 112, 121, 129, 142–146, 149, 169–170, 172; and competence 144
curriculum: anthropology and curriculum 72–73, 84; as contested term 1; crafting curriculum 9–10, 186–187; curriculum design 125–136; definition of 8–9, 50–51, 54; development and curriculum 86–87, 98–99; dispositions and curriculum 151–153; learning and curriculum 156; layered curriculum 13, 15, 54, 57–64; macro level curriculum 100–105; potentialities and crafting curriculum 120–123; strands of a coherent curriculum 6; Waldorf curriculum 50, 93, 106, 173–178

Dahlin, B. 14, 50, 53, 64, 190
development: a developmental approach 5, 6; personal development/development of the person 2, 16, 33, 39, 43, 51, 69, 92, 96, 100, 105–106, 109, 149
Dewey, J. 15, 18, 30–31, 85, 162, 182, 189
didactics 5, 6, 12, 17, 34, 51–52, 54, 62, 161
dispositions/predispositions 2, 4–5, 6, 13, 16–17, 34–35, 40, 46, 50–51, 57, 60–61, 75–76, 101, 104–105, 114–154, 156, 163, 167–169, 183; dispositions to wellbeing 61; habits of mind 51; innate dispositions 80; learning dispositions 54, 151, 161; teacher dispositions 183–185

educational aims 2, 4, 6, 22, 54–56, 61, 99, 109, 164
European Council of Steiner Waldorf Education 58, 106, 175, 193

generative principles 5, 13, 58–59, *155*, 156, 163, 179, 183, 189
Goethe, J.W. von 26–28; Goethean observation 185, 190; Goetheanum 97

Hattie J.A.C. (and learning) 34, 185
Hay, D. & Nye, R. 68
Herbart, J.F. 12, 17, 28–30, 37, 158–159; Herbart's *General Pedagogy* 28; theory of aesthetic judgement 17

Holzkamp, K. 43, 52
human flourishing 2, 30, 48, 61, 147, 189, 192; *see also* wellbeing

Ingold, T. 10, 14, 41, 52, 66, 84, 89, 103, 111, 143

Lave, J. 41, 52–53, 95, 178
leadership (school) 20, 50, 52, 90, 164, 179, 187–189
learning, learning and teaching *155*, 156–179; defensive and expansive learning 43, 159, 169; learning as processing experience 4; learning communities 127–136; learning needs 2; learning processes 6, 33–34, 112, 114, 116, 118, 137, 152, 156, 163; learning systems 2; self-directed learning 145; stages in learning process 158–170; transformative learning 5, 6, 33, 105, 117, 120, 123, 142, 149, 152, 156, 161
learning needs, holistic learning 51
life processes (and transformation into learning processes) 101, 112, 114–123, 137, 139, 141, 149, 163
lifelong learning 33–35

Marx, K. 94–95

needs (learning and developmental) 2–3, 9; needs of society 23, 36, 47, 51

pedagogy (definition) 12; history of 24; implications for curriculum 109, 142, 146, 149; implications for teaching and learning 80, 106, *155*, 156, 165; implications for teacher skills 180–181, 183, 186, 188; pedagogy 8, 14, 28, 31, 43, 50, 61; pedagogy and Bildung 26; pedagogy and knowledge 146; pedagogy and pedology 91–92; pedagogy and structure of book 13, 49–50, 59–60, 65–87, 92, 99–100, 114, 121, 138–139; pedagogy as art, craft and science 63; pedagogical (educational) anthropology (definition 3–6) 8
potentialities 2, 4, 6, 13, 51, 114–137, 146, 151, 192

Rawson, M.P. 14, 64, 85, 111, 113, 137, 153, 179
Reis, M.J. & White, J. 64
relaxed/calm alertness 156–158
resilience 3, 5, 13, 21, 39, 44–45, 52, 54, 57, 61, 101, 103, 108, 121, 130, 157; *see also* salutogenesis; sense of coherence; wellbeing; dispositions to 124, 151
Rogoff, B. 52, 89, 91, 95, 103, 111–113, 153–154
Rubicon 107

salutogenesis 45, 53, 137, 163–164; *see also* Antonovsky; sense of coherence
Scharmer, O. 1, 13, 84, 186, 188–190
Schieren, J. 14
Schiller, F. *Aesthetic Letters* 28; and pedagogy 26–28, 37
senses (i.e. sense organs) 18, 25, 107, 110, 117–118, 139; connoisseurship and senses 31; cultivation of the senses 26–27, 150, 158; sense experience 26, 71, 74–75, 79, 150; senses and learning 118, 135; senses and potentialities 118–119, 121–122, 128; senses and theory of knowledge 182; underdeveloped senses 116
sense of coherence 44–46, 50, 120–121, 130, 157, 163–164; *see also* resilience; salutogenesis
skills; *see also* constrained/unconstrained skills; cultivating/learning skills 41–43, 89–90; knowledgeable skills 2, 4–5, 6, 13, 16, 21, 23, 50, 62–63, 75, 102; potentialities as basis for skills 114–137; skills and competences 103; skills and curriculum 54, 56–57, 59–61, 84, 86, 109–110; skills and developmental tasks 99; skills, capacity and dispositions 25, 138–153; soft skills 70
spirit (also spiritual) 18, 68–69, 73, 84; body, soul and spirit 120, 123, 137; definitions of spirituality 74, 85; free spiritual and cultural life 49, 63; Marx and the human spirit 94–95; mind as spirit-soul 73–74; spirit and mind 140–141; spiritual activity 28, 48; spiritual core and potentialities 118; spiritual thinking 182; spirituality 7–8, 16, 21, 23, 47, 49, 69–71, 108, 152; spirituality as potentiality 121, 130–132; Steiner and spirit/spiritual science 108, 139–141, 187; the human spirit/Self as spiritual core of being/spiritual nature of the human being 5, 46, 65, 68–74, 76, 79–80, 85, 95–96, 106, 115, 122, 124, 150–151
Steiner, R. (education) 2, 4, 14, 53; aesthetics and Steiner 28; forgetting and recalling 167; methods of observation 185; social theory 31, 46–50, 53; Steiner and curriculum 57–58, 64; Steiner and spirituality 69–71; Steiner and Waldorf 7; Steiner's pedagogical anthropology 31, 71–77, 85, 107, 116–117, 130; Steiner's theory of growth of abilities/dispositions 139–142, 149–151, 153; teaching economy 163; theory of knowledge 182, 187–190

teaching 4, 12, *155*, 156–178; block teaching 56, 147; didactics and teaching methods 17, 42, 45, 55, 58, 60, 62–63, 110; explicit teaching of constrained skills 143–144; generative principles of teaching 59; learning societies to teaching societies 16–17; teaching and pedagogy 4–5, 8, 12–13, 67, 75, 131, 134–135, 152; teaching as art and craft 56, 78, 105, 182; teaching economy 163; teaching for the test 3; teaching profession 20, 189–190; transformative learning 5, 6, 33, 105, 117, 123, 142, 149, 152, 156, 161–162, 165

Ubuntu 23, 37

Vygotsky, L. importance of teaching 89; pedology 91–95

wellbeing 3, 5, 10, 13, 21, 23, 39, 44–45, 52, 56, 61, 67, 107, 121, 125, 130–131, 147; *see also* resilience; salutogenesis; sense of coherence; memory and wellbeing 167; sense of wellbeing/sense of life 75

Wulf, C. 25, 84

For Product Safety Concerns and Information please contact our EU
representative GPSR@taylorandfrancis.com
Taylor & Francis Verlag GmbH, Kaufingerstraße 24, 80331 München, Germany

www.ingramcontent.com/pod-product-compliance
Lightning Source LLC
Chambersburg PA
CBHW060300240426
43661CB00060B/2850